BICESTER

NCOTT
ARD
Arncott "Regulator"

site of
"Regulator" (Removed)
d to Bicester

STORES SIDINGS, Nos 1, 2 & 3
& 2 Removed)

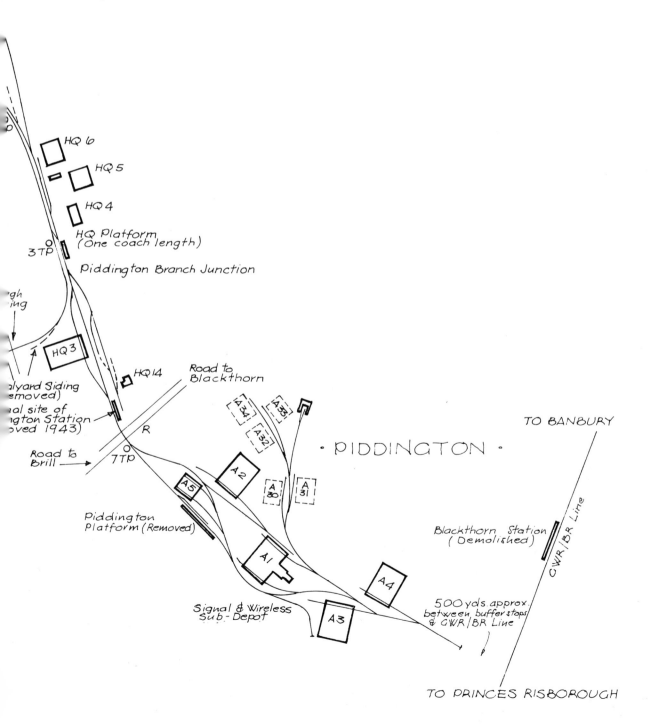

HQ 6

HQ 5

HQ 4

HQ Platform
(One coach length)

3 TP

Piddington Branch Junction

gh
ing

HQ 3

HQ 14

Road to
Blackthorn

A 34   A 33

A 32

· PIDDINGTON ·

TO BANBURY

lyard Siding
emoved)
al site of
ngton Station
oved 1943)

R

7 TP

A 30   A 31

A 5   A 2

Road to
Brill

Piddington
Platform (Removed)

A 1

Blackthorn Station
(Demolished)

GWR/BR Line

Signal & Wireless
Sub-Depot

A 3

A 4

500 yds. approx.
between buffer stops
& GWR/BR Line

TO PRINCES RISBOROUGH

Bicester Military Railway

Waggoner "Army 92" (Hunslet 3792 of 1953), one of the Army's standard "Austerity" 0-6-0 saddle tanks was used on many occasions to illustrate the work of the Royal Corps of Transport, Central Workshops, Bicester. The locomotive is seen here on display at Rushmoor Arena, Aldershot in 1973. It is now on permanent exhibition at the Museum of Army Transport at Beverley, Humberside.

Authors' collection

Bicester Military Railway

by

E. R. Lawton

and

Major M. W. Sackett

Oxford Publishing Co.

The scene today in Graven Hill locomotive shed on the Bicester Military Railway with four of the five Thos Hill "Steelman Royale" 4-wheel diesel hydraulic locomotives present.

Peter Nicholson

A catalogue record for this book is available from the British Library.

ISBN 0-86093-467-5

Library of Congress catalog card number
92-81445

Oxford Publishing Co. is part of the
Haynes Publishing Group PLC
Sparkford, Near Yeovil, Somerset BA22 7JJ

Haynes Publications Inc.
861 Lawrence Drive, Newbury Park, California 91320, USA

Printed by: J. H. Haynes & Co. Ltd
Typeset in Times Roman Medium 10/11 pt

Contents

Acknowledgements

No account of this kind could possibly have been written without the help of many organisations and individuals. This especially applies to the story of the Bicester Military Railway which serves an operational Ministry of Defence establishment where access is, rightly, severely restricted. The Second World War period was particularly difficult to chronicle as many local records were lost and the priorities of the period allowed little time to maintain meticulous files. The fact that both authors worked on the system, at various times, has helped, but neither could have written the entire history without the assistance of others. To these patient, kind and co-operative people the authors accord their most sincere thanks.

Special acknowledgements are due to the following for their outstanding efforts:

S.W.G. Daniels, Depot Railway Officer, Bicester.

A.P. Lambert, former Operating Manager, Sealink, now Southern Area Representative, Museum of Army Transport.

The late Major W.H. Mounsey, former Officer Commanding, Bicester Detachment, No.1. Railway (Home) Group RE.

T. Pinchen, Deputy Defence Land Agent, Ministry of Defence, Aldershot.

G.P. Roberts, The Industrial Railway Society.

Bill Simpson, author of the *Oxford to Cambridge Railway (Vols 1 & 2,* OPC) and other publications.

Paul Sutton, owner of WD 191 and former Joint Editor of the *Tenterden Terrier* the house magazine of the KESR.

John C. Woods, Deputy Chief Librarian, Ministry of Defence Library, London.

Several of the following have, at some time, either worked on the BMR or BR, or have possessed knowledge of the system. Some have spent many hours tracing documents and information which has helped to complete the narrative. Others have forwarded their recollections and photographs. All the contributions have proved invaluable: John Bentley, Tony Bracewell, Mrs Daisy Bloomfield, the late H.T. Buckingham, R.H. Carter, the late Major Clarke MC, the late Captain Harry Forbes, Colonel G.K. Gilbery RAOC, N.J. Haymen, Jimmy Higgins BEM, Roy H. Holford, Jack Iles, Harold N. James, the late Lt Col. N.H.D. Prendergast RE, David H. Mather, S.C. Robinson, David Rouse, R.H.G. Simpson, Lt Col. M.E. Stone RAOC, A.F.G. Styles, A.L. Tibbs, Eric Tonks and A.J. Walker,

Museums and Record Offices
David Jenkinson and John Edgington, both formerly of the National Railway Museum, York.
Gordon Kobish, Rutland Railway Museum.
The courteous, kind and helpful staff of the Public Records Office, Kew and the National Army Museum, Chelsea, London.
J. Morley-Clarke, Assistant Curator, RAOC Museum, Camberley. Ellen Schwartz, Librarian, California State Railroad Museum, USA.

Newspaper and Journals
John N. Slater, Editor, *The Railway Magazine.*
Editors of the *Bicester Advertiser*, *Oxford Mail* and *Rail News.*
Colonel E. Ridgeway OBE, *RAOC Gazette.*

Railway Equipment Manufacturers
Andrew P. Mott and David Chalkley, D. Wickham & Co Ltd.
D.M. Robertson, Westinghouse Signals Ltd.
W.R. Souster, Baguley-Drewry Ltd.
Ian A. Edley, Managing Director, Thos Hill (Rotherham) Ltd.

Also, thanks are due to Dr E. Liana Sakelliou-Schultz, BA MA for reading the manuscript and Captain Alan Potts, formerly of the RCT, for the drawings and track layout plans.

Abbreviations

ARP	Air Raid Precautions	NS	Nederlandse Spoorwegen (Netherlands Railways)
BAOR	British Army of the Rhine		
BR	British Railways/Rail	OD	Ordnance Depot
BMR	Bicester Military Railway	P&EE	Proof & Experimental Establishment
CMR	Cairnryan Military Railway	PLA	Port of London Authority
COD	Central Ordnance Depot	RAF	Royal Air Force
DE	Diesel electric locomotive	RCE	Railway Construction Engineer
DH	Diesel hydraulic locomotive	RCH	Railway Clearing House
DM	Diesel mechanical locomotive	RCT	Royal Corps of Transport
EQ	Exhaust quenched	RE	Royal Engineers
ESD	Engineers Stores Depot	REME	Royal Electrical & Mechanical Engineers
GWR	Great Western Railway	RN	Royal Navy
hp	Horse power	RNAD	Royal Naval Armament Depot
KESR	Kent & East Sussex Railway	ROF	Royal Ordnance Factory
KWVR	Keighley & Worth Valley Railway	RPS	Railway Preservation Society
LMR	Longmoor Military Railway	SA	Spark arrested
LMS	London, Midland & Scottish Railway	SNCD	Société Nationale Chemins de Fer Belges (Belgian National Railways)
LNER	London & North Eastern Railway		
LSWR	London & South Western Railway	SMR	Shropshire & Montgomeryshire Railway
LT&SR	London, Tilbury & Southend Railway	SR	Southern Railway
MMR	Melbourne Military Railway	TP	Telephone Post
MMMR	Martin Mill Military Railway	UK	United Kingdom
MOD	Ministry of Defence	WD	War Department
MOF&P	Ministry of Fuel & Power	WO	Working order
NCB	National Coal Board (now British Coal)	WR	War Reserve
N/K	Not known	WWII	World War Two
NRM	National Railway Museum, York		

The driver's eye-view of the approach to 'A' blockpost. The modern building on the right is the Railway Headquarters, Graven Hill, which overlooks the Sorting Sidings, served by the line branching to the right.
Peter Nicholson

Introduction

The large Ordnance Depot at Bicester in Oxfordshire, like many existing army installations in United Kingdom, was a product of the 1939-45 war. Similarly was 'Railway Group', the organisation which had the overall responsibility for the operations of military railways in Great Britain. An exception was the well-known Longmoor Military Railway in Hampshire which was separately administered until the last few months of its existence.

We cannot deal in depth here, or in any great detail, with the vast military railway activity which has operated in Britain overall. Instead we will attempt to paint a broad brush picture into which the Bicester story can be slotted.

In 1830 the military authorities realised the advantages offered by rail transport and arranged for the movement of a Regiment of Foot over the newly opened Liverpool & Manchester Railway. The movement took two hours compared with a march of two days after which the soldiers would have arrived exhausted and with some 20% stragglers. Since then the armed forces have taken full advantage of the civilian railway system both in the UK and overseas. Additionally they have developed their own railway expertise in the Corps of Royal Engineers and since 1965, in the Royal Corps of Transport. This knowledge enabled the Forces to utilise, develop, build and operate railways in various theatres of war. Initial training and experience was gained following the build up of the Woolmer Instructional Military Railway (which was to become the Longmoor Military Railway) in Hampshire from the turn of the twentieth century. Furthermore, it was soon recognised that railways had an important part to play in the running and organisation of military stores depots. Not only did they make connections with the civilian railways for the transfer and transport of military stores but also provided internal transport for the movement of goods within the depot.

In 1805 Lt Col. Henry Shrapnel RA (whose name was adopted for the kind of shell he invented) came to Shoeburyness in the County of Essex to carry out trials of the new shell. Special screens were erected on the mud flats to be used as targets to evaluate the projectiles. By 1849 a Detachment of the Royal Artillery arrived in the tiny village of Shoeburyness to set up a School of Gunnery, together with Sappers, to erect the necessary buildings, to construct the ranges and so on. Furthermore the Sappers constructed a standard gauge tramway to connect the various installations and facilitate the transport of equipment and stores. By 1854 the Government had decided it was advantageous to separate proof experimentation from instruction and practice. Consequently they brought into being the Proof and Experimental Establishment (P&EE) which has continued until this day.

The War Office was troubled by the fact that the London, Tilbury & Southend Railway terminated at Southend, some four miles from the Ranges at Shoeburyness, necessitating the provision of horse drawn transport for the conveyance of military supplies over very indifferent roads, not only with conventional stores, but also heavy and bulky items of ordnance. The High Street at Southend was a major problem in the way of extending the LT&SR and the Company also had serious doubts with regard to the viability of such an extension. An alternative existed in the shape of the River Thames and so a barge pier was constructed in the range area in 1859 enabling heavy ordnance to be conveyed from Woolwich Arsenal by barge, and onwards over the military tramway.

Although this water route was of great importance it was still clearly necessary to have a railway connection. Eventually the War Office was able to cajole The LT&SR to extend their line to Shoeburyness so as to connect with the Tramway and this was completed in 1884. The size of the guns increased, the ranges were expanded as was the Tramway which was involved not only in the transport of guns, ammunition and targets (some of the latter weighing up to 25 tons) but it was also required to provide a quite intensive passenger service. The Tramway is still in use today, with the exception that passenger services are limited to the conveyance of visiting officers and occasionally the movement of personnel to the site of artillery trials. It was originally operated by Royal Engineers, then a mixture of Sappers and locally trained civilians, and eventually by civilian staff only under the direction of the Deputy Chief Royal Engineer (DCRE) for the district until 1961. Then 'Railway Group' accepted responsibility for military railways in all the P&EEs.

There were many other similar railways, with different purposes of course, Messrs Vickers made use of Eskmeals in Cumbria as a Test Range which was eventually taken over by the Ministry of Defence as a P&EE. The authority for the construction of the London & South Western Railway line to Aldershot included a caveat for the provision and subsequent shunting arrangements for the Government sidings there. The sidings, besides handling normal military stores traffic were also used for passenger trains conveying visitors to the Searchlight Tattoo, which for many years, was held in the Rushmoor Arena. A large covered platform was constructed to handle such trains. The LSWR also constructed a line to serve the military establishments at Amesbury and Bulford.

During the war of 1914-18, in answer to a national scandal over the short supply of shells, a depot was built in 1915 at Chilwell, just outside Nottingham, which by 1916 was producing shells in great quantities. By the end of that war the railway serving the Depot had moved some 227,000 inwards loaded wagons and despatched 224,000. It was just one of six such installations. With the end of the war the Depot began to be run down until 1934 when the decision was taken to convert it to a mechanical transport supply centre, in which role it achieved enormous success, eventually becoming the headquarters of the Army's Vehicle Organisation and controlling many motor transport depots throughout the country.

In 1917 at Bramley, Hampshire the construction of an Ammunition Depot was commenced by prisoners or war employed by His Majesty's Office of Works. It was handed over to the War Office on completion in 1920. It contained some 28 miles of railway track serving the numerous ammunition sheds. Again the civilian staff were under the control of the local Deputy Chief Royal Engineer but with the advent of the Second World War, railway troops from the Royal Engineers were drafted in to augment the civilian staff, control subsequently being exercised by 'Railway Group'.

By the mid-thirties it was becoming increasingly likely that there would be another major war and the War Office began to plan new depots to meet the situation. In some cases construction was commenced, such as the underground ammunition depot at Corsham and the large Ordnance Depot at Donnington. Amongst those planned was that at Bicester, the subject of our book, Kineton (Ammunition), Long Marston (RE Stores), Longtown (Ammunition), Steventon & Lockerley (Motor Transport), West Moors (Petroleum), Cairnryan and Marchwood (Military Ports). Some were entirely new projects, others the adaption of an existing industrial facility. In the case of the Ammunition Depot at Nesscliffe the War Department took over the Shropshire & Montgomeryshire Railway in 1941 with a detachment of officers and men from 193 Railway Operating Company RE. The Depot was built alongside the main line with connecting lines to the various sub-depots and in addition to providing the military railway requirement the Royal Engineers continued to run a minimal public freight and passenger service. The line experienced the busiest period of its entire life!

With the upsurge of military railways following the declaration of WWII a great variety of locomotives, passenger and freight rolling stock was acquired from the major railway companies, for use on military railways systems by detachments of railway operating troops under the control of a War Office Staff Branch - 'TN 3'. As the size of the task grew this form of control became impracticable and in 1942 the many small units were brought together as a United Kingdom based organisation called the No.1 Railway (WD Depots) Operating and Maintenance Group, Royal Engineers which eventually became No.1 Railway (Home) Group RE.

By this time the Group was operating some 39 military railway systems, ranging in size from a depot with 70 miles of track serving 290 sheds, to those with but a few miles of track. In total there was approximately 600 miles of track and over 200 locomotives. Additionally, the Group had responsibility for a further 200 odd locations and sidings where an agency carried out the railway work on its behalf. Some 2,400 personnel were controlled from the Group Headquarters at Hampstead, London through six Divisional Commanders with the rank of Major. Alongside the Group there were additionally six Railway Construction Groups.

During 1945 Railway Group was converted into a largely civilian organisation to free troops for other purposes. The message was sent out to transportation troops throughout the world offering employment on demobilisation, but the response was insufficient and in the immediate post war years there was a countrywide recruitment campaign resulting in some 90% of the establishment being filled. The remaining 10% took many years to complete.

With the war finished, besides continuing to provide the railway services required by the various depots, there was an immediate attempt to rationalise the locomotive situation, raise the standard of rolling stock, much of which was old in the first place and by now, run down by heavy wartime pressures. Additionally the authorities had to improve the quality of the permanent way, mostly laid down in haste under difficult wartime conditions and then subjected to extremely heavy use. Many of the locomotives were old and varied as could be spared by the civilian railways, but the admirable 'Austerity' 0-6-0 saddle tanks which had come forward in ever increasing numbers since 1943, greatly eased the problem until by 1946/7 they were virtually the only steam type in use. The stores, spares and maintenance problems were considerably eased. Diesel locomotives were, however, making their presence felt and the Group was already laying the foundations for a wholly diesel locomotive fleet. Unfortunately efforts to obtain standardisation were to take many years to achieve.

In parallel with this activity by the Group, the War Office was anxious to reduce the number of depots by running down holdings and to centralise the remainder in a lesser number of locations. It is perhaps not surprising that the very first depot to be closed was the Royal Engineer Hutting Depot occupying the site of Newbury Race Course. It is hard to imagine now, the main line running the circle of the race track and contained within it some 28 miles of track with stack upon stack of hutting stores! Some years later the Ministry of Defence was formed and after a slow start began to achieve some of the original objectives, including the rationalisation of service interests. The Royal Navy for example became responsible for provisions for all three services, expanding their own organisation for victualling, but making redundant the Army's food depots. Similarly the Royal Air Force took responsibility for barrack accommodation, the Army for motor transport.

The peacetime changes and the reduction of quantities of military stores led to a similar run down of the associated military railway systems and staff. By 1965 only two Divisions remained in No.1 Railway Group RE, one covering the area south of Stratford-on-Avon, the other the remainder of the country. In various stages the Group had lost the "Home" from its title and then when it was realised there was only a single Railway Group, the "No. 1" was deleted. In 1963 the military port at Rhu was absorbed into the organisation with a resultant change of title to Transportation Group RE. The next major reorganisation came in 1965, consequent upon a Ministry of Defence examination of the overlapping roles of various Army Corps. As a result the Royal Corps of Transport was formed, taking from the Royal Engineers the responsibility for railways, maritime and movement control; from the Royal Army Service Corps it absorbed road and water transport. The remaining responsibilities of the RASC ie food supply and barrack accommodation, were given to the Royal Army Ordnance Corps, both much later being handed over to the Royal Navy and Royal Air Force respectively, as already noted.

Additionally, in the 1965 re-organisation it was decreed that all Government building and associated works, including the construction and maintenance of permanent way, should be concentrated under the new Department of the Environment as a result of which, although the railway tracks remained in the ownership of Railway Group, work on it was under the direction of the DOE.

The newly formed Royal Corps of Transport centralised its Movement Control functions in a unit known as the Army Freight Organisation, using the Colonel rank of Railway Group as its Commander, and establishing the railway organisation as a Railway Wing, Army Freight Organisation. However, further and wider re-organisations were taking place with the MoD decision to centralise the whole of its military logistic functions in a new Headquarters located at Andover, Hampshire and known as 'Logex'. This Headquarters encompasses the logistic functions of the RAOC, RCT, REME and RE. The railway organisation was absorbed into the new HQ as a unit with the title 'Army Department Railway Staff' with a civilian Superintendent in charge. The two Divisions were disbanded, a small outstation being left at Carlisle to ease the problems of management of the military railway systems in the North of England and Scotland.

From the inception of the Corps of Royal Electrical and Mechanical Engineers they had steadily taken responsibility for all aspects of the Army's mechanical engineering. As a result of the 1965 re-organisation the Corps became responsible for those aspects of army railway work, and the Central Workshops at Bicester came directly under their control. They also assumed responsibility for overall control of all railway mechanical matters, together with the financial justification. However, the direct control of work outside Workshop overhaul was left in the hands of the Railway Group Motive Power Department.

Researching the history of the Bicester Military Railway was made especially difficult because of the loss of many of the local official records. The authors would be grateful if any readers who may be in possession of any additional information to please contact them, via the publishers.

The story of military railways continues and without doubt, further changes will take place. It must be made clear, however, the ensuing account is an attempt to chronicle the history of the Bicester Military Railway and, not in any way, to represent the story of the other military units which served in the Garrison.

1

Building the Line – The Birth of 'X' Depot

In the late 1930s with the possibility of war looming ahead the authorities realised the existing ordnance depots in Britain were totally inadequate, and could not possibly cope with the enormous task of supplying a wartime army. Only five Central Ordnance Depots existed, each dealing with a particular type of equipment. Branston stored clothing, Chilwell motor transport and spares, Didcot general stores, Weedon small arms and machine guns and Woolwich artillery, engineers and signal stores.

Amongst the five only Chilwell could be considered as up to date, the others lacking sufficient transport and modern handling equipment. When mobilisation took place in 1939 there was an even greater need for increased storage and supply depots to serve the rapidly increasing size of the Army. Construction of an entirely new depot at Donnington in Shropshire had already begun. In other parts of the country temporary sites were being taken over quickly and covered space in the existing depots increased

An aerial photograph taken from above Arncott in 1942 whilst the railway was being constructed. The trackbed can be traced from the line of black ash ballast.
1. Main Line to Piddington
2. Arncott triangle formed by the main running line, West Curve and South running line.
3. No.3 Camp HQ and accommodation of the BMR staff and Patrick Haugh Road.
4. Site of the original locomotive shed which was later the paintshop of the Central Workshops.
5. South Running line.
6. North Running line.
7. Track to junction of South and North Running lines, just before crossing the Arncott to Murcott road at White Cross Green.   *COD Bicester*

An aerial photograph taken from above Piddington in 1942, again the trackbed can be traced from the lines of black ash ballast.

1. Main line to Ambrosden and Bicester.
2. South Running line
3. West Curve.
4. Site of Arncott station.
5. Sidings Nos RE 1 & 2 (No. 3 was added later)
6. Main line to Piddington.
7. Foundations for Shed 'HQ3'.
8. Site of original Piddington station. (Main line later extended to serve 'A' sites, formerly Signals & Wireless sub-depot).
9. Thame to Bicester road.
10. Palmer Avenue.
11. Patrick Haugh road.

COD Bicester

as resources would allow. Despite these desperate measures it became increasingly clear the construction of another large depot was imperative and reconnaissances for this were put in hand.

The project, code named 'X' Depot, was for various reasons to be located in the Southern part of England, with a layout that would permit the rapid processing of large, unprecedented quantities of stores with easy access to rail and road networks, aerodromes, electricity and water supplies.

A further requirement was the location of a nearby sizeable town for the supply of civilian labour, which at the time, was considered an essential element for constructional and operational purposes. During this period favourable sites were hard to find and the problems in building a depot of the size envisaged were immense. Many Government departments were already building factories to supply the armed forces; the construction of new airfields was being actively pursued and, in addition,

large tracts of land had been acquired for barracks and training areas.

At the beginning of 1941 the then Director of Warlike Stores, Major General L.H. Williams CB, MC (later knighted) nominated Colonel (later Major General) G.W. Palmer as the Commandant (Designate) of the 'X' Depot project with a remit to plan its location and layout. Colonel Palmer, with a small staff, commenced work in offices at Beeston, near Chilwell, Nottinghamshire. Eight potential sites were examined, the choice finally falling on a large area of land south of the small town of Bicester in Oxfordshire. The area was flanked by the LMS Railway's, Bletchley to Oxford line and the Great Western, Princes Risborough to Banbury Railway. The City of Oxford and Aylesbury were each just twelve miles away.

On 9th April 1941 it was confirmed that this site, with its suitable communications and good natural camouflage, would be ideal for 'X' Depot. Further advantages were claimed by the location of two low lying hills at Graven Hill and Arncott which, in the terms of warfare in the 1940s, would restrict the possibility of low level bombing by the enemy. The area was vulnerable to flooding in the winter months but sufficient space was available without spoiling too much good quality agricultural land.

From the outset it was planned the installation would also be the premier post war depot of the Royal Army Ordnance Corps and its construction would enable other smaller depots to be closed. With this is mind the building of the storehouses was to be of a high order with light and heavy overhead cranes, good office and general equipment.

The LMS Railway, then under the overall control of the

Arncott yard in June 1943 showing ramp board and on the right the original Arncott Regulator hut. One of the first drivers, Sapper Cooke, is standing near the front buffer beam on 'Austerity' 0-6-0ST.

Major W.H. Mounsey

Wartime description	Current description
(1) Signals & Wireless	'A' site
(2) Engineering Stores	'B' site
(3) Motor Transport (spares and tyres)	'C' site
(4) Armaments	'D' site
(5) Small Arms	'E' site

With its associated rail and road facilities the depot was described as the largest single military project ever launched in the United Kingdom.

A Chief Royal Engineer, (Lt Col. J.P. Haugh) was specially appointed to supervise the depot building work, which was to be carried out by military labour, supplemented by civilian specialists for certain specific items such as the erection of steel work for the large storage sheds, construction of roads etc. The demand for stone was such that a quarrying company worked for a long time at Woodstock for the project. About one thousand Italian prisoners of war were also employed eventually in the constructional work.

1941

The first step to be taken was the provision of tented camps for the personnel engaged on the building work. Whilst this was being planned the 165 Railway Survey Company, Royal Engineers, commenced a preliminary survey of the line on 22nd April 1941. The whole of the railway work was under the control of the Royal Engineers Railway Construction Engineer No.5. (Southern) and on 11th July the Officer Commanding 601 Railway Construction Company, Royal Engineers was appointed Resident Engineer for construction of the track. By May the Survey Company had already completed the preliminary survey and Treasury sanction had been obtained, when an order was issued from the War Office that construction was to begin immediately.

The acquisition of the areas of the required land was the responsibility of the former War Department Land Agent based in Oxford. By July he was able to confirm that requisition notices had been served on the various owners or occupiers. The Compensation (Defence) Act 1930 provided the means for acquiring lands required for strategic wartime needs and included provision for payment of the necessary compensation to persons who held title deeds to such areas.

These included well-known local families such as Mrs A. Calcutt, Mr C.E. Chilton, Mrs E.E. Cook, Messrs W.S. & R.A. Deeley, Miss S. Hadlan, Mr J. Haskings, Mr F.A. Harper, Mr C.J. Herring, Mr S.J. May, Mr J. Tredwell, Mrs R. Wakefield and Mr W.T. Wilkins. Some of these had farmed in the locality for several generations.

Organisations and companies included were Hall's Breweries, Oxford, who held title to land adjacent to the Plough Inn at Lower Arncott, Jack Olding and Co. Ltd, Wadham College, Oxford, Reverend A. Gatehouse, Vicar of Ambrosen (glebe lands) together with charities named Arncott Poors Peace and Woodstock Municipal Charities.

Later, in the mid to late 1940s and early 1950s the land areas were purchased and the negotiations were conducted on behalf of Her Majesties Principal Secretary of State for

wartime Railway Executive Committee, was far from pleased with this decision and in April 1941 they sent an urgent communication to the Ministry of War Transport (MOWT) pointing out there were no marshalling facilities in the immediate neighbourhood. They also argued that the existing yard at Bletchley, some twenty miles to the east, was completely inadequate to deal with any large increase of traffic. Furthermore, the Oxford-Bletchley-Cambridge railway was a crucial part of an emergency belt line which was to be used in the event of the bombing of London termini and their rail connections.

In 1940 new connections had already been built at Calvert and Sandy providing links with the London & North Eastern Railway main lines and at Oxford with the GW Railway, for this eventuality. However, the fact that the events had moved swiftly, planning was so far advanced and the other seven sites were definitely unsuitable, led to a Ministerial decision that the site must be maintained. The Ministry stated, however, that additional sidings and/or other connections required by the Railway Executive Committee would be favourably considered to cope with the estimated increase of traffics to and from the new depot. Accordingly the Ministry of War Transport authorised the construction of a new 660-wagon capacity, yard at Swanbourne on the 'up' side of the Oxford-Bletchley line, approximately 3½ miles from Bletchley.

'X' Depot was therefore re-titled Bicester Central Ordnance Depot, the estimated cost of construction being in excess of £5 million. Later additions increased the sum to £6½ million. This would provide 6,739,000 square feet of covered storage, 5,177,000 square feet of open storage, approximately fifty miles of railway track and 24 miles of new road. Accommodation was to be provided for 9,450 military personnel, 2,900 Auxiliary Territorial Service (ATS) and 1,500 civilians.

The installation was to be sub-divided into six sub-depots, later reduced to five ie:

Concrete plaque at entrance to No. 3 Camp, Lower Arncott during the war years. The letters 'R.O.&.M.D.' represents 'Railway Operating & Maintenance Detachment'. The plaque was sculptured by an Italian prisoner of war.

Authors' collection

the War Department. The original requisition notices were converted to formal legal conveyances. The title deeds are now held by the Treasury Solicitor with copies retained by the Property Services Agency of the Department of the Environment, Estate Office in Abingdon, Oxfordshire as successors to the War Department and Land Agents Service.

Following the issue of the requisition notice, authority was given for a final survey and a pegging out of boundaries. At the same time decisions were being taken to determine the exact location of the great storage sheds the construction of which was expected to commence in October 1941. The LMS Railway was asked to commence installation of the rail connections from its Oxford-Bletchley line at milepost 20 (from Bletchley) at the Oxford end of Bicester station. Work on the trailing connection was completed by 13th July. The connection was controlled from a ground frame with trap points to protect the main LMS line from any unauthorised traffic movements from the sidings. The LMS also informed the military authorities that ballast could not be supplied in any large quantities unless the BMR had priority over the planned new marshalling yard at Swanbourne.

Soon after, the ground was prepared for the laying of Exchange Sidings which consisted of five tracks which were eventually connected at each end with the LMS line. Four of these tracks had a capacity to hold a fifty-wagon train, while the fifth formed a part of the principal BMR running line and was also used as a run-round loop to release locomotives after working arriving freight and passenger trains.

Correspondence was also proceeding over the urgency of facing connections but it was agreed this could wait until the signalling work would be completed in September.

Meanwhile the site engineers requested that locomotives, rolling stock, coal, water supplies and operators for the construction be sent immediately. On 30th July the

War Office stated that six flat wagons and two ferryvans had been despatched to Bicester followed, a week later, by four more ferryvans.

In August the first estimated costs of the railway emerged:

LMS	Railway connections and signalling.	5,000
Part 1	Exchange sidings.	12,000
Part 2	Main line from Exchange sidings to start of Motor Transport Depot including Sorting Sidings.	25,000
	Locomotive Depot.	2,000
	Main line from start of Motor Transport Depot to start of the Signal & Wireless Depot.	9,000
	Line to Transit Shed.	4,000
Part 3	Bridges.	3,000
Part 4	Motor Transport Sub-Depot.	25,000
Part 5	Armaments Sub-Depot.	18,000
Part 6	Small Arms Sub-Depot	7,000
Part 7	Mobilisation Store siding.	1,000
Part 8	Engineering Sub-Depot.	18,000
Part 9	Signal & Wireless Sub-Depot.	14,000

General

Water supply, lighting, drain, fencing to Railway (other than sub depot fencing).	4,000
Signalling (excluding LMS).	1,000
Traffic offices, buildings, lavatories, messes.	5,000
Loading mounds (track only).	3,000
Total:	£156,000

Following the pattern of other large engineering projects these were revised in March 1942 by which time, with additions, the total cost had risen to £216,000. The estimates applied to materials only, the labour being supplied from the various military units and prisoners of war.

During August plans were drawn for the 2.6 miles Armaments and Small Arms loop which encircled Graven Hill and during the same month pegging out of the route commenced.

A report from the Director of Fortifications and Works in September stated good progress had been made on the railway construction and a borehole, location not specified, for water was producing 5,000 gallons per hour.

Early in the planning stages the use of concrete sleepers had been specified for use throughout the system and the LMS had been duly informed of this decision. A specifications for 'philplug' sleepers using bearing plates and 'dog' spikes had been drawn up and a firm called Bells engaged to manufacture these for the Ministry of Supply. The firm were provided with a site and siding on War Department land at the east end of Exchange Sidings, later the location of Langford Farm station. The first batches of sleepers were found to be unsatisfactory, of a low quality and uncertain strength. A meeting was held on the site attended by the Resident Engineer at which it was ordained that sleepers already laid should be lifted and replaced, whilst inspection procedures would be intensified.

A few months later the first Operating Officer, Lt (later Major) W.H. Mounsey chartered a small aircraft to view the progress of the works. He was concerned to find the railway vividly outlined from the air by the white lines of the concrete sleepers. As this would aid identification by German bombers orders were quickly issued to cease production of the concrete sleepers and revert to the conventional wooden pattern.

The Transportation Directorate at the War Office had also laid down certain standards to be observed:

1. Minimum radii for running lines to be 495 ft (the same radii as in standard Army turnouts).
2. Minimum radii for shed spurs to the 462 ft.
3. Maximum grade to be 1 in 150.
4. Spurs from the running lines to storage sheds to fall towards the sheds at 1 in 150.
5. If for any reason a shed spur had to rise, a grade of 1 in 400 would be permitted.

In the event exceptions had to be made on some running lines and in the case of the spur to storage shed 'D7', where there were exceptional level and layout problems, a down grade of 1 in 75 was authorised.

In September the LMS had made arrangements for the War Department locomotives to run to Oxford for coal, water and servicing as to this date no facilities existed on the BMR.

The pace quickened in October as the main line from Exchange Sidings was pushed beyond Ambrosden. In the early stages it was intended the locomotive shed would be built adjacent to the Motor Transport Sub-Depot but after further consideration it was agreed this would be built near the village of Lower Arncott alongside the South Running line.

Construction of the Armaments and Small Arms Sub-Depots loop commenced and 165 Railway Survey Company, Royal Engineers had prepared plans for the MT Yard.

Personnel from the Royal Corps of Signals (No. 1 Railway Telegraph Company) were hard to work laying the overhead railway telephone lines and installing temporary telephones.

The War Office were engaged in tracing the location of the side tipping wagons which were urgently needed for the conveyance of spoil and ash ballast.

By November the main line had reached the village of Lower Arncott, and crossed the Arncott-Murcott road. The lead in for the locomotive shed was also installed.

The main line between 'A' and 'B' blockposts was almost two miles in length and twisted and turned. The survey company, mindful of the urgency, had chosen the ground which was above the flooding level. Between Ambrosden and Arncott the roadway and fields would often be under eighteen inches of water and the decision lessened the amount of fill required. This lead to particularly sharp curves some quarter of a mile south of Ambrosden which were to give endless trouble to the permanent way staff for many years. Two streams were crossed on this section, the River Ray nearer Arncott yard and a minor tributary just a quarter of a mile from Ambrosden. These were crossed by standard army stock

span bridges of twenty feet length. A single span sufficing for the tributary and three spans in the case of the River Ray. The bridges were built within the estimated cost of £3,000 but few details of their construction plans survive. A Lt Mickey Russell RE was in charge of the project and it was popularly alleged that more effort went into the River Ray bridge than the famous Forth Bridge! For many years afterwards it was known as 'Mickey's Bridge'. Elsewhere in this book can be found details of the troubles that beset this structure until remedial work in 1957 proved successful.

A permanent way maintenance force of Royal Engineers, consisting of one officer, four sergeants and 93 Sappers were provided to work on the completed portion of the new railway.

At the end of the year a two-inch water main to the locomotive shed yard was laid and track was in place to the Engineers Stores at Arncott serving the urgently required siding at 'RE Nos 1, 2 & 3'.

1942

By the commencement of the New Year some 1,500 Royal Engineers, 607 Royal Pioneer Corps and 550 Italian prisoners of war were engaged on the construction of the vast depot and its rail network. Despite snow, ice, and appalling ground conditions created by the churned up clay, the construction companies forged ahead surrounded by new roads, the din of rapidly rising steelwork and the laying of seemingly endless tons of concrete and brickwork.

Private adjoining landowners were demanding additional occupation crossings to give access to the fields divided by the railway. These were reminded their land had been requisitioned and compensation paid with severance in mind and no further crossings would be provided.

A camp at Lower Arncott, consisting of a collection of Nissen huts, cookhouse and office facilities was reported in January as being 80% complete. This was designated as 'No.3. Camp' and was to house the railway operating and maintenance personnel for the BMR. Small wooden huts were also requisitioned for the keepers at the principal level crossings at Ambrosden, Arncott Main and Piddington. This followed a decision that passenger train services were to run on the new railway.

The LMS was demanding telephones at Exchange Sidings and stated that proper operations could not function unless these were provided forthwith.

Side tipping wagons were sent from Scotland, 22 being supplied from No.1 Military Port at Faslane to carry thousands of tons of spoil and ballast.

Track laying on the 'B' and 'C' sites loop was in hand by May. These were served by a 3.3 mile long running line which encircled Arncott hill, throwing off numerous spurs at various points for the storage sheds.

Problems regarding capacity and layout were delaying plans for the completion of the MT Yard and these were not finalised until 1943. Plans for a new signal box were drawn by the LMS to control the connections to the BMR. These resulted in the building of Bicester No.2 signal box.

Jimmy Higgins BEM

A small group of Army railwaymen who were ordered to operate the fledgling BMR in November 1941, included Lance Sergeant Jimmy Higgins. The group was detached from 154, Railway Operating Company, Royal Engineers and found the main line had reached Arncott with two sidings laid to serve the Royal Engineers Stores depot. A connection to the proposed site of the Arncott locomotive shed was also in position.

Jimmy Higgins, who had joined the Royal Engineers in 1939, proved to be a tireless and enthusiastic military railwayman. When traffic conditions warranted additional effort he often worked lengthy hours to ensure that marshalling and passage of freight trains was conducted in a highly efficient manner. Promotion to Company Quartmaster Sergeant followed, during which he took charge of one of the turns in the Sorting Sidings Control, among the busiest of centres on the system. He often led by example rather than direction and would frequently assist in the intensive 'loose' shunting operations which were such a feature in the operation of this busy, congested yard.

Mr Higgins received further promotion to Warrant Officer Class 1 and became the Regimental Sergeant Major of the Railway Operating and Maintenance Detachment where he kept a close eye on the running of the BMR and its personnel. After demobilisation from the Army in July 1947 he was appointed civilian Yard Master at Bicester and afterwards was promoted to Operating Officer at Kineton. He returned to the BMR in a similar capacity early in 1960 and in January 1962 took charge of the Shoeburyness Military Railway from where he retired on 8th February 1979.

After eight years as a serving soldier and 32 years civilian service on military railways he was awarded the BEM in the 1979 honours list. This was presented by Lord Strathcona, Ministry of State for Defence. Mr Higgins now lives in Mollington, Nr Banbury Oxfordshire.

'End of steel' at Piddington - the buffer stops are approximately 500 yards from the BR Princes Risborough - Banbury line.

E.R. Lawton

The labour force was augmented by additional Companies of the Pioneer Corps and the 3rd Non Combatant Corps (NCC) supervised by the Royal Engineers Construction Companies. The NCC, known as 'Conchies' by the personnel of the other military units, proved to be hard and tireless workers and their output of work surpassed all previous expectations. Although failing to quote specific dates a report written years later by their Officer Commanding the late Major G.W. Clarke MC included:

"I have stated that at Arncott we were regarded as 'Less than Nothing'. I should have added 'except by the Engineers'. It fell about that on a day when I was visiting the job at the Depot while Arncott was still a detachment, the Engineer Officer in charge came up to me and said 'I have been waiting to meet you, Sir. There is something I want to say about this job'. I braced myself against some trivial complaint and I could see Lt Andrews, our Works Officer, edging close and opening both his ears.

What this RE officer wanted to say was simple enough, 'I want to thank you' he said 'for the way your men are working on this job. They have got us out of a jam'.

This is the story he told: During the winter a single railway track had been built from Bicester station (sic) through the depot, past Ambrosden and finishing at Arncott. It joined on to the main railway line connecting Bicester and Oxford. But practically all constructional material had still to be delivered by road. These Oxfordshire roads in the old village areas are narrow and winding and to add to the confusion, they were now in course of being widened and re-surfaced. So the railway job at Bicester had been first priority on the Home Front for some time. But before a single line could be used to any great extent a marshalling yard, shunting yard or Triage, had to be constructed. Immediately it was ready for use the Supply people could supply a thousand tons of steel a day, but delivery could not start until it was finished. Progress had fallen hopelessly behind schedule. The War Office was gingering the RCE.

The RCE was gingering the Railway Construction Company. The Officer Commanding the Sappers was gingering his subs, who passed it on to their NCOs, who in turn were tearing strips off the men. 'And then this detachment of NCC arrived'. I want to remind you that this is the story told me by the Sapper Officer - not my story. What he probably did not know was that before these various sections of NCC - culled from the various detachments where each had a pride in work output bordering on fanaticism - left for Bicester the full situation was explained to then and the urgency of the job made clear. 'Let each man do his damndest - you have earned a reputation for good work - take it with you. From the first go off on this new job you can establish a reputation for working hard you will get away with murder!'

If for 'murder' some of them substituted '36 hour week-end Passes', obviously that was not my responsibility. It was the challenge of the job, not any thought of week-end passes that drew the best out of these - the first arrivals at Bicester. To return to the story of the Sapper Lieutenant, 'What made the situation worse for us', he continued 'is that our Company was due to march out in a fortnight's time - and to leave this job before 'Triage' was finished would be a terrible blow to the O.C., in fact to all of us. It would be equivalent to getting a black mark'. When these 'gluttons for work' arrived, men who knew every detail of the job, the situation changed. The O.C. took on a bet of

5s (25p) with the Colonel that 'Triage' would be finished before our time was up. The Colonel had taken on a guinea (£1.05) with his opposite number in the War Office. 'There is no doubt about it', he continued confidently, 'We are to finish in time'.

As he was telling the story I looked round. The third long siding was being constructed. Streams of ashes were pouring from a score of wagons. Sleepers were being unloaded practically on to their final resting place. Two squads were carrying heavy thirty-foot rails. The siding shivered, shook itself together, took shape and literally sprang to life before our very eyes; and what was of National import, steel girders, columns and roof trusses for the numerous huge store hangars that had not yet commenced were being unloaded and piled alongside. Hammers were flashing and the clang of steel meeting steel filled the air. Engines were slowly moving empties and shunting in full wagons, and on the two long sidings already completed, buffer stops were being constructed. Everywhere bustle and movement, purposeful and pointed, as every man knew his job. Every man seemed to be working with gusto! Though that is a word rarely applied to WORK! Well they did finish in time. Whereas the RE Company was due to march out on Saturday, 'Triage' as then planned, was finished on the Thursday evening. One thing of great importance is that everybody on the job knew they had beaten the clock. There was one sentence that this Sapper Officer said that intrigued me very much; for he had continued, 'Besides they have set a standard and our Sappers and other working parties are having to work twice as hard to keep up with them."

The 'Triage' referred to in the late Major Clarke's story was in fact the Up Siding which consisted of four roads, with buffer stops, each over 450 yards long. The Operating Officer requested its urgent construction and the Royal Engineers Construction Company and the 3rd Non Combatant Corps levelled, laid and ballasted the whole yard in less than one week.

Another part of Major Clarke's account included:

"Our period at Arncott - or in more general terms - our period at Bicester, falls naturally into two sections. First, the period of new construction. Second, the period when our work consisted solely of maintaining the existing track. With new construction to stimulate the mind and add variety to the daily drag, there is no excuse for any Company being other than efficient. Of the actual construction of the railway system little more need be said. In summer and in good weather the job was - of its type delightful; in winter, or during spells of wet weather - not so delightful. Then it was a case of gum boots or waders - a fight against mud and water that seemed to lay in each pocket. Obviously, deep extensive drainage was the key, not only to stability of the railway track but to the security of the depot as a whole. Oxford clay 'ates a'. quoting once again the oldest inhabitant whose farm and fields the depot had absorbed.

So, keeping up the Company tradition, we turned out our own special surveying and drainage team. It was so much easier to look through a level - if you know how to do it - than dig clay with a spade. 'Andy' (Lt B. le M.

Andrew, better known later as Garrison Welfare Officer, who arranged divorces or reconciliations with equal dexterity), organised this team in the first instance, had in his early days surveyed in the Yukon and enjoyed renewing his youth. The Engineers welcomed this surveying team with open arms, but alas could only supply a dumpy level at rare intervals. Dumpy levels were in short supply. So Captain Peach went up to London on short leave and from his headquarters at the 'Strand Palace' scoured Westminster in search of one. A needle in a hay stack; but by an amazing coincidence spotted one in an instrument maker's window - it had only been there four hours - walked in, wrote out a simple chit to the effect that the level was to be used on military work, signed it, paid for it there and then and brought the level back with him to Upper Arncott. He refused to have the money refunded; his reward being that the surveying team had constant work from then onwards. It was finally employed helping to set out the new buildings, roads, dry standings etc., which became necessary owing to the great increase in the capacity of the depot, which followed the arrival of the American troops anticipating the 'D' Day.

Later, a RE Major at a routine conference at the War Office, on being informed that surveying instruments were absolutely impossible to obtain, countered by asking how it is that a NCC Company could go to London and pick one up - just like that. But then he did not know the persuasive capacity of our Captain Peach, for of course it was not the NCC which accomplished the impossible - it was Captain Peach.

Clay or not clay, we got quite a lot of fun out of it - even the work of cutting drains or railway levels was lightened by keeping a look out for fossils in which the Oxford clay is particularly rich and which eventually formed quite an interesting collection."

Bolero

With the entry of the United States into WWII during December 1941 it became imperative to plan and construct facilities for the accommodation of American troops and their equipment. The Combined Chief of Staffs coined the codeword 'Bolero' to describe this operation.

So far as Bicester was concerned this involved additional storage and associated railway facilities. As a result, the so-called 'Bolero' layouts were designed for various sites within the depot, all to be served by the BMR. These consisted of a central feed rail track with several short spurs on either side, each spur feeding a group of five Romney sheds of corrugated iron sheeting which were also provided with road access. On the layout plan (see endpapers) these are depicted by dotted lines such as the layout serving 'B40' to 'B48'. The tracks serving the 'Bolero' sites were taken up and the sheds removed when they had served their purpose in the 1960s. The 'Bolero' scheme and the resultant extra rail traffic and shunting necessitated the provision of extra sidings in the planned MT Yard at Arncott. The latter eventually consisted of eight loops, in excess of 700 yards in length and a long shunting neck approximately 270 yards long.

Other additional work was the building of sidings and

coal stacking areas for the three large boiler houses at 'E14', 'B14' and 'HQ14' which supplied heat to the whole depot and another end-loading ramp at 'C6' that served the large REME workshops.

1943

On 16th January some 30¼ miles of track had been laid and seven locomotives were at work. There was little time for the track to become consolidated and it was immediately brought into use.

The Railway Operating and Maintenance Detachment of the Royal Engineers, the personnel of the BMR, consisted of 136 officers and men, all of which were busily engaged dealing with the ever increasing flows of traffic.

The facilities at No. 3 Camp, although adequate for wartime conditions, were somewhat basic. The Nissen huts were overcrowded with 'double decker' bunks with straw palliasses. No cupboards or lockers were provided for the 'other ranks' and personal kit was stored in redundant ammunition boxes. Toilet facilities consisted of a line of standard army latrine buckets surrounded by a corrugated iron screen. Ablutions were spartan and carried out on a bench in the open air with tin bowls and cold water. Showers were allocated, on a once per week basis, in a compound shared with the Pioneer Corps, a few hundred yards away. The conditions inside the Nissen huts used by train crews and operators working on lengthy shifts, can best be left to the imagination. Coal fired stoves in the centre of each hut were kept supplied by coal purloined from the locomotives, which kept the temperature and the unhygienic conditions at a high level.

The majority of the train crews and operators of the BMR had previously been employed by the civilian main line railways before enlistment into the RE. They were augmented by staff from various private industrial railway installations such as the former Stewarts & Lloyds steelworks at Corby and the famous York confectioners Rowntrees in York. One fireman, in civilian life, was the driver of a showman's traction engine and had a wealth of interesting stories about the perils of hauling caravans and fairground equipment around the country. Yet another fireman had previously driven a steam roller for a highway authority in Shropshire.

All had received basic military training with parade ground drill, weapon and courses in the use of explosives before posting to military railway units at home or overseas. The majority had also received railway technical training at Longmoor or the Melbourne Military Railway and had qualified in an army railway trade test. The drivers and firemen were issued, in addition to the usual army uniforms, with two-piece blue overalls complete with a dark blue peaked cap bearing the RE badge. Thus equipped, particularly in the 'blackout', they were often confused with civilian footplate screws. One in particular, during his leave periods, made fraudulent free rail journeys to his home by posing as a civilian locomotive driver.

The brakesmen/shunters, blockmen and permanent way staff wore standard army denims when engaged on rail duties. A common irreverent remark was often made that

The late Sapper Bernard Whicher showing the working uniform of a Royal Engineers locomotive driver (1944).

Authors' collection

if army denims fitted a person he was certain to be deformed! When the brakesmen/shunters worked as guards on the passenger services they invariably had blue peaked caps with an RE badge.

The merging of staff from the former 'Big Four' companies the LMS, LNER, GWR and Southern resulted in many heated arguments over the respective merits of their previous employers. Each maintaining their railway was the best and the other three were merely glorified tramways with inferior locomotives, equipment and methods of operation with useless staff. Any failure or delay was always explained by "what do you expect from ex-LMS men" or whatever company was being reviled. The names of locomotive parts were also deeply entrenched in this partisanship. The plates fitted inside the upper portions of the firehole directing cold air under the brick arch and protecting the tubeplate were variously called deflector, smoke or scoop plates, depending on which railway company the person concerned had been employed. This line of argument often led to raised tempers and a torrent of rather rich barrack room language.

In the early construction days all the storage shed spurs were linked to the appropriate running line at both ends, providing a through run for the construction trains. As the sheds were completed it was planned that the facing points would be removed, but the BMR operators put in a special plea for their retention in order to ease the shunting problems and supply of wagons to the sheds. As a result the two-way levers were replaced with one-way spring levers with treadles and this practice continued until February 1943 when removal was ordered. A few exceptions were made including the Transit Shed at 'E15' and at 'C9' where the possibility of shunting from both ends was considered essential to speedy working. At that time, where the facing points had been removed, it was decided the spur left beyond the shed should be equal in length to the wagon holding capacity of the shed. This remained the situation until the 1970s when, in order to save maintenance, the spurs were shortened to a point just clear of the level crossings over the roadways circling the sheds.

Still more sidings were requested in January to cater for the tremendous amount of armament equipment consigned to the Gun Park at Graven Hill.

No water column had been constructed near the locomotive shed at Arncott and reliance was still placed on the two-inch main and hose pipe. Repeated requests were made for the column to be built quickly to avoid the lengthy delays occasioned by engines taking water.

Plans for the final layout of the Arncott triangle were submitted at the end of January and included the proposed site of Arncott platform to which approval was given and construction commenced in February.

As supplies flooded into the Depot over the newly laid tracks more requests were made for additional sidings. These included a spur to serve a domestic coal dump at No.4 Camp, Arncott and at other storage sheds which had not been planned with rail access in mind.

In June passenger services were running from Arncott to the former Bell's siding re-named Langford Farm. No engine run-round loop had been built at the latter point and the engines of incoming trains had to propel the empty coaches back into Exchange Sidings in order to run round. The cost of the proposed loop was estimated to be £950 and a month later approval was given for this to be constructed.

Delays to construction trains were reported in mid-1943, created by the run down condition of the internal freight rolling stock, which had been used heavily, carrying track materials, and were now in need of extensive repairs.

The War Office sent an order to the LMS for 1,300 tons of ashes for track maintenance purposes. The ash was to be supplied at the rate of 100 tons per week at a cost of 5s 10d (29p) per ton delivered.

Although the actual date was not recorded, towards the middle of the year the main line had reached Piddington, 5¾ of a mile from Bicester and terminated at buffer stops some five hundred yards from the Great Western, Princes Risborough-Banbury line, to which it was intended to connect. This was never carried out and instead military passengers were accommodated at a six-coach length single platform bearing Piddington name boards. A large camp nearby housed several units of the Auxiliary Territorial Service (the womens' forces).

Last minute plans to extend the line from Langford Farm to a point near the LMS at Bicester was surveyed by the 602 Railway Construction Company, Royal Engineers in November 1944, but like the connection to the GWR line at Piddington, this was not built and passengers continued on foot to and from the two main line stations.

At the end of the year the BMR system, comprising some 47½ miles of track and 234 turnouts was largely complete. The control of the remaining work had been handed over by Railway Construction Engineer 5 (Southern) to RCE 4 (South Eastern) on 17th February.

Four months later, 956 Railway Survey Company RE replaced 165 Company. 600 Railway Construction Company RE finally left the BMR on 18th November when all responsibility for track maintenance was taken over by the Bicester Railway Operating and Maintenance Detachment.

An inspection by a senior Royal Engineering Officer on 30th December revealed that in the hurried construction period insufficient attention had been given to drainage. The subsoil of heavy clay was of such a nature that efficient drainage was of first priority. Labour had to be diverted from track maintenance to the building of more outlets from the trackbed and the digging of additional drainage ditches. A further six months heavy work was needed to complete the task, which was accomplished without serious interference to the intensive rail services.

It is nevertheless a credit to the builders that the barely consolidated track immediately took the strain of heavy and continuous flows of vital traffic needed by a nation at war.

Without the aid of mechanised track laying equipment the Corps of Royal Engineers, Royal Pioneer Corps, Royal Corps of Signals, the 3rd Non Combatant Corps and the Italian prisoners of war built a railway network which did its arduous job so well.

2

Controlling the Line

The arrival of the first two locomotives in 1941 preceded any form of traffic control. It was a generally agreed procedure that one locomotive would work at the Arncott end of the system and the other in the Exchange and Sorting Siding area. When the first locomotive departed for Arncott, no further movements were made through the single main line section until the Arncott engine returned to the Bicester end, and proceeded at caution through the principal sidings area. This was a similar arrangement to that practised on early American railroads, often described as operating on "smoke orders" ie watching for the exhaust of other trains and taking timely action.

The Regulator System

The rapid build up of traffic and the arrival of additional engines made a traffic control system essential and Lt (later Major) W.H. Mounsey devised the 'Regulator' system. This required the running lines to be divided into 'block' sections of varying lengths which, during normal circumstances, only one train was allowed to occupy at any one time. A telephone point (TP) was provided at the entrance to each section from which the train crews obtained permission to proceed from a control or regulator point.

Each locomotive was allocated a target number carried on a metal disc on the front and rear lamp brackets. On

Major William Henry Mounsey RE
Almost from the date when the main line had reached Lower Arncott one of the best-known key figures, the first commissioned officer William Henry Mounsey, more commonly known as Bill Mounsey, arrived at Bicester. He took command of a small detachment of railway troops from 154 Railway Operating Company, RE. This detachment consisted of one Lance Sergeant, a Traffic Operator, three RED (railway engine drivers), three firemen (locomotive) and six brakesmen/shunters.

He had commenced his railway civilian career with the Great Western Railway at James Street, Liverpool, now an underground station on the electrified 'Merseyrail' (Wirral Line) network. He was just of sufficient age to serve two years in he Royal Navy, from 1917 to the end of the First World War in 1918.

He returned to the GWR and for a time served as a passenger train guard at the now closed Woodside station, Birkenhead. He later became a traffic inspector and also enlisted in the Supplementary Reserve with 154 Railway Operating Company, RE, which was largely composed of former GWR staff.

At the outbreak of WWII he was called for full time service with the 154 Railway Operating Company, first on the Longmoor Military Railway and then on armoured trains in the Canterbury and Tonbridge areas of Kent. At the latter place he was commissioned and promoted to Lieutenant. He was posted to Bicester to take charge of the small band of military railway personnel engaged on running the partially completed system.

Lieutenant Mounsey developed the 'Regulator' system of traffic control and endeavoured unsuccessfully, to implement two other improved signalling projects. In addition to being heavily involved in administering the rapidly growing railway and the increasing number of trains he encouraged the 'Dig for Victory' campaign, utilising all the spare areas of land around the huts at No.3. Camp, Arncott. So successfully was this carried out that, as well as providing a source of fresh vegetables, the flower display won the Army's Southern Area Garden Competition in July 1945.

All his energy and enthusiasm were directed to the problems of running the extremely busy BMR. It became his personal pride to ensure the great volume of wartime traffics were dealt with expeditiously. His drive and initiative resulted in the BMR being widely known as 'Bill Mounsey's Railway'.

Major Mounsey returned to railway service in Liverpool at the end of hostilities, joining the LMS, later BR. He passed away at the age of 87 in Mill Lane Hospital, Wallasey, Merseyside on 10th October 1986.

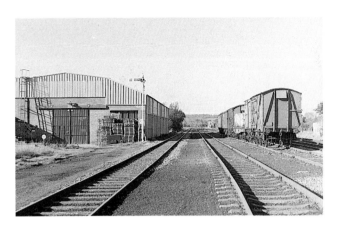

The main line to Bicester with Arncott Yard on the right and 'C9' storage shed to the left, October 1987. 'B' blockpost is in the far distance.

E.R. Lawton

arrival at a TP the brakesman/shunter, or fireman in the case of a light engine, announced the target number of his train, the number of the TP from which he was calling and requested authority for the next move, usually to proceed into the next section. According to the traffic position the regulator then granted or refused permission to proceed. The train crew member repeated the message to ensure it had been understood correctly.

During slack periods when sections were not occupied, trains could be instructed to pass several TPs and run to the next section in rear of an occupied block. There were two Regulated areas, the first covering A, B and C sites, called Arncott Regulator, from an Office in Arncott Yard, the second covering Exchange Yard, D & E Sites and called Control (in order to avoid any telephonic confusion). Metal discs, 3 in in diameter, bearing the corresponding target numbers were displayed on line diagram boards in each on the control points. The discs were hung on pegs and moved to indicate the position of trains. By this basically simple method the movement of trains on the running lines serving the various sub-depots was plotted, traffic expedited and accidents prevented. On arrival back in the Arncott locomotive shed the target disc was removed from the running line diagram and placed in an 'On Shed' position. The Regulator system worked well in practice and few accidents occurred from failure of this operating method despite blackout conditions, very heavy flows of traffic, hand-operated points and loose coupled freight trains interspersed with passenger trains.

The door of each telephone box was marked with its appropriate number, while a round hole in the upper part of the door enabled the light from an oil lamp mounted on the rear panel, to give an indication of its location to approaching trains during the hours of darkness. The hand-worked point levers were also fitted with discs showing the number of the storage shed, siding or spur served.

The Regulator system controlled all the running lines with the exception of the two-mile single tracked main line from Arncott Yard to the junction of Bicester Sorting Sidings.

Flagboard Signalling

At the time military railway working was governed by the Military Rulebook (MRRB) which was based on the, then, Railway Clearing House rules, but amended to take note of the requirements of military working. For example it allowed the possibility of having to run railways where the signalling system had been destroyed by enemy action and when there was neither time nor equipment to replace the installations. With this in mind a system was devised whereby the entrance to a block section was controlled by a Station Limit Board and Flagboard (Figs 1 & 2) which could be the equivalent of outer and inner home signals.

The Station Limit Board was situated 200/300 yards in advance of the Flagboard which displayed two metal flags about two feet square: one immediately above the other. One side was painted red and the other green. When two green flags were displayed this indicated the line was clear through the section. If the top flag was red and the lower grccn, trains could proceed past the Station Limit Board and stop at the Flagboard which was situated adjacent to the blockpost. If both flags were displayed red, trains stopped at the Station Limit Board. The display of only one red flag also indicated that drivers must stop at the Station Limit Board. At night the flags were replaced by oil handlamps, identical to those used by brakes-

The Telephone Point (TP) No. 6 at the junction of the South Running Line and the main track to Piddington. Locomotives leaving the shed obtained permission to proceed from this TP. The round hole in the door enabled a beam of light from an oil lamp to illuminate the position of the TP at night. This scene, taken in June 1943, shows the improved condition of the permanent way.

Major W.H. Mounsey

View of 'up' home signals at 'A' blockpost. Connection to the right leads to the Sorting Sidings.

Courtesy of Bucks & Herts Newspapers Ltd

men/shunters mounted on wooden brackets fitted behind the Flagboards, and displayed the required aspects through round holes in the flagboard.

Telephone and Ticket working

Permission to proceed was obtained by the blockman from his colleague at the other end of the section in accordance with Rule 26 in the MRRB (1938). This took the form of a verbal request by telephone, "This is 'B' blockpost, is line clear for passenger/freight/light engine etc to proceed from 'B' to 'A'?" If the section was clear this was acknowledged by the message "Line is clear, etc" or "No, the line is blocked". If clearance was obtained the blockman then completed a white coloured 'Line Clear' ticket (Fig. 3) handing this in a pouch and hoop to the engine crew. If the train was double headed or banked the rearmost engine took possession of the ticket. If there was a need to caution a driver in the event of a temporary speed restriction or other engineering work, an orange coloured 'Caution Ticket' (Fig. 4) was issued showing the reason for the caution. In certain cases where an obstruction was known or suspected, such as enemy action or heavy engineering work necessitating the use of lineside

machinery, a red 'Special Caution' ticket (Fig. 5) was issued, bringing to the driver's attention that extra vigilance was called for and that he should be prepared to stop clear of any obstruction. The ticket was surrendered to the blockman at the other end of the section who then informed his opposite number that the train had arrived. Rule 43(d) instructed the driver to reduce speed to 10 mph when exchanging ticket carriers.

Flagboard signalling, together with telephone and ticket working, as described, was employed on the heavily-used single two-mile stretch of line between Arncott Yard and the south end of the Sorting Sidings.

Small, ground level brick blockposts with 'ARP' type concrete roofs were built at each end of this section. No names were ever allocated to these, which have been known throughout the entire history of the system as 'A' and 'B' blockposts. 'A' was located at the junction of the Sorting Sidings and the 'up' and 'down' running lines at Bicester, while 'B' blockpost controlled the junction of the main line to Arncott and Piddington, the connection to the North Running Line and the branch to Motor Transport (MT) Sidings.

Trains running from the Bicester direction approaching 'B' blockpost were faced with three sets of flags, side by side, showing which route was set. The left was the running line to Arncott and Piddington, the centre flags to the North Running Line and the right to MT Sidings.

Freight trains running towards Bicester after leaving 'A' blockpost joined the double tracked running line to Exchange Sidings, usually stopping alongside the Sorting Sidings control office for further instructions. Often, outward bound freights were re-marshalled according to destination in the Up Sidings before transfer to Exchange and the civilian railways.

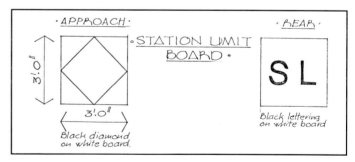

Fig 1 Station Limit Board.

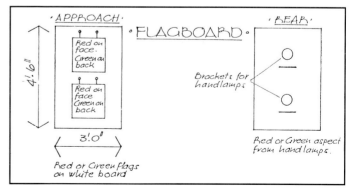

Fig 2 Flagboard.

23

Passenger trains bound for Langford Farm, Bicester or Oxford were reported by telephone from the Sorting Sidings control to Exchange Yard, the entrance to which was controlled by a short arm upper quadrant semaphore signal, operated by a ground frame adjacent to the yard foreman's office at the Oxford end of the yard. This semaphore also protected any movement out of Exchange Sidings to the 'down' LMS line. All trains leaving Exchange Sidings for the Bicester and Bletchley direction were controlled by Bicester No.2 signal box (see Chapter 6) and an upper quadrant semaphore at the Bicester end of the yard protected the connection.

Proposed New Signalling Schemes

Ever increasing traffic, both conveying military stores, constructional material and additional passengers, placed further demands on the new railway. It was inevitable, therefore, that thoughts would be given to improved, more sophisticated methods of signalling.

Early in 1943 a plan was proposed to provide an electro-mechanical installation between Piddington Branch Junction and Arncott Yard. This scheme included two aspects (100 volt) colour light signals controlled from a new nine-lever mechanically interlocked ground frame. The latter to be constructed on the site of the existing TP (No.3) at Piddington Branch Junction. At this stage consideration was still being given to the proposed connection with the Great Western line between Princes Risborough and Banbury, as one of the advantages claimed for the new scheme was that "it improves main junction which will be necessary when connection with the Great Western Railway is made".

The estimated cost of the project makes interesting reading today:

"Scheme using two aspect colour light signals (as shown on the plan, page 27) with simple electrical detection on the point shown by "X" and using a nine-lever mechanically interlocked ground frame at "A", to

Looking in the 'down' direction with 'A' blockpost on the right. The building to the left is built on the site of the original Sorting Sidings control. To the right is situated the Up Sidings.

E.R. Lawton

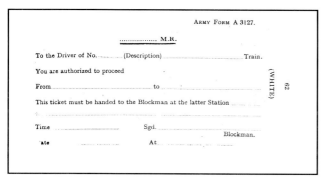

Fig 3 White - Line Clear ticket.

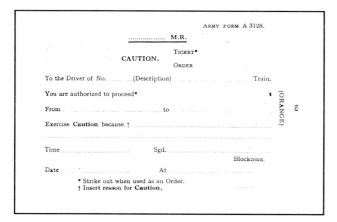

Fig 4 Orange - Caution ticket.

Fig 5 Red - Special Caution ticket.

control all the signals and points marked "B":

Equipment	Estimated cost
	£
7 M.E. type signals @ £10 each.	70
3 point detectors type CC4 @ £4 each.	12
7 signal lever controllers @ £2 each.	14
1 nine-lever ground frame, mechanically worked.	120
7 relays and rectifiers, type S2 @ £5 each.	35
1 Westinghouse transformer 220-110 volts.	5
1 Westinghouse transformer 110-112 volts.	5
100 terminals.	5
20 fuses and boxes.	2
30,000 ft 1061 Ancolite cable.	180
Total cost of materials:	£448

The labour was to have been supplied by the Royal Engineers and Royal Corps of Signals. The project was, however, never implemented and the frequent freight and passenger trains over this section of the line continued to be controlled by the 'Regulator' system based in Arncott Yard.

In March 1945 consideration was again given to improving operating methods and another re-signalling plan was discussed, covering the area of line from 'A' blockpost to Exchange Sidings together with the exits and entries to the Sorting and Up Sidings.

The plan involved construction of a new signal box 350 yards in the 'up' direction from the existing 'A' blockpost and sited between the Sorting Sidings and the 'down' main running line. The new installation was to be equipped with a 36-lever (three spare) mechanically interlocked frame controlling all movements on the running lines with ground discs at the connections with the Sorting and Up Sidings. Presumably telephone and ticket working was to be continued through the single line to 'B' blockpost as no mention was made of this on the plan.

The plan shown on page 27 is drawn from the sole

The 'down' home signals at 'B' blockpost.

M.W. Sackett

25

The fireman of a 'down' freight hands over the hoop carrying the 'Line Clear' ticket to the blockman at 'B' blockpost. The line on the left is the main running line to Arncott and Piddington. The North Running line is straight ahead and the track to the MT Yard curves to the right.

Authors' collection

where he was able to fulfill the pipedreams of his predecessors by designing and installing a semaphore signalling project to replace the flagboards and a miniature electric token system, taking over from the telephone and ticket method.

One of the frames, with fourteen levers, was installed at 'A' blockpost. Unlike the 1945 scheme it was considered only necessary to control the exit from the Sorting Sidings to the single main line and the connection to the 'up' and 'down' running lines to Exchange. The remaining frame was fitted with sixteen levers and was installed at 'B' blockpost. Both frames had three channels for the locking bars.

In the 'down' direction the single line at this point lead into four possible routes:

(a) Entrance to Arncott Yard.
(b) Main line to Arncott and Piddington.
(c) Northern Running Line.
(d) MT Yard.

To give a clear passage to freight trains it was desired to control the Arncott Yard points from the frame. It was, however, not possible within the limitations of the frame to accomplish this with complete interlocking. Thus a compromise had to be made. Two home signals were erected, one controlling the main running line and the other covering entry to Arncott Yard, Northern Running Line and the MT Yard. By this means it proved possible to utilise 'B' blockpost as an extension of the 'Regulator' office and, if necessary, a train could be brought to a stop at the home signals and precise instructions regarding destination, marshalling details etc., to be passed to the train crew.

A starting signal was also installed on the Northern Running Line enabling the blockman to shunt a train clear of the main line, and to bring it back when the main was clear.

surviving records which were probably preliminary drawing produced to obtain rough estimates of the cost. Obviously there would have been problems for the blockman to issue and collect tickets for trains departing or arriving in the Sorting Sidings owing to the distance between the blockpost and the connection to the yard.

For the first time on the BMR semaphore distants and detonator laying machines were envisaged with a fixed 'up' distant on the approaches to Exchange Sidings. Although evidence exists the scheme was submitted to No. 1 Railway (Home) Group Headquarters for financial authority, nothing further was heard and the existing control methods continued in use for a further four years.

By 1947, one of the co-authors, Major M.W. Sackett, then Operating Officer of the BMR, heard of the forthcoming closure and projected disposal of the military railway at Cairnyran port, near Stranraer and consequently he sought and obtained permission to lay claim to the ground frames at Luffnol North and South blockposts. This equipment, together with a quantity of signals, posts, ladders and point rodding was transferred to Bicester,

The interior of the second 'B' blockpost which was built in 1948, containing the 16-lever interlocking frame transferred from the Cairnryan Military Railway. The civilian blockman is Bert Ebbsworth.

Authors' collection

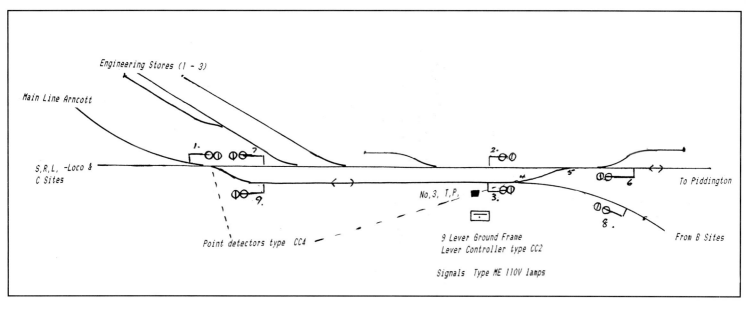

Proposed Signalling - Arncott 1943

Owing to the shortage of levers, arrangements were made for the 'up' ground signals controlling the exit from the Yard lines Nos 1 and 2 to be operated from one lever, the appropriate disc coming clear according to the setting of the points.

Only one spare telephone wire was available to link the electric token instruments and, due to the financial restraints, it was not possible to install a further line. An earth return was the only feasible alternative, and this, at first, proved a failure. A solution was eventually found by sinking copper firebox stays some 10 ft into the ground and this has worked satisfactorily ever since.

The existing 1942 ground level blockposts were demolished and replaced by larger structures, also on ground level, to accommodate the 'new' frames. The structures were fitted with large windows to facilitate observance of train movements and at the beginning of 1949 the familiar flagboards, a feature of the BMR since its inception, vanished forever.

The 'Regulator' system remained to control the rest of the running lines, the only change being replacement of the discs bearing target numbers by magnetic type discs and deletion from the line diagram board of several spurs which had been removed.

Further Changes

In the early 1970s money became available to re-build or improve some of the depot buildings and amenities, many of which were built in the war years and were either worn out or outdated. The Operating Department of the BMR requested new blockposts to replace the 1948 ground level structures at 'A' and 'B' which were totally lacking in staff facilities. The proposals included larger, higher buildings similar to those used by the main line civilian railways, with washing, toilet and cooking facilities. The principal problem concerned the interlocking frames which could not be converted to the vertical pull required by a frame sited on a higher level.

Accordingly, the Westinghouse Brake & Signal Co. Ltd were asked to design new frames with similar or improved

'B' blockpost in January 1988. The track on the left leads to MT Yard, centre route to North Running Line with the main line to Arncott and Piddington on the extreme right. View taken looking towards Ambrosden.

Courtesy of Bucks & Herts Newspapers Ltd

27

'B' blockpost looking towards Ambrosden at the commencement of the two mile single-line block section, on a very wet Wednesday, 5th April 1989.

Peter Nicholson

interlocking. With the advent of highly sophisticated methods of signalling it appeared the Company had not designed or constructed a new mechanical frame for many years, and were only too eager to undertake a task as a nostalgic labour of love! When completed, the job was highly regarded by the BMR authorities.

Westinghouse Signals Ltd, a subsidiary of the Westinghouse Brake & Signal Co. Ltd of Chippenham, Wiltshire, installed the Type A3d locking frames in May 1978. A nine-lever frame was built at 'A' blockpost and a similar type with sixteen levers at 'B'. The 'S' type,

Pattern 'C' electric token instruments supplied by the Railway Signal Co. Ltd of Fazackerley, Liverpool for the Cairnryan Military Railway were retained. The blockposts are also linked by telephones, with other lines giving access to the yard Foremen's offices and the level crossing keeper at Ambrosden.

In 1951, following difficulties with shunting at the storage sheds together with staffing problems, the night shift was discontinued. For several years the system operated with two turns of duty until falling traffic levels reduced the requirements and a single shift sufficed. The blockposts are now manned from 07.30 to 16.15hrs (15.00 on Fridays).

The Control and Regulator systems utilising target numbers at the Sorting Sidings and Arncott were discontinued in 1961. Traffic control at each end of the system is now supervised by Yard Foremen at Graven Hill and Arncott via the Telephone Points. Arrangements are also

The Arncott Regulator building, looking towards 'B' blockpost in October 1987. The ground frame controls the points at the junction of the main running line and the West Curve. The original Regulator cabin stood on the opposite side of the main line.

E.R. Lawton

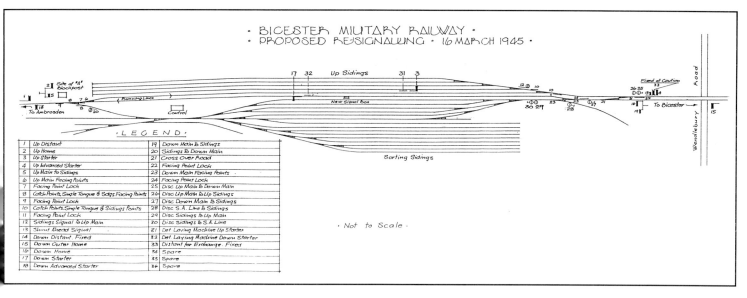

· BICESTER MILITARY RAILWAY ·
· PROPOSED RE-SIGNALLING · 16 MARCH 1945 ·

· Not to Scale ·

	·LEGEND·		
1	Up Distant	19	Down Main to Sidings
2	Up Home	20	Sidings to Down Main
3	Up Starter	21	Cross Over Road
4	Up Advanced Starter	22	Facing Point Lock
5	Up Main to Sidings	23	Down Main Facing Points
6	Up Main Facing Points	24	Facing Point Lock
7	Facing Point Lock	25	Disc Up Main to Down Main
8	Catch Points, Single Tongue & Sdgs. Facing Points	26	Disc Up Main to Up Sidings
9	Facing Point Lock	27	Disc Down Main to Sidings
10	Catch Points, Single Tongue & Sidings Points	28	Disc S.A. Line to Sidings
11	Facing Point Lock	29	Disc Sidings to Up Main
12	Sidings Signal to Up Main	30	Disc Sidings to S.A. Line
13	Shunt Ahead Signal	31	Det. Laying Machine Up Starter
14	Down Distant, Fixed	32	Det. Laying Machine Down Starter
15	Down Outer Home	33	Distant for Exchange. Fixed
16	Down Home	34	Spare
17	Down Starter	35	Spare
18	Down Advanced Starter	36	Spare

Proposed Re-Signalling - Bicester Military Railway 16th March 1945.

in force whereby one locomotive can operate over the entire system when all the Yard Foreman's offices and blockposts are closed.

In 1978 the administration centre, which had previously been sited at Lower Arncott, was replaced by a new complex at Graven Hill overlooking the Sorting Sidings.

This new headquarters' building was officially opened on 1st March 1978 by Major General P.H. Benson CBE, Director General of Transportation. The brick-built building houses the Depot Railway Officer, Yard Foreman and administrative staff with messroom and toilet facilities for train and yard personnel.

At the beginning of 1990, concurrent with the re-laying of track in the single-line section between blockposts 'A' and 'B', two Tyer No. 7 electric key token instruments were installed in the blockposts. These included a remote operation facility for use when one of the blockposts was switched out.

Operating Instructions

Regulations for the operation of the BMR and other military railways were, from the outset, contained in the Military Railways Rulebook published by His Majesty's Stationary Office in 1938, priced 4d (1½p). This was supplemented by local instructions, which at Bicester, have been re-written three times. On each occasion the volume was reduced to be compatible with the staff situation and unnecessary orders and instructions deleted. No copy of the original 1942 instructions appears to have survived. The 1938 Rulebook consisted of 121 pages which included regulations for operation, observance of signals, block working, station work, shunting, duties of engine and train crews, miscellaneous and emergency procedures.

The Rulebook was based on the principles embodied in the (then) Railway Clearing House book used by the civilian railways, although the numbers of the various rules differed in each case. For example, the well-known Rule 55 (Railway Clearing House) which laid down the procedures to be adopted when trains were detained at stop signals, became Rule 23 in the Military Rule Book. Many of the block signal codes and hand signals in the

The Railway Headquarters building at Graven Hill.

E.R. Lawton

The BR (Western Region)-type level crossing gates still in use at White Cross Green in October 1987.

E.R. Lawton

military version were identical to those used in the RCH publication. Protection of trains, in the event of breakdown or accident, by use of detonators differed from civilian practice as only one detonator was placed 440 yards, and two (twelve yards apart) 880 yards from the obstruction. Under the civilian rules then in force, one detonator was required at ¼ mile, one at ½ mile and three ten yards apart, at ¾ of a mile from the disabled train. This difference of course, took into account the higher speeds of trains on the main line civilian systems.

Instructions applying to locomotive head lamp codes (Rule 82 in the military version) were more basic and required only a white lamp to be placed on the leading bracket, the position of which was not specified. This contrasted with the civilian method of utilising the position of headlamps to denote the type of train being worked, ie one lamp over each buffer describing an express passenger train. BMR trains traversing civilian metals carried headlamps in accordance with the RCH practice. In such instances the military engine and train crews were obliged to be familiar with both sets of rules.

The 1938 Military Railways Rulebook, apart from a few minor amendments, remained in force throughout the whole of WWII and beyond. By the late 1960s and early 1970s some of the instructions had become outdated and no longer served any real purpose. With the change to civilian personnel transfers of staff between military railways seldom occurred. To take but one example there was little point in teaching and testing, every six months, the staff on all military railways the principles of double line block working, when in 38 instances there were only single line block sections.

Consequently, during this period, pressure was growing for a revision of the Rules and the idea of a Ministry of Defence Rulebook was born. The regulations in the new documents would be applicable to all UK military railway personnel irrespective of their location. These would be supplemented by a new set of Local Railway Instructions applicable only to specific locations. For the greater proportion of the smaller railway systems these would be very simple and consist only of some five to six rules covering, for example, maximum train loading, arrangements for the exchange of traffic with BR and important local telephone numbers etc. In the case of the larger railways these instructions would be rather more detailed describing such arrangements as the 'Regulator' system and enumerating the telephone control points. So far as the BMR was concerned, provision was made for single line block working, operation of public level crossings and so on.

The lifting barriers at Arncott Main level crossing. October 1987.

E.R. Lawton

30

The gates at Ambrosden level crossing are closed behind MOD No. 275 *Sapper* as it proceeds, light engine, to Arncott. The curved platform and twin-lever ground frame controlling the gate semaphores are clearly visible on 5th April 1989.

Peter Nicholson

The new publication, known as the General Railway Rules, was issued on 1st July 1973 together with the appropriate Local Railway Working Rules in a pocket-sized loose leaf format for the easier introduction of any further amendments.

All these Rules were produced in liaison with the Department of Transport, Railway Inspectorate whose advice and comment was invaluable. With the passing of the Health and Safety Work Act 1974 the Railway Inspectorate assumed the same responsibilities for MoD railways, as they already had for BR.

The 'Regulator' system, as used on the BMR created difficulties when adopted by other military railways, especially those at ammunition depots where numerous closely spaced TPs were installed. Thoughts were then given to using a system of radio control instead of telephones, but retaining Regulator points in the same position as the previous TPs to mark the entry to the various block sections.

Experiments were carried out at Kineton in 1947 but had to be abandoned because of interference with radio signals to aircraft from a local Royal Air Force station. In the 1960s fresh experiments were carried out on the BMR and later at Bramley, using a variety of systems. These were somewhat unsuccessful owing to 'blind' spots and difficulties of overcoming noise from the locomotives. Eventually equipment used by the Royal Navy and manufactured by Messrs Storno was tried and found to be successful. This method was installed at the three major ammunition depots and a new supplement to the General Railway Rules was compiled. The radios supplanted the previous telephones but the same Regulator Points, previously TPs, continue to be used in exactly the same way. This obviated the need for a member of the train crew to dismount and call the Regulator. In practice the system was found to have advantages in operation not considered at the time of introduction. Train crews are now acquainted with the location of other train movements and their direction of travel, and fresh orders can be given immediately as a result of unexpected traffic demands.

Level Crossings

The BMR, with just under fifty miles of track, boasted something like 180 level crossings, possibly a greater number than any other railway system of comparable length. Of course many of these were service roads crossing tracks serving storage sheds. Road and rail vehicles use the same shed door to gain entrance, thereby posing a problem to operators and train crews alike.

During the war years with peak traffics being worked,

White Cross Green level crossing keeper's cabin. When the line was built no gates were provided and trains were hand signalled over the road.

E.R. Lawton

the crossing problem was not too acute. Private cars were a rarity and the drivers of army lorries were generally well acquainted with the layout of the Depot and its frequent rail services. Privately run buses were not introduced until 1944 and road traffic on the whole was much lighter than today.

From the completion of the railway there were crossings over public roads at Piddington (Thame-Bicester road), White Cross Green (Arncott-Murcott road), Arncott South and Main (Ambrosden-Arncott road) and Ambrosden (Ambrosden-Merton road). Three level crossings also exist over army roads external to the Depot proper at Patrick Haugh road in Arncott and Pioneer and Westacott roads in the Graven Hill area. Because of the increasing use of these roads by public vehicles it was decided in 1946, for railway rule purpose, to treat these as public crossings.

Initially no gates whatsoever were provided but whenever possible, crossing keepers armed with flags and lamps, were on duty at Piddington, Arncott and Ambrosden. By means of hand signals and prolonged whistles from approaching trains road traffic was halted to allow the frequent trains to pass. When the crossings were not manned, train crews were instructed to stop and exhibit red flags or lamps to road users before proceeding (see Chapter 3).

Owing to the tremendous number of crossings inside the perimeter fences of the various sub-depots rail traffic was accorded priority, and notice boards at depot entrances warned road users of this fact and the necessity of ascertaining the tracks were clear before crossing. It was a continuing problem and many accidents occurred. Additional warnings were put up at the approaches to crossings and eventually 'St Andrews Crosses' were installed at each site.

During the war years very little could be done to alleviate the crossing problem, all the resources of staff and materials were directed at the vital task of moving immense quantities of military supplies and delays could not be tolerated.

When peace descended, a different climate prevailed, road traffic was on the increase, private cars began to appear, there was no longer the urgency of moving Army freight and the level crossing situation became the subject of serious complaints from local councillors, MPs and parliamentary questions. In 1947 the Royal Electrical and Mechanical Engineers were requested to fabricate experimental gates using mild steel angle to protect Piddington

'A' Cabin

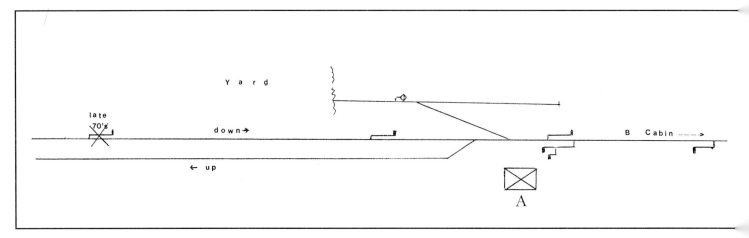

The Industrial Railway Society's special train crosses Arncott Main in April 1972. Looking towards Arncott Yard the lifting barriers and colour light signals, together with the crossing keeper's cabin are shown.

G.P. Roberts

crossing. This was done and the gates were installed to be operated manually by a keeper. A War Office working party examined them, pronounced the arrangements satisfactory and ordained that four more sets should be produced for the remaining crossings. Unfortunately, failure of communication resulted in the additional four sets of gates being manufactured to exactly the same design and length. When the Arncott gates were fitted, the road being much wider, the gates failed to meet! Extension arms were quickly welded on but the extra weight caused the gates to sag and the latches became inoperable. The gates would often swing, and on one occasion when this occurred during the night, the extension piece struck the windscreen of an approaching car, passed through the vehicle and out of the rear window. Fortunately no one was hurt but the incident led to further criticism and provided the spur needed to release funds for the provision of standard railway-designed crossing gates. The Western Region of British Railways undertook the design, construction and installation of five sets of gates covering all the public roads. There was an immediate improvement in both road and rail behaviour to everyone's satisfaction.

In 1971 a motor transport garage was constructed for the Royal Army Ordnance Corps on the North side of the South Running Line in 'C' sites, the entrance road creating a new level crossing adjacent to 'C9' storage shed. Since a serious hazard had been created by the fact that all the road vehicles allocated to the depot would be using the new crossing, an automatic signal system operated by track trips was installed. The colour light signals were of the two-aspect type accompanied by a loud sounding bell. The South Running Line served one side of many of the 'C' site sheds and with the new crossing being only two hundred yards from 'B' blockpost, there was little problem in regulating the speed of trains to 10 mph, and to then set the track trips to provide an eight-second warning before a train arrived at the crossing.

The BR, Western Region, type gates at the public level crossings had served their purpose well but began to deteriorate and proved increasingly difficult to repair. Eventually the BMR authorities were informed that it was no longer possible to replace the long gate timbers, consequently authority was given to install electrically operated lifting barriers at two principal crossings, namely Arncott Main and Piddington. With the cessation of the four-times daily passenger trains conveying the WRAC personnel from Piddington to 'C2' platform, there was little justification for the retention of that part of the South Running Line, from the Workshop's area to the junction with the West Curve and accordingly, the level crossing was abolished. Sufficient timber was, however, found to maintain White Cross Green which retained its BR type gates.

The planning of the proposed electrically-operated barriers was carried out in close co-operation with the Railway Inspectorate of the Department of Transport which also co-ordinated with the local authorities. The crossings are equipped with loud sounding bells, amber and red 'wig wag' signals for the road users with red and green colour light signals for the railway. The barriers and associated signals are timed to operate exactly as those on British Rail but are operated by a five-position switch located in the crossing keeper's cabin. The central position (No. 1) raises the barriers, puts the railway signals to red and turns off road signals. Position Nos 2 and 3 on one side operate in respect of 'down' movements with Nos 4 and 5 for the 'up' movements. The switch positions operate as follows:

Position 1	Barriers raised, rail signals at red.
Position 2	In sequence - amber signal, red 'wig wag' signals and loud sounding bell, lowering of the nearside barriers in either direction followed by the offside barriers.
Position 3	Rail signal in 'down' direction to green.
Position 4	As for position 2.
Position 5	Rail signal in 'up' direction to green.

In the special case of Arncott, due to its proximity to the yard and the junction with the West Curve the Yard Foreman has a master switch controlling the aspect of the signals at Positions Nos 3 and 5. Owing to the difficult sighting of the crossing by train crews approaching in the 'up' direction, a repeater signal is provided at the south end of Arncott platform.

The barriers were installed on 25th February 1972 and inspected by Major Peter M. Olver, Inspecting Officer for

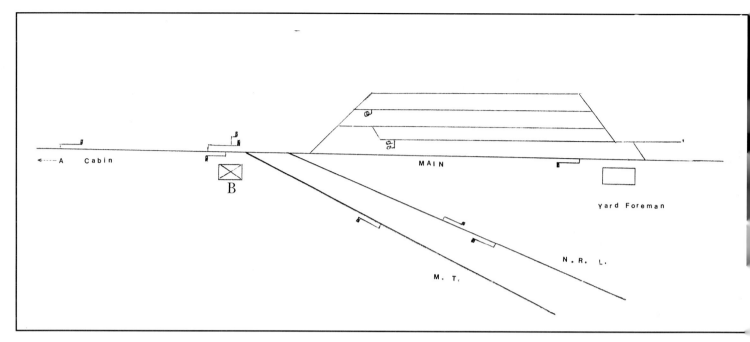

the Department of Transport. Major Olver approved the installations on 27th March 1972.

The level crossing over the Ambrosden-Merton road had always proved a problem, being in the centre of the single line controlled by 'A' and 'B' blockposts. Additionally, the line from Graven Hill is a long down gradient ending with a 1 in 100 at the crossing, which is blind to train drivers. The problems of wartime crews is mentioned in another chapter. At the same time as the installations of semaphore signals at 'A' and 'B' block-posts, stop signals were also erected either side of the Ambrosen crossing, operated by the crossing keeper from a ground frame situated outside his cabin. The working instructions provided that 'line clear' would not be given until the crossing keeper had confirmed that the gates were open. This caused difficulties with the public because it was found that Yard Foremen, particularly at Graven Hill, were asking the blockman to send a train through the section, whilst the train was still being marshalled, with the result of a ten or more minutes' hold up of traffic. The rules were changed to say, that with the exception of railcars, 'line clear' would not be requested by blockmen until the train was approaching or at a stand at his blockpost.

3

The System at Work

Freight – World War II

When the railway was first planned it was estimated that two hundred wagons would be received, and a similar number despatched each day. In practice the maximum number of wagons handled greatly exceeded these figures and over double the number of estimated wagon loads were handled on peak days. Indeed the numbers of freight trains ultimately required surpassed by far the initial estimates which, when first formulated, could not have possibly foreseen several factors such as the "Bolero" project, ie the entry of the United States into the Second World War and the subsequent need for considerable additional accommodation, or the date and period of the Second Front and the unexpected vast flows of internal rail movements. Even later events added to the burden on

the Depot's rail system including the disbandment of the Home Guard and the return of its equipment to ordnance sources.

The BMR carried a bewildering array of war traffic including tanks, spares and tyres for every type of army road vehicles both British and American, Bren Gun Carriers (fast tracked vehicles), armaments and small arms such as Sten guns and rifles, wireless and signalling equipment, generating sets and 'wading' equipment. The latter resulted from a method of waterproofing army tanks which could then travel through several feet of water. The bulky 'wading' equipment alone required some 400,000 square feet of storage space. These operations demanded many thousands of internal rail movements as stores and equipment were sorted, labelled and packed for issue to units in the field or preparing for the invasion of Europe.

In the final build-up to 'D' Day BMR locomotives laboured night and day marshalling and running heavy freight trains, from all parts of the Depot, with its near fifty miles of track to Exchange Sidings where they were

One of the many 'Warflat' wagons used for carrying military road vehicles and tanks. A 'Warwell' wagon, also used for similar purposes, can be seen in the background.

Authors' collection

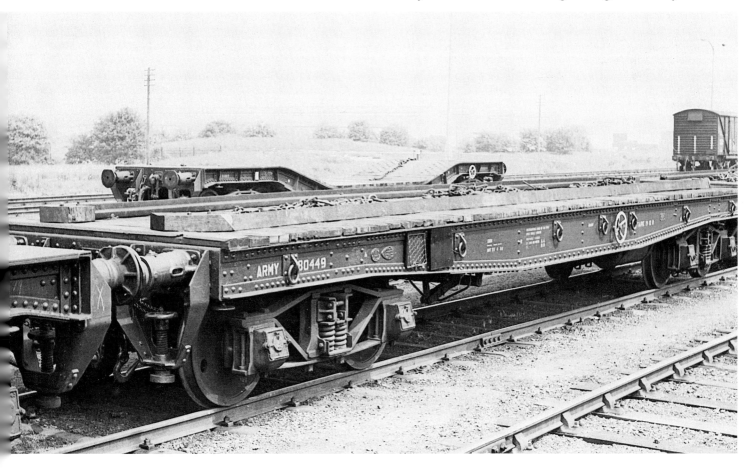

handed over to the main line railways for onward transmission to the ports.

During a specimen week in October 1944 a comparison of traffic figures on several of Britain's military railways revealed the BMR as the busiest system under the control of No.1 Railway (Home) Group, Royal Engineers:

Military Railway	Track mileage	Total wagon movements	Passenger journeys
BMR	48	5,535	29,273
Donnington	17	4,877	Nil
No.1 Military Port	27	3,074	Nil
Long Marston	35½	3,038	Nil
Shropshire & Montgomeryshire	84¾	2,974	9,002
Bramley (Hants)	31½	2,360	Nil

The planning of traffic requirements on the system was centralised in the Traffic Headquarters situated at 'HQ7' (later 'E15' located on the Armaments and Small Arms loop near its junction with the Sorting Sidings). It was staffed by the Royal Army Ordnance Corps Traffic Officer, the Senior Railway Transport Officer of the Royal Engineers (Movement Branch), representatives of the BMR, the Depot's Motor Transport Officer and the Royal Army Service Corps. In wartime there was also a representative of the Ministry of War Transport. Each day every officer in charge of every storage shed throughout

A ramp wagon, used to unload road vehicles and tanks from 'Warflat' wagons. Hand-worked screw jacks lifted or lowered the end of the vehicle when one axle was removed or replaced.

Authors' collection

Tanks on a train of 'Warflats' amply illustrating the superiority of rail transport to convey large quantities of these heavy fighting vehicles.

Authors' collection

the Depot would submit his requirements for work to be undertaken, and at the daily conference of all the representatives, a decision would be made on what transport would be used to meet the demands and translate this into action. The Depot Traffic Officer also had a representative at Exchange Sidings whose task it was to receive incoming trains and label each wagon for its particular destination on the BMR. This task had to be completed before the train departed for marshalling in the Sorting Sidings. The Senior Railway Transport Officer also had responsibility

Although this view was taken on another military railway it illustrates the use of the ramp wagon and Vickers tractor for off-loading earth-moving vehicles from a train of 'Warflats'.

Authors' collection

for advising the BMR operators on which trains the outward traffic would be conveyed, a task particularly important in the case of shipping consignments.

With the 'Regulator' system of operation used on the BMR each locomotive in traffic was allocated a target number used both as a reporting number for operational control, and as a means of identifying its basic duties. The regular, wartime, scheduled targets were:

Target	1	Passenger services and some freight trips.
	2	Passenger services and some freight trips.
	3	Sorting Sidings Pilot.
	4	Arncott Yard Pilot.
	5	MT Yard and sub-depot. ('C' sites)
	6	Engineering sub-depot. ('B' sites)
	7	Armaments sub-depot. ('D' sites)
	8	Small Arms sub-depot. ('E' sites)
	9	To work as required.
	10	Stand by.

Inwards trains worked from Exchange into the Sorting Sidings for re-marshalling into:

(a) Shed order for the Armaments and Small Arms loop.
(b) For the MT and Arncott Yards.
(c) Bulk traffic for the Engineers' Stores Depot at RE Sidings Nos 1, 2 and 3. Arncott.

Traffic destined for the two main loop lines at Graven

Hill and Arncott was worked in an anti-clockwise direction and, where possible, picked up outward bound vehicles and empties before detaching inwards loads at each of the storage sheds.

Heavy trains containing roadstone and other building materials were run daily from the Sorting Sidings to Arncott for the Engineers' Stores Depot. These trains required careful handling by the train crews as from 1941 to 1950 no brake vans were in use and the sole brake power was provided by the steam brakes on the locomotive. Furthermore, after passing 'B' blockpost a good turn of speed was necessary to run successfully through Arncott platform with its tight curve and upgrade. Off duty personnel billeted in No.3 Camp at Arncott, often listened in the late evening as the loud exhaust blasts of the engine, usually a saddletank, could be heard approaching Arncott Yard and fighting its way round the curve. The beats became louder as it climbed through the short 1 in 90 gradient in Arncott platform and onto the 'down' running line towards Piddington. This train was known throughout the system as 'The R.E. Park' and staff would sometimes comment "R.E. Park has only just managed it tonight". Pleas to double head this train went unheeded and it was left to the redoubtable saddletanks and their crews to do their best to clear the main line and run the 'Park' to its destination.

Target No.3, the saddletank allocated to shunt the Sorting Sidings, proved to be the hardest worked engine and was employed continuously throughout the day and night, seven days a week. Sometimes on Sunday nights the pace seemed to slacken but at all other times the only

Roy Holford
Roy Holford, (on the right) was a well-known figure on the
BMR. Born in Broadway, Worcestershire on 1st November
1921 he started work in 1937 with the former Great Western
Railway at Winchcombe station as junior porter.

He entered the world of military railways at Longmoor in
November 1941. After military and technical training he
was posted to the Cairnryan Military Railway as
brakesman/shunter, blockman and eventually as a traffic
operator.

After leaving the Army he was appointed civilian yardmaster at Cairnyan in February 1947 and transferred to the
BMR as a traffic inspector, where he remained until
promotion to Depot Railway Superintendent at Long
Marston. In 1966 he gained further promotion as Depot
Railway Officer, Bicester and served until 1982 when he
retired.

He has since occupied his time with railway preservation
and gardening. Mr Holford is married with two children and
resides in Bicester.

COD, Bicester

included in the rulebook but remained as always, an unofficial arrangement between engine and yard staffs.

Making the work of Target No. 3 even harder was the
shunting neck which sloped away from the Yard and
required a lot of additional power from the engine to start
the wagons being shunted. The Yard was contrary in other
ways as the dead end sidings sloped towards the buffer
stops and if a cut of wagons escaped the attention of the
brakesmen they would strike the buffer stops or other
vehicles in the same siding with a resounding blow. This
situation remained until the 1960s when the various roads
were lifted 2 ft 6 in, forming a slight upward rise towards
the buffer stop. The shunting neck was similarly treated
and levelled.

Initially it had been intended that Target No. 3 would
return to the locomotive shed at Arncott at the end of each
shift for servicing. Due to the pressure of work however, a
wagon of coal was placed at the end of the shunting neck
and the bunkers topped up by hand, during which time the
fire was cleaned and water taken. This lessened the need
for trips to the locomotive shed and enabled the work to
be carried on, after a short interval. The engine then only
visited the shed once every 24 hours for full servicing.

Relief crews for the Sorting Sidings were brought from
Arncott by a Wickham railcar hauling an open trailer
conveying the relief blockmen for 'A' blockpost and yard
staff. When relief crews were not available the work
continued and this often meant long hours of duty, stretch-
ing to 14 or 16 hours, at the end of which a badly
clinkered fire, choked ashpan and smokebox had to be
cleaned, together with some three tons of coal hand-
loaded into the bunker.

A Royal Engineer Company Quartermaster Sergeant
situated in the Sorting Sidings Control Office was in
charge of each turn with a junior NCO assisting. They
controlled the network from 'A' blockpost to Exchange
Sidings, the Armaments and Small Arms loop, Sorting
Sidings and the Up Yard. The usual train crew consisted

stops were to obtain water (a column having been
provided for this purpose), and short halts for the weary
crew to obtain a hurried meal. Most of the work involved
'loose shunting' the brakesmen/shunters aided by the yard
staff making the necessary 'cuts', uncoupling the wagons
at the required place and giving the engine crew a rapid
side to side swing of the arm or handlamp at night. This
was colloquially known as the 'hit 'em up' signal and
required the engine to start as rapidly as possible and stop
just as promptly on another handsignal ie both arms held
high over the head, or red lamp at night. The detached
wagons would then, hopefully, run on their own
momentum into the required siding. The operation was
then repeated and the points re-set until the whole train
had been sorted into the required order. Loose shunting
thus obviated the need for the engine to be reversed after
each 'cut'.

Needless to say the 'hit 'em up' handsignals were not

The last surviving example of American built rolling stock at Bicester
was AD 47984. This was formerly part of a military workshop train and
was built by the Pullman Standard Car Manufacturing Co. in 1941. This
vehicle was in regular use on freight services until 1986 when it was
scrapped.

E.R. Lawton

of an RED (railway engine driver), fireman and two brakesmen/shunters, the senior of which was regarded as being in charge. The driver was responsible for obtaining the food supply before the commencement of each turn. Food was strictly rationed and the allowance for a full crew of four was a loaf of rather hard bread, a tin of herrings, a small amount of margarine, tea and sugar with tinned milk. The tea was brewed in 7lb metal tins which had formerly contained jam. The crew fitted the tin with a makeshift wire handle and suspended it from a metal rod inside the firebox. The first question always asked by relief crews was "have you a brew tin and rod?"

When a train for the Armaments and Small Arms loop was marshalled, other engines, usually Targets 7 or 8, would couple on and run, in an anti-clockwise direction, placing wagons at the appropriate storage sheds in the 'D' and 'E' series, removing the empty and any outward wagons. These would then be worked back to the Sorting Sidings for disposal. If more than one train was working in the loop permission to proceed would be obtained from Sorting Sidings Control by using the Telephone Points Nos 1, 2 and 3. A good knowledge of the route was essential, especially during the hours of darkness, the whole area being 'blacked out', the only lights being the oil lamps on the engine, inside the Telephone Points and

the handlamps carried by the brakesmen/shunters.

Until the track forming the loop had become consolidated derailments were frequent. Most of these were, fortunately, minor and involved the four-wheeled wagons, some of which were still running with grease lubricated axleboxes. Steel re-railing ramps were placed on the trackside at strategic points around the loop marked with white notice boards bearing the legend 'Ramps'. The majority of the derailments were dealt with by the train crews using the ramps, aided by sundry bits of wooden packing. The more serious incidents necessitated the attention of the breakdown train located at Arncott locomotive shed. No heavy lift cranes were provided until the post war years and the breakdown outfit consisted initially of one of the original ferryvans carrying jacks, packing, tools and lamps. Later, when this was required for internal passenger services, use was made of several four-wheeled steel bodied vans. One carried packing and ramps, others tools and jacks including two heavy, massive 35-ton hydraulic lifting and screw traversing types. The former Kent & East Sussex Railway 'Pickering' coach was pressed into service as a riding vehicle for the breakdown crew (See later section on Passenger Services). A later, much vaunted, possession was a petrol-driven generator purloined from a battle wrecked tank which supplied power to lights in the vans, and to three ex-army lorry headlamps mounted on steel

Two examples of the internal wagon fleet in the Sorting Sidings, April 1972.

G.P. Roberts

tripods. This equipment proved a boon and saved time and trouble starting the paraffin pressure lamps used previously.

Trains for the 'B' and 'C' sites at Arncott were worked from the Sorting Sidings to the MT Yard where remarshalling in shed order took place. When complete these were run, again in anti-clockwise direction, round the Arncott loop. Trains of empty wagons were run into Arncott Yard from the loop, either for holding until required at other points, or tripped back to Exchange Yard.

At night, several heavy trains of outward loads originating from the 'A', 'B' and 'C' groups of storage sheds were run from Arncott Yard to Bicester, where they were propelled into the Up Sidings for remarshalling into destination order. Many of these were formed of seventy loaded wagons and proved a substantial load for a single saddletank, especially on the approaches to Ambrosden station, where various hazards were encountered, including the level crossing which, during the war period, was not provided with gates or telephones. A crossing keeper using lamps and/or flags protected the

crossing and was aroused by prolonged whistling from approaching trains. If this failed to attract his attention, or owing to shortage of personnel no one was on duty, the rule in the Military Railway Rule Book (No.103) was explicit:

"At all main road crossings ... drivers must stop two engine lengths before the crossing unless signalled over by an authorised person. Where no one is on duty ... the brakesman/shunter or fireman must go ahead onto the road and after the crossing is clear and that approaching road traffic is at a stand ... signal the train over the crossing."

The rule then went on to specify that two red lamps would be used, one for each direction of the road or a red flag by day.

In the absence of the keeper, which happened fairly frequently, considerable difficulties would have been faced it this procedure had been carried out to the letter. Starting such a train on a tight curve up a short 1 in 100 gradient would have been a task, if not impossible, with a wet rail. It would have certainly involved full gear and second valve of the regulator together with a thick heavy fire and possible breakage of drawgear. Thus faced with such a dilemma most drivers 'took a chance' and charged over the crossing with whistle screaming. Fortunately, in those days road traffic through Ambrosden, especially during

A general view of Graven Hill locomotive yard with the shed on the left. The various diesel locomotives are in store and are not allocated for regular use on the BMR. To the right there are Wickham railcars Nos 9038 and 9032. The large building on the right is the 'E15' boilerhouse, one of three supplying heat to the storage sheds. In 1985/6 the boilerhouses were re-fitted to burn coal after several years of oil firing.

G.P. Roberts

During the war years MT Yard was the scene of intensive activity as thousands of wagons were marshalled for distribution or onwards despatch to Exchange Sidings. Today it is held under a minimum maintenance procedure ready for any emergency which may arise.

E.R. Lawton

the night, was very light by present day standards and surprisingly few accidents were reported. What the residents of this one time sleepy village thought about their lot is not recorded, but the exhaust blasts of heavily loaded locomotives must have cost them many sleepless nights.

Trains passing through Exchange Sidings were examined by a Royal Engineer Carriage and Wagon Examiner to ascertain their suitability for proceeding onto the civilian main lines. The military examiners were themselves given an examination by an LMS Railway Carriage & Wagon Inspector who assessed their capability to detect rolling stock defects and to take the required procedures to remedy the fault. Most of the BMR rolling stock repairers and examiners had held similar posts on the civilian railways before enlistment in the Royal Engineers and were already proficient and very capable of holding such posts.

The civilian locomotives working freight trains in and out of Exchange Sidings included O4 Class 2-8-0s from the LNER, 0-8-0 "Super Ds", Class 8F 2-8-0s, "Black Five" 4-6-0s, Class 4MT 2-6-4Ts and 4F Class 0-6-0s from the LMS. Occasionally a British 'Austerity' 2-8-0 would also put in an appearance.

Consignments of sundry traffic destined for the Depot (less than a single wagon load) were also received by normal scheduled freight trains at Bletchley LMS Railway depot. These were then loaded into wagons for despatch to the BMR, where considerable re-sorting was necessary to ensure the various packages were delivered to the correct storage sheds. This often involved wagons being moved several times before finally being emptied of their cargo. To speed these consignments, it was arranged for several, specially trained, RAOC personnel to be located with the Railway Transport Officer at Bletchley. Here they assisted the civilian rail staff to make up composite loads, correctly labelled, to the appropriate storage sheds resulting in a minimum number of internal railway movements. This lessened the amount of shunting required and generally speeded up delivery.

In February 1943 the fleet of 22 side-tipping wagons used on the construction of the line were no longer required and disposal to other installations was ordered.

The number of wagons received on the system by May 1943, both for constructional and ordnance needs, exceeded 57,000 and gives an indication of the traffic handled.

The movement of tanks also increased and the Royal Electrical and Mechanical Engineers 9th Central Workshops located at 'C6' was stated to be the largest installation of its kind in the United Kingdom. Here, tanks from the United States were fitted with turrets and guns and generally made ready for action. The majority of these were carried by rail on 'Warflat' wagons. The 'Warflat' vehicles were double-bogied with a flush wooden

Almost new Thos Hill 'Steelman Royale' No. MOD 272 stands at 'B' blockpost before working an 'up' freight from Arncott Yard on 28th October 1987.

E.R. Lawton

Thos Hill 'Vanguard' No. 253 *Conductor* marshalls wagons in the Sorting Sidings during a sunny day in October 1987.

E.R. Lawton

deck 40 ft x 8 ft 6 in, just over 4 ft above rail level and could carry a load of 50 tons or 45 tons centrally loaded. As far as possible these heavy trains were hauled by vacuum-fitted locomotives and were often double headed.

Shortly before Christmas 1943, owing to unusually light rainfall, a serious water shortage was experienced at the Depot. Thus the Buckinghamshire Water Authority was forced to reduce the supply from the normal 380,000 gallons to 170,000 gallons per day. Water was immediately rationed, the main valves were closed for most of the 24 hours and supplies to washing and toilet facilities were severely restricted. The toilets for the military railway staff were not affected as these consisted of latrine buckets and no flushing was necessary!

The shortage also affected the supply of water for the locomotives, and as it was vital to maintain the rail services, the Depot fire brigade was called in to pump water from the River Ray. Locomotives were then brought to a halt on the River Ray bridge between Ambrosden and 'B' blockpost to enable the tank to be filled by means of the fire hose. A portable fire pump was positioned on the parallel Arncott road. This procedure required

the locomotive fireman to climb onto the top of the tank with the fire hose and to grip the handrails firmly whilst the engine proceeded onto the bridge because no walkways were provided at that time. The driver then signalled with a handlamp to the waiting fire pump crew to commence pumping. A frenzied whistling from the engine was the signal that the tank was full. As the engine taking water occupied the single line block sections between 'A' and 'B' blockposts, considerable delay to trains was experienced and it was a relief to the BMR operators when supplies returned to normal in March 1944.

To enable BR to carry out clearance tests the Carriage & Wagon Shop at 'C1' was asked to produce a template representing the outline of a 'Chieftan' tank mounted on a 'Warwell' wagon. Syd Hopcraft the Chargeman and his staff constructed a 'snap stick' jig, seen here outside the 'C1' Shop. Syd Hopcraft is shown on the left with Major M.W. Sackett, the Operating Officer, on the right. Much later BR modified this to have hinged arms and it was used at many main line locations.

Authors' collection

'Vanguard' locomotive Army 252 couples on to the first 'Freightliner' train to traverse BMR tracks. It is believed this was also the first time that a 'Freightliner' train was hauled by motive power other than a British Rail engine. Snow covered the tracks on 9th February 1979 when this view was taken in the Exchange Sidings.

Lt Colonel G.K. Gilberry

During this period the Armaments and Small Arms sub-depots were dealing with over 50% of the country's total of small arms, including thousands of Sten guns and the entire manufacturer's output of six-pounder guns. The storage sheds served by this loop comprised 491,000 sq ft of covered accommodation, with the greater proportion of railborne traffic being moved at night.

Military stores from the United States were received at the Inland Sorting Depot at Kirkby, Liverpool. When sorted the stores were despatched to the appropriate Central Ordnance Depots. Trains for Bicester from this source were usually worked direct to the MT Yard and marshalled into shed order. By close liaison with the Kirkby authorities a scheme was developed to label the wagons direct to the appropriate shed at Bicester, and this again helped to reduce the number of internal shunting movements. Up to the end of May 1945 some 14,000 wagons containing over 1¼ million case of stores from Kirkby were hauled over BMR tracks.

In between running passenger trains, Targets 1 and 2 were often require to haul freight trips between Piddington and Arncott Yard and from Arncott Yard to the Up Sidings at Bicester. The 'Dean Goods' locomotives performed these duties in an efficient manner. The engines were fitted with blackout curtains between the cab and stanchions on the tender cut down the glare from the fireboxes when being fired. On occasions these engines were also used on freight trips around the 'B' and 'C' sites at Arncott. Their performance

MOD No. 272 crosses the River Ray bridge with an 'up' freight from Arncott Yard to the Sorting Sidings, October 1987.

E.R. Lawton

'Vanguard' locomotive No. 253 *Conductor* marshalls freight in the Sorting Sidings. 'E14' boilerhouse is on the right.

E.R. Lawton

round this loop was less satisfactory because of the tight curvature and the numerous level crossings. When the 'Deans' received heavy repairs at Swindon Works they were, of course, returned with the correct tolerances between the axleboxes and horn cheeks, which made them very prone to derailment on the loop lines, especially when running tender first. When fresh from the shops every effort was made to roster their duties on the main line.

On one occasion in 1944, during daylight, a freight train working round the Arncott loop was attaching additional wagons to its 45-vehicle train adjacent to 'B4' shed when, owing to an error by the brakesman/shunter, the train standing on the running line was hit violently by the additional vehicles and commenced running away, in the wrong direction, down the falling gradient. The brakesman/shunter endeavoured to pin down brakes but tripped and fell, the runaway gathering speed in the direction of White Cross Green level crossing. No.2 TP was fortunately adjacent to the scene and a hurried telephone call was made to the Yard Foreman at MT Yard. Points were quickly set into an empty road. The runaway had by this time gained considerable speed, estimated by a soldier near the crossing, to be approaching forty miles per hour, but more likely to be 25 to 30 mph, and roared over the crossing, which, by an act of provi-

dence, was temporarily clear of road traffic. The track levelled out at this point and the speed was reduced to such a degree that the whole of the runaway entered MT Yard, where the yard staff pinned down sufficient brakes to halt the train completely clear in the empty road.

Also in 1944, on one notable day, the 'B' and 'C' sites received an extraordinary number of trains conveying inwards stores, and only by outstanding efforts had many of these wagon been discharged. By nightfall many of the storage sheds were full of empty wagons awaiting clearance before it was possible to accommodate further loaded vehicles. The crew of Target No.6, working round the loop, were valiantly trying to pick up as many empties as possible and in the early hours of the next morning Target 6, worked by the usual saddletank, re-appeared in Arncott Yard hauling 127 empty wagons. The efforts of the crew were, however, unrewarded as the Operating and Locomotive officers were far from pleased with this example of overloading and the senior brakesman/shunter and driver were both reprimanded. Thereafter trains on the Arncott loop were limited to a maximum of 60-70 vehicles.

With the threat of an invasion largely removed by the successful advance of the allied armies in Europe, the Home Guard (the citizens' army) was stood down on 1st November 1944. This defence force reached a strength of 1,727,000 of which 142,246 were on anti-aircraft gun duties, 7,000 on coastal defence artillery and 7,000 on bomb disposal squads. Practically all the volunteers were armed with rifles or machine guns and large quantities were then handed back to the regular army ordnance sources, much of which was despatched by rail to Bicester.

Initially it had been hoped to store this equipment in Arncott Gun Park which, in the event, proved inadequate. A larger and more suitable site was found in 'B52' storage shed situated on the Arncott loop line. In just over twenty days over one thousand wagon loads of this material were off-loaded in 'B52', greatly adding to the internal rail movements required over the five monthly period. This flow of traffic was reduced to a trickle by March 1945.

In the summer of 1943 a total of 67 miscellaneous freight vehicles, mostly four-wheeled open and box vans, requisitioned from the main line railways constituted the internal freight rolling stock fleet. No records remain of their origin, type or numbers.

For approximately eight months prior to 'D' Day in June 1944, the BMR carried its highest recorded traffics, the limits of which are hardly likely to be exceeded. All leave for the army railway staff was cancelled and the only opportunity for rest was between one lengthy turn of duty and the next. Warlike stores of every description were prepared for the invasion of Europe and all available engines and rolling stock pressed into service.

May 1944 witnessed the busiest month in the history of the Depot and the rail system was worked to its maximum capacity. Some military units were obliged to use valuable petrol to collect certain supplies by road, the BMR being unable to cope with any further loads. It may be thought this avalanche of traffic was mainly confined to outward bound trains, but the volume of inwards trains was equally as heavy. One item alone gives an indication of the sheer volume: approximately 3,600 barrels for the six and seventeen-pounder guns were received and placed in reserve stock in the 'D6' storage shed in a single month. Some traffic statistics have fortunately survived to illustrate the level of traffic during this period and to reveal that 78,623 wagons were received and 77,896 despatched through Exchange Sidings from all parts of the Depot

The boilerhouse at 'E14' is one of three which supply heat to the vast storage sheds. The installations were originally coal-fired, then converted to oil and finally new coal-fired equipment was fitted. The coal is brought to Exchange Sidings by BR Railfreight in HEA, bottom door discharge wagons and then conveyed over the BMR direct to the boilerhouses.

E.R. Lawton

On 10th June 1945 WD No. 70094, one of the BMR's Dean Goods hauls a Piddington (BMR) to Oxford (Rewley Road) troop train past Port Meadow on the approaches to Oxford.

The locomotive is carrying the express passenger headlamps code and the BMR Target No. 1 at the base of the chimney. This train was worked entirely by a Royal Engineers crew who had to have knowledge of both civilian and military operating procedures and rules. On this occasion the driver was one of the authors, E.R. Lawton and can be seen in the cab. The former GWR Worcester and Birmingham lines are on the left of the picture.

R.H.G. Simpson

during 1944. Additionally, there were 135,034 internal wagon movements, giving a grand total of 291,554 wagons dealt with during the twelve-monthly period.

From 25th July 1942, with 22 miles of track completed and five locomotives in use, construction reached a total of 48 miles with a maximum number of 17 engines in use by October 1944. The number of railway personnel ranged from 241 to 300. It must also be noted that in addition to the figures quoted, all the wagons required extensive marshalling to cater for the near eighty destinations or forwarding points within the Depot area. A large proportion of this traffic was delivered or collected from the storage sheds during the night hours, in totally blacked-out conditions. Although showing a reduction, the total number of wagons handled during 1945 was in excess of 200,000 and it was not until the end of that year that a decline in carryings was recorded.

United States of America - Rolling Stock

Large numbers of freight vehicles manufactured in the United States were shipped to Britain during 1942 and 1943, including four-wheeled opens, box vans and tank wagons. These were received in kit form for assembly in the United Kingdom. Manufacturers included the Magor Car Corporation of Passaic, New Jersey, the Pullman

Standard Car Manufacturing Co. and others.

Several of the four-wheeled wagons and vans were used on the BMR. All were fitted with automatic Westinghouse air and hand brakes. The latter were applied by side wheels with chain linkage. In practice the handbrakes were found to be ineffective and the American wagons were always marshalled between British built vehicles which had simple but positive hand brake gear.

As none of the locomotives working on the BMR were equipped with Westinghouse air brake equipment, the hoses on the USA wagons were removed and placed in store. A stencilled legend "WH Hose in Store" was painted on the ends of the vehicles.

During the invasion of Europe many of the American wagons were shipped to the Continent replacing war-damaged rolling stock. It is thought that few if any examples were used on the BMR after 1946.

In March 1966 a complete train consisting of six former military workshop vans was transferred from Longmoor to Bicester. This train had been in storage for many months in the 'Apple Pie' depot at Longmoor and consisted of five USA built vans and one of British construction. All were unmarked except for their numbers 20578, 20548, 20570, 20131 and 20571. The sole British example was an ex-Southern Railway vehicle registered as SR 1132/1943.

The vans had been completely stripped of the former workshop machinery before being sent to Bicester. On arrival two of the vans had the sides removed and replaced by curtains. These were then utilised for conveying palletised traffic throughout the BMR, the loading and unloading being performed by fork lift trucks.

The remainder were absorbed in the conventional internal user fleet and, with one exception, were gradually scrapped.

The sole remaining example, No. 20548, later AD 47984, was regularly used on internal freight services until 1986 when it too was scrapped unfortunately. Its details were as follows:

Army Dept. No. 47984.
Builder - Pullman Standard Car Mfg. Co. No. 20548, 1941.
Tare weight - 9 tons. Maximum load - 20 tons.
Overall length - 29 ft. Height - 11 ft 3 in. Width - 8 ft 8 in.
Wheelbase - 13 ft. Wheel dia. - 2 ft 8 in.
Frame - steel channel. Body - box steel frame with laminated wooden panels.
Two hinged doors on each side.

Freight - Post War Years

The cessation of hostilities in Europe and the VE Day celebrations on 8th May 1945 ended an era on the BMR. Gone was the frenzied rush of the previous four years, supplies were of course, still needed in the Fast East but problems for the war-torn system remained compounded by the following:

(a) The condition of the permanent way which had been hurriedly constructed and now needed extensive repairs.

(b) An Ordnance Depot with some 34 very large store sheds stacked to the roofs with military equipment, together with seven groups of 'Bolero' sheds (see Chapter 1) similarly stacked.

(c) Practically every piece of open ground covered with equipment.

(d) Nine 'Austerity' saddle tanks, some of which required workshop attention. Three 'Dean Goods' locomotives of considerable age.

(e) About 500 internal freight vehicles in varying states of repair, many unlisted as to type and number, and some 40 passenger coaches.

(f) The commencement of demobilisation for many skilled army railwaymen.

(g) Comparatively little in the shape of accommodation and facilities, with everywhere the debris and aftermath of war.

(h) Five ungated level crossings over public roads which were to be the subject of frequent parliamentary questions.

A policy decision was taken to civilianize the activities of the then No.1 Railway (Home) Group Royal Engineers and Bicester became the Bicester Railway Operating Detachment, in name at least. In name because very soon

The only ex-LSWR A12, 'Jubilee' class 0-4-2 allocated to the BMR was No. 625, shown here being turned on the manually-operated turntable at Oxford (LMS) depot. This locomotive retained its Southern Railway livery throughout its WD career and is being prepared by its RE crew for a return troop train from Rewley Road station at Oxford to Piddington on 4th February 1945.

R.H.G. Simpson

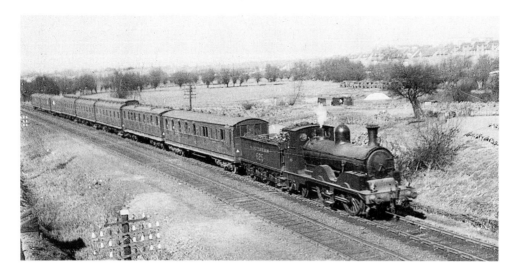

Polished, fired and driven by Sapper crews A12, 'Jubilee' No. 625 coasts past Port Meadow on a WD worked troop train from the BMR to Oxford (Rewley Road) on 26th March 1944. The train is composed of ex-Midland Railway and LNWR vintage coaches and the locomotive is working the Bicester Target No. 2 diagram. This locomotive had excellent steaming qualities and despite its 0-4-2 wheel arrangement rode extremely smoothly.

R.H.G. Simpson

there were less than a handful of skilled railway staff with approximately 130 untrained staff recruited from all over the country and even then, largely perhaps because of poor accommodation arrangements, they were leaving at something like ten per week to be replaced with new recruits. The Headquarters staff, with the assistance of the various railway Operating Officers, were touring the employment exchanges in an endeavour to recruit the necessary staff, not only for Bicester, but for all the other Railway Units.

Throughout 1946 and most of 1947 the BMR was being run by a few military railwaymen assisted by 40 German prisoners of war. This produced the strange situation of former enemy soldiers running military freight trains for the British Army. At least one complete train crew, including the driver, were prisoners of war. Through their interpreters the Germans had mastered the Military Railway Rule Book, BMR operating procedures and passed the locomotive and traffic examinations. In the main the Germans where ex-railwaymen and proved to be excellent engine and traffic staff. The railway rules had to be written in German whilst the daily Operating Notices were issued in English and German. Amongst the many problems besetting the newly appointed Operating officer was the training aspects. Could the new recruits be trained in time, before the prisoners of war were repatriated?

These difficulties were perhaps a microcosm of identical problems faced by the main line companies and eventually British Railways in post war Britain.

The immense stocks of war equipment laying in the store sheds, together with hundreds of tanks and vehicles all placed as reserve supplies for the allied armies which had defeated the Nazis, for the continuance of the war in the Far East and the military campaign which followed, provided a major task for the Bicester RAOC authorities. The disposal of stores not now required continued to offer considerable traffic for the BMR. Sales of surplus equipment occupied some ten years, but all led to an enormous amount of internal rail movement. The tanks were cleared fairly quickly, many of these being American Shermans conveyed on trainloads of 'Warwell' vehicles. Many special trains carrying ten tanks each were despatched, but surplus armaments took much longer to clear and remained in store for many years.

The traffic requirements could therefore be summarised as follows:

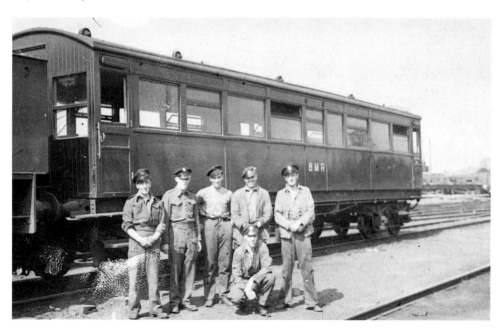

A group of Royal Engineers taken alongside the former KESR coach whilst it was used as a push-pull unit. The year was 1946 and the train is standing on the South Running Line.

A.L. Tibbs

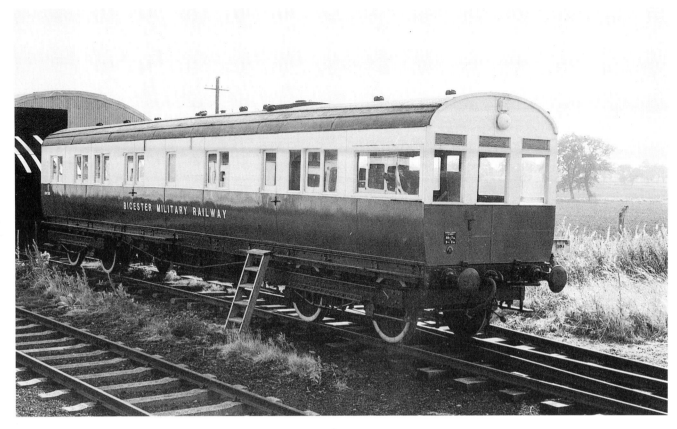

The Royal coach, ex-ambulance vehicle, No. 3018 is pictured in pristine condition, in the Up Sidings on 16th May 1981. This is the last remaining passenger vehicle on the BMR.

Bill Simpson

(a) The handling of military stores received and forwarded via British Railways (London Midland Region).

(b) Coal (washed duff) for the three boiler houses supplying heating for the whole depot.

(c) Food supplies and engineers' equipment for the maintenance of buildings, roads etc.

(d) The rapid increase in internal rail traffic.

(e) To provide a passenger train service from and to varying parts of the depot as the need required.

In the case of (d), for several reasons, the internally generated traffic on many occasions proved greater in quantity than the external movements. Many of the storage sheds held stores in bulk which had to be broken down in to smaller parcels and sent to other sheds, where the now much smaller demands from military units could be met quickly. Then for some ten years there was the task of analysing the huge amounts of stores held and making decisions as to retention or disposal, the latter in particular leading to transfer to the 'Sales' areas for disposal by auctioneers. The completion of that task, the clearance of all stores from grassed open areas and the removal of the 'Bolero' sites were not the end of internal movement story. The Ministry of Defence then progressed with its centralisation of effort between the three services (Navy, Army and Air Force) in which each took new responsibili-

ties (see Introduction). Bicester became responsible for all service clothing and this meant selection of suitable store sheds, some consequential re-organisation of other sheds, followed by transfer of stores to empty the selected sheds.

For the first time brake vans were introduced in 1950 and used on all freight trains proceeding through the single line section between 'A' and 'B' blockposts. Prior to this white discs by day or red tail lamps by night had been used to denote the last vehicle. The brakesman/shunters had formerly been conveyed on the footplate. Four, vacuum-fitted vans, numbered 49000, 49001, 49005 and 49019 were transferred from BR Southern Region of which three are still in use.

The newly constructed civilian organisation had started with some 500 'internal use only' wagons. These were of all shapes and sizes, some dating from the 19th century and in varying states of repair. Because of the exigencies of war and the urgency of the more pressing matters of meeting freight movement demands, the recording of freight rolling stock detail was patchy and haphazard. It was not known how many wagons or their types were located on the BMR. Special 'number taking' exercises were organised, and every three or four months all supervisors, often accompanied by senior officers, would spend a Sunday walking every part of the track recording the numbers of every wagon found. It was some years before the Operating Officer could put his hand on heart to HQ and say "I now have complete and accurate record of wagons on the BMR"! A small example of the problems was revealed on one such occasion when there were several rakes of wagons in Arncott yard being recorded by the Yard Foreman, Bill Bracewell and the Operating Officer. By mistake they walked down either side of the same rake of forty wagons. Comparing lists afterwards it was found that each had one wagon the other had not. On re-checking the rake they discovered that one vehicle, which was numbered 53702 on one side was 53703 on the other!

Railway Group HQ maintained a fleet of main line vehicles (ie fit to run over BR metals), consisting of 'Warwells', 'Rectanks' and later on vans and opens, their use on BR being controlled by the Senior Operating Officer at HQ. The maintenance of these vehicles was the responsibility of the Railway Workshops which had its own C&W Department, and revolved round an intermediate inspection and then a complete overhaul. The Operating Officer was responsible for keeping the workshops fed with work, holding the incoming vehicles and the overhauled, until required. Whilst on BMR tracks they could of course be used for internal work and of particular use were the 'Warflats'. So much so, that as 'Warflats' aged and became unable to meet BR standards, they were transferred to internal use, and to make sure they were not fed out on to the BR line in error, they had a white line painted along the edge of the solebars. Other depots began to find a use for such vehicles and as they became available were re-allocated.

In addition to determining the size and nature of the existing fleet of wagons, two other exercises were in hand. First a continuing exercise to ascertain the numbers and types of wagons which would be required to meet the

HM The Queen and officers of Bicester Garrison at the original Graven Hill station, later 'D4', on 16th May 1978. Thos Hill 271, MOD 253 is formally named *Conductor*. The station was later re-named 'Queen's Halt' to commemorate the occasion.

RAOC Museum

Barclay 0-8-0 diesel No. 894 (later Army 623) Class D3 hauls the Royal Train conveying HM The Queen, through Ambrosden on the 16th May 1978.

M.W. Sackett

Depot's future requirements, and secondly, to determine the condition of existing vehicles to discover which would be suitable and economically repairable to meet the requirements. This last decision was taken against a background of the availability and cost of repaired secondhand wagons on offer from the civil market. Those not worth repairing were scrapped on site, or together with those no longer required but still usable, were put up for auction through the Ministry of Defence, Directorate of Disposals. It was soon realised that some of the wagons had an interest for railway preservation societies and these were annotated by the Operating Dept for the Directorate, so that such organisations could be included on the distribution list of tender forms.

Experiments were carried out with the movement of internal transfer traffic by conveying unlashed stores on 'Warflat' vehicles, and eventually became an accepted method of moving stores from one shed to another. Not only did the scheme utilize some of the large numbers of 'Warflats' available but more importantly had the advantage that stores could be loaded using fork lift trucks and conveyed without the need for securing. Understandably, it took a long time to convince RAOC loading staff that this was a viable proposition. The change came about when a sudden order from on high demanded that many thousands of rifles had to be moved to another location forthwith. The initial plan was to use a Scammel tractor with a trailer but it was slow and caused difficulties with the trailer suspension. BMR were asked if they could assist, and an hour later, at about 14.00hrs, arrived with a locomotive and twelve 'Warflats.' Eight were placed in the loading shed, and as soon as the first

four were loaded, were taken off to the receiving shed. The locomotive returned, removed the next four, irrespective of loading state and placed four more empties, taking the loaded to the receiving shed. In effect this created a moving platform almost on 'merry-go-round' principles, the loaders and unloaders were continuously at work and only the train crew had to stand by waiting for the next move.

The Scammel tractor and trailer were dispensed with almost immediately and the task was completed early the following morning. The 'Warflats' rode very smoothly, and if the situation dictated, could be close-coupled and vacuum-braked for even steadier movement.

During the seven month period from 1st March to 30th September 1963 some 45,080 wagons were handled on the system, of these 7,645 were received and 6,762 were forwarded through Exchange Sidings, the remainder being internal movements. Five locomotives and two railcars were in daily use. By then the number of staff required had reduced to 79, of which 29 were platelayers.

The outwards traffic from the depot consisted either of complete wagon loads, or part loads and smalls which needed to be assembled, if possible, into wagon loads. For this purpose, in the original design of the depot, the lead shed in each site was designed as a Transit, or Traffic shed, of which the most important was 'E15' since this was also the HQ of the RAOC Traffic Officer and the offices of all the transport services. It is not known to what extend the others were used during the war but in 1946/7 only 'C9' and 'E15' were being used and 'C9' was soon given over to other storage requirements. The movement of stores from sheds to 'E15' was either by road or by under utilisation of internal-user wagon capacity, which caused another problem with a concentration of such wagons at 'E15' for a comparatively small amount of traffic. Part of the problem was solved by

'Freight-liner' trains which had been introduced by British Rail on 15th November 1965 for conveyance of bulk container traffics at high speeds. The first 'Freightliner' to run on BMR tracks consisted of five vehicles, each carrying two 30 ft open containers of barbed wire. It ran from Exchange Sidings to 'C' sites hauled by AD No. 252 *Greensleeves,* a 'Vanguard' diesel locomotive. This was claimed to be the first time a 'Freightliner' train was hauled by motive power other than a British Rail locomotive.

In addition to the BMR Operating Officer and the Chief Planning Officer of the Central Ordnance Depot the train was accompanied by representatives of British Rail and Freightliner Ltd on its journey over the system. The chief concern was whether such a train composed of long, bogie, flat vehicles would safely negotiate the sharp curves of the BMR. The train was fully air-braked and the experiment was a complete success. A few days later two similar trains ran, and since then, further 'Freightliner' trains have been handled, without difficulty.

On several occasions the BMR has been used for the Royal Engineers, now Royal Corps of Transport, Territorial Army/Volunteer Reserve during their annual training fortnight. The personnel of this voluntary unit are composed in the main of experienced railwaymen and once they have studied the Depot Railway Working instructions and the layout, they can take over many of the functions, working alongside the civilian staff. The Operating Officer withdraws the latter as he considers appropriate, with the exception of the level crossing keepers.

In some instances it has been necessary to 'manufacture traffic' for the exercises, there being little worse from a training aspect than moving trains of empty wagons needlessly from place to place. With the co-operation of the RAOC it was usually possible to delay non-urgent stores until the reservists took over operations, which then provided the necessary traffic for the training period. Other 'incidents' would be introduced to tax the skill of the operators, such as an imagined derailment at a vital point.

On one such occasion, early on a Friday morning, the Squadron arrived and the majority of the volunteers were

arranging a daily railcar run throughout the system on booked timings to each shed to pick up small consignments to deliver to 'E15'.

By 1955 the quantity of small, sundry consignments had again shown an increase and road transport was arranged to convey these items to 'E15' but was proving laborious with the considerable handling necessary and the poor utilisation of personnel and vehicles.

The problem was eventually resolved by the use of what became known colloquially as the 'Whistle Stop' or 'Milk Train'. It comprised a diesel locomotive, an ex-Southern Railway Bulleid designed coach equipped as an office with tables, chairs, filing cabinets etc., in which a small team of RAOC traffic staff travelled. Eight or nine BR box vans, together with a number of ferryvans for overseas destinations, completed the consist, each labelled for the particular day's range of destinations.

The RAOC Traffic Officer, in constant touch with the officers in charge of each shed, was able to decide each days requirements and draw up an appropriate plan. The 'Whistle Stop' service departed from 'E15' at 08.30hrs each day and visited all storage sheds on the prepared schedule. The loading platforms in each shed were marked and despatches laid out according to the destination of each wagon, so that when the train was propelled in and stopped, the stores for despatch were opposite the appropriate wagon for loading. Vouchers and other documents were handed to the 'on train' staff for immediate processing. At the end of the day the train departed for Exchange Sidings and handed to British Rail for onwards despatch to Oxford and the ultimate destinations. This method reduced by half the handling required and consequently reduced the cost of transporting small consignments. However, with the continuing reduction in requirements and changes in work-load the 'Whistle Stop' service was withdrawn early in 1986.

On 9th February 1979 an experiment was undertaken to assess the suitability of conveying military supplies by busily engaged in setting up camp. The senior operating staff received a briefing from the BMR officers on the proposed exercise and were despatched on a reconnaissance of the system. As it was planned the volunteers would operate the railway from 18.00hrs without assistance from the regular staff and by 16.00hrs members of the Squadron would be arriving at the locomotive depot preparing to take over.

The reconnaissance team were discussing their final plans with the BMR Operating Officer, who considered they had formulated an excellent plan of operation. However, as the final decisions were being made the Operating Officer was called to attend a telephone call from the Depot Traffic Officer who explained there was a military emergency and at least one locomotive would be required all night to load and assemble an urgent special freight train. The Sergeant Major of the Squadron thought at first it was a hoax to test the abilities of his unit, but was persuaded it was a genuine emergency. Once convinced, the Squadron sprang into action and within a few minutes, was on its way to the scene of operations. Not only was the emergency dealt with efficiently but the planned exercise was also carried out exactly according to the programme.

Senior RAOC officers later complemented the Squadron for a job carried out in the best traditions of the Army.

The term 'Operating Officer' was perhaps a slight misnomer in terms of Railway Group organisation, as he was in practice a 'general manager' of his particular railway system. Each Divisional Commander controlled a number of railway systems and according to size, with an Operating Officer, Yardmaster, Yard Foreman, sometimes a chargehand in charge. Within the Divisional HQ there was a Locomotive Officer, originally Paddy Forbes, followed for many years by Ted Lees, then Alec Martin and finally Ron Hoyle; staffed with an inspector, fitters,

and boilermakers who worked mainly in the depots without such staff.

Similarly, with the Permanent Way Officer and his inspector, Operating Officers were responsible directly to the Divisional Commander for the whole operation of the railway system, including the maintenance of locomotives, wagons, permanent way and the administration of staff. Whilst Operating Officers listened and took note of the advice given by the Divisional Locomotive and Permanent Way Officers their prime concern was the safe, economical operation of the system, bearing in mind the needs of the service, but of course they accepted responsibility for action taken out of line with the advice being given. An example is a telephone call from the Senior Locomotive Officer at Group HQ saying it is noted that Bicester is using twice as many coupling rod brasses as any other depot. The answer, "we are taking up to one hundred loaded wagons through the section per train, instead of the theoretical 50 - double the number of locomotives and train crews, and we will conform to your target". Hush from the other end - and then "Carry on as you are."

As in the war years there were several problems to overcome which do not necessarily appear on BR. For example, with the peace-time decreasing work load, and especially the cessation of the Oxford Passenger trains worked by Army crews, it was not possible to allocate locomotives and crews solely for passenger train work. Freight work had had to be planned to be interrupted whilst a locomotive went off to run a passenger train, this often meaning a stop for water as well. Then the system was not bounded by fencing (other than the single line between 'A' and 'B' blockposts) which opened the railway system to all in the Depot. No amount of regulations seemed to prevent personnel using the railway track as a pathway, when so often it was the shortest distance between two points, and turnout levers were something to pull on the way.

Drivers had to be on the constant lookout for stray walkers, for turnout settings, and when road transport became more dense, for those drivers who, seeing a 'slow' moving train, thought they could beat it across the next level crossing. The Caution signing of

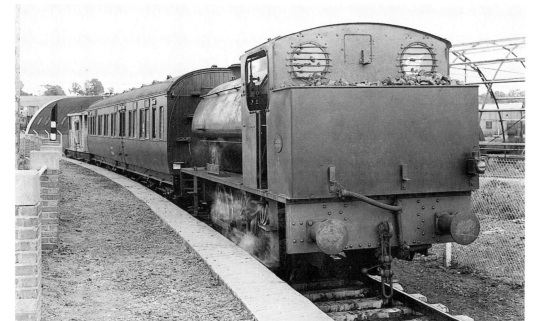

WD No. 113 *Royal Pioneer* enters Arncott station on the 'up' BLC enthusiasts' special of 3rd June 1956. The Central Workshops complex was situated on the right of the picture.

John Edgington

An 'Austerity' saddle tank hauls the Royal Coach through Ambrosden station with members of the Railway Enthusiasts Club and Industrial Railway Society in April 1969. The special is travelling in the 'up' direction.

G.P. Roberts

crossings has been discussed elsewhere but the Operating Officer in his efforts to caution road users requested permission to copy the level crossing signs on an American railway which read, "Our trains take 20 seconds to cross this road, whether your car is on it or not". Permission denied!

On one 'sad' occasion a recreational passenger train was running on a Sunday night from Piddington to the Graven Hill Theatre to take troops to a dance. The Foreman had asked whether the newly returned 1928 Wolverton stock (it had just been in for overhaul) could be used and with some reluctance permission was granted. On the night, the train left Arncott Platform and as it gathered speed and disappeared in the darkness Bill Bracewell, the Foreman on duty, heard a sound like rapid machine gun fire but the train kept on going. When it reached Westacott Road it was found that none of the doors on the platform side could be opened. There were no door handles! At the points leading from the north end of 'C9' shed there was a pile of door and grab handles. It was subsequently found that store staff had been ordered to clear the area north of the shed of rubbish. The party saw a permanent way trolley parked on the line which would be ideal for moving the rubbish and to take advantage of it moved an empty railway wagon further up the line towards the main, leaving it there on completion of the task. In fact it was so placed that the bolts on the corner stanchion just caught the handles as the train passed, so exactly placed that there was not a scratch on the new paintwork of the five or six coaches comprising the train.

The Depot railway and store sheds had been designed in the main with a down gradient into the shed, the idea being that wagons would be braked on the gradient by the train crew and run into the shed by gravity by the shed staff. Certainly in the post-war years this was a very bad practice, the shed roads were unlit and the sheds were not manned because the Ordnance staff worked on a day shift. The result was innumerable shed doors damaged by runaway wagons, either the train crew proceeding too far, not pinning down sufficient brakes, or by brakes being released by shed staff before the shed doors were opened and then being unable to halt them. There was a fear that day shunting of sheds, with locomotives placing wagons right to position would lead to a great loss of work due to staff stopping to watch the locomotive, but eventually it was agreed that the day from a railway point of view would be 12.00hrs one day to 12.00hrs the next. Shed commanders would advise the Traffic Officer by 11.00hrs

54

each day of their requirements for wagons and be advised of receipts coming to them. The main shunts would take place from 12.00hrs to early afternoon, other shunting only being carried out to meet special requirements. Outwards traffic from these shunts would be sorted and placed in Exchange Sidings, either that evening or the following morning as required. The change resulted in a great improvement in efficiency and much less damage to shed doors.

In the early post war years derailments, mainly due to the poor condition of the track, were very frequent with the resultant interruption to traffic and deployment of staff, especially since for many years all heavy re-railing had to be done with 35-ton hydraulic jacks. In many places the water table is but inches below the track level and on one such occasion, when a locomotive was derailed across the track, sleeper beds were laid out, and the jacks operated, but it was the following day before the greatly increased sleeper bed stopped going down, and the locomotive began to rise. What a relief when the system was provided with a heavy breakdown crane.

Mention of the water table reminds of a time when the railcar fitter asked whether he could have a pit to work under the cars. A suitable old water tank was obtained from the local DCRE, and with difficulty, because of water, it was sunk in the four-foot on the spur adjacent to the south running line. Come one winter's morning to find the tank had risen on a block of ice, taking a railcar up with it!

Passenger Services

Although the BMR was constructed primarily to carry military supplies throughout the large Ordnance Depot, the need for passenger train services was quickly realised. This was dictated by the sheer size of the Depot, together with the impossibility of providing living accommodation for all the thousands of military and ATS personnel within marching distance of their places of work.

At the outset no public transport facilities of any kind existed within the 20 square miles of the area occupied by the Garrison. Army lorries were occasionally used to convey military parties to and from the various sites and were also used to bring parties from the two main line stations in Bicester to the Depot.

With the rapid increase in the numbers of troops, plus the shortage of petrol and diesel fuels, it became apparent

Once a busy congested yard, Exchange Sidings was devoid of any freight trains on 16th May 1981 as an Oxford Publishing Company's special travels on the 'down' main running line to Graven Hill on its tour of the system. The Oxford-Bletchley line of British Rail is on the left with Langford Farm station situated on the extreme right.

Bill Simpson

A view taken in October 1980, of 'A' blockpost showing the second (1948) structure alongside. The scene looks towards Bicester and the connection on the right with a 5 mph restriction leads into the Sorting Sidings. The 'Up' Sidings are to the left with an RCTS dmu special halted on the 'down' line outer home signal.

Bill Simpson

that rail passenger services would be essential to the efficient operation of the installation, both as a means of conveying large numbers of persons to and from the working sites, proceeding to and from leave, or being sent to other units.

The passenger trains could, therefore, be divided into three main categories:

(a) External leave and recreational services (trains starting or finishing their journeys at points outside the BMR).

(b) Internal recreational services (confined to BMR tracks).

(c) Works trains (conveying staff to and from their places of duty.)

The first instance of a passenger train occurred on 16th February 1942 when a locomotive hauling several open wagons filled with soldiers engaged on construction duties, ran from Arncott to Langford Farm. No platforms existed and the hapless troops were forced to scramble over heaps of clay and indescribable mud to reach Langford Lane and the road to the town of Bicester. This operation was reminiscent of the pioneering days of the railways when passengers with 3rd class tickets were carried in open vehicles.

Later, in February of the same year, the first timetable provided a service of five trains daily between Arncott and Langford Farm, seven on Saturdays and four on Sundays. Details of the times and rolling stock used have not been traced, but it is believed the nine former ferryvans used during the construction days were utilised, hauled by one of the 'Dean Goods' and sometimes by the O2 class 0-4-4 Southern tank engine.

In the following month the passenger rolling stock fleet was augmented by an interesting six-coach set of six-wheeled compartment vehicles. These had originally been part of an eleven-coach set built by the former London & North Western Railway in 1911 for the Birmingham-Sutton Coldfield service. The coaches had elliptical roofs, a body length of 30 ft and a tare weight of 15 tons. As built, the set had consisted of two brake thirds, six thirds, each with five compartments and three firsts. All were originally illuminated by gas, later converted to electric lighting. The six coaches sent to Bicester included two brake thirds and four thirds numbered 26435 to 26440 in the final LMS Railway numbering scheme. One of the five compartment thirds, No. 26435 is shown in the accompanying photograph. Why the six-wheeled set was constructed is hard to determine. Large numbers of bogie rolling stock was in use by the turn of the century and four and six-wheeled vehicles, although still running until the late 1930s, were regarded as distinctly old fashioned. After this batch left Wolverton Works it is thought no further attempts were made to produce any more examples.

Nevertheless under the spartan conditions applying on the early BMR the vehicles were highly regarded, despite the fact that neither lighting not heating were supplied. The six-wheelers, did, however, provide a reasonably comfortable ride and their upholstered seats were a distinct improvement to the seatless ferryvans. These coaches were confined to BMR tracks and not allowed to venture forth onto the neighbouring LMS metals. The ancient six-wheelers ran continuously throughout the war years on the internal services and were eventually maintained in a good condition. At the end of the war the bodies were removed and the frames and wheelsets were used as flat wagons. Their comparative light weight created a propensity for the wheels to 'pick up' when

braking, especially on the down grades entering Ambrosden and Arncott stations. Drivers frequently overshot these platforms until experience brought about an improved braking technique.

As well as the timetabled services many short distant trains were unrecorded and ran only on request from the various military units stationed within the Depot area, when large numbers of troops needed to be moved at short notice. It was often necessary to detach locomotives from freight work to run these 'on request' trains, utilising either the ferryvans or the ex-LNWR six-wheeled set. Frequent trains of this kind worked round the Graven Hill loop line which, during the war period, was not provided with any platforms and required passengers to clamber in and out of the coaches into pools of water, sticky clay and mud. Some of these trips were hauled by the newly acquired saddletanks which, at first, were not equipped with vacuum brake fittings. The braking effort was confined to the engine steam brakes and the handbrakes of the train. This primitive and risky operation continued for many months until two of the saddletanks were fitted with vacuum ejectors enabling most of the internal services to be fully braked. Even then the ferryvans continued to run, without automatic brakes, conveying full loads of troops,

Former London & North Western Railway six-wheeled coach, one of six, used for internal passenger services during the Second World War. All were scrapped at Bicester in the 1950s, the frames and wheelsets being used as six-wheeled flat wagons. The coaches were 30 ft long and had a tare weight of 15 tons.

Authors' collection

prisoners of war and civilian workers.

As the Depot developed, it was to be expected the numbers of passengers would increase and the summit was reached during the years from 1943 to 1946. Over this period every item of rolling stock was pressed into passenger service, including for one short period in 1944, a train of twelve four-wheeled, loose-coupled box vans running once daily between Arncott and Graven Hill.

The following table of passenger journeys illustrates the growth and eventual decline in the carryings:

No. of weeks	Week ending		No. of passenger journeys
4	25th July	1942	34,271
5	29th August	1942	40,845
4	26th September	1942	24,357
4	24th October	1942	27,750
4	21st November	1942	45,575
4	19th December	1942	49,962
5	23rd January	1943	51,956
4	20th February	1943	39,646
5	27th March	1943	61,700
4	24th April	1943	54,589
2	8th May	1943	25,286
5	26th June	1943	115,528
4	24th July	1943	105,016
5	28th August	1943	159,663
4	25th September	1943	128,738
4	23rd October	1943	133,485
4	20th November	1943	146,840
5	25th December	1943	167,395
4	22nd January	1944	113,541
4	19th February	1944	107,756
4	18th March	1944	100,229
4	15th April	1944	111,599
5	20th May	1944	124,751
4	17th June	1944	94,412
5	22nd July	1944	138,670
4	19th August	1944	118,735
4	16th September	1944	107,822
4	14th October	1944	118,615
4	11th November	1944	145,286
5	16th December	1944	162,789
4	10th January	1945	Not known
4	10th February	1945	136,900
4	10th March	1945	144,936
4	7th April	1945	151,810
4	5th May	1945	138,785
5	9th June	1945	154,559
4	7th July	1945	117,390
5	11th August	1945	156,758
4	9th September	1945	115,870
4	6th October	1945	119,951
4	3rd November	1945	106,144
4	1st December	1945	120,470
5	5th January	1946	106,570
4	20th February	1946	89,677
5	9th March	1946	107,298
4	6th April	1946	113,099
4	4th May	1946	108,486
6	15th June	1946	167,706
4	13th July	1946	103,608
4	10th August	1946	85,243
4	7th September	1946	75,687
4	5th October	1946	77,760
4	2nd November	1946	75,755

Several hundred women serving in the Auxiliary Territorial Service (ATS) later renamed the Women's Royal Army Corps (WRAC) were billeted in a camp at Piddington. Many of them were employed in the MT sub-depot located on the Arncott loop line. Army lorries were used to convey the ATS on the short, two-mile journey. This method was time consuming, uneconomic in terms of manpower and utilisation of vehicles. Furthermore, this movement required use of rationed petrol supplies.

In April 1943 an experiment was carried out to move these personnel by rail. New platforms were constructed near the Piddington camp, replacing an earlier structured of concrete sleepers near the level crossing and at 'C2' storage shed. A six-coach set of bogie, compartment rolling stock was requisitioned from the LMS Railway. After several day's trials the experiment was pronounced a success, with the entraining and the discharge of passengers being accomplished without a hitch, while valuable time was saved in transporting the women in a single train load. The ATS also found the journey more comfortable than standing, packed tight in army lorries.

When staff were available the junction points from the Up to the South Running Lines were manned and the Arncott (South) level crossing provided with a part time keeper. This enabled the train to run non stop to and from 'C2' and Piddington. If the rolling stock was not required for other purposes it was stabled in the 'C5' lay-by and formed the 18.10hrs return service from 'C2' to Piddington. The morning train departed from Piddington at 07.35hrs Mondays to Saturdays and at 08.10hrs on Sundays. In the event of the ATS being required to work later in the evening 'Q' paths (to run if required) locomotives and rolling stock were available to leave 'C2' at 21.05hrs for Piddington, the six-wheeled stock being ear-marked for this purpose.

Other trains for the ATS were provided from Langford Farm at 07.30hrs calling at all stations and returning from Piddington at 18.00hrs. The ATS trains became a BMR institution and during the war years ran seven days per week. In an amended form the services continued four times daily after 1948 until January 1959, thus achieving the record of the longest running passenger trains on the BMR. The 'Dean Goods' and vacuum brake equipped saddletanks provided the haulage through the 16 years period.

Services to Oxford

The town of Bicester offered little in the way of leisure facilities for a large garrison of troops. One cinema, two service canteens run by voluntary organisations, and several pubs, although well run and much appreciated by the military, could hardly be expected to cope with thousands of soldiers thrust upon the once peaceful locality. Most of the personnel worked very long, hard hours. An escape from the confines of the depot for short intervals was regarded as essential by the Commandant, Brigadier Palmer. The City of Oxford, over 17 miles from the Piddington terminal, offered more amenities, albeit restricted by food and drink rationing. After many overtures by the Garrison authorities, in May 1943, the

LMS and GWR railways agreed to provide additional services on Saturdays and Sundays between Bicester (LMS) and Oxford (Rewley Road) stations. The journey was made over LMS tracks utilising GWR motive power.

The first of these trains was run via Bicester (LMS) station where the GWR locomotive ran round and proceeded to Exchange Sidings, and where the BMR engine and crew took over for the remainder of the journey to Piddington, stopping at all stations en route. After several months some BMR train crews were given an examination by LMS Railway Inspectors and authorised to run in and out of Bicester (LMS) station. This removed the necessity for the civilian engine to run round, and reduced the overall journey time.

Troops travelled free on the BMR and paid only 6d (2½p) for the return journey between Bicester and Oxford. The balance of the fare 1s 4d (7p) being paid to the civilian railways by the various military units from their 'Imprest' (petty cash) account. A 35-mile journey for such a small sum, even by 1940's standards was a remarkable bargain, and one which was extensively used by the men and women from the Garrison.

A report from the Operating Officer of the system, dated 7th August 1943 stated that twelve passenger coaches were in use, ie the six-wheeled set and the six requisitioned LMS bogie coaches. Only four of these were in sufficiently good condition to run over LMS metals. This report gives an indication of the growing requirements for even more passenger trains between the Depot and Oxford, which had already been provided with extra services on Saturdays and Sundays. By August 1943 these had become inadequate to cater for the heavy traffic and it was evident that a proposal had been made by the LMS Railway for the Army to work extra trains utilising military crews and locomotives. This seemed a reasonable request when considering the great strain under which the railways were placed during wartime, when resources of all kinds were at a premium.

By the end of 1943 the Garrison had doubled in size and comprised of 43 units and approximately 14,000 personnel. The adjacent RAF station and the influx of many hundreds of airmen also added to the transport problems. Efforts were made to widen the vicinity in which off-duty troops could travel without permits or leave passes and Banbury was eventually included in the permitted area. The GWR then scheduled extra trains from Blackthorn in an effort to ease the pressure on Oxford. These measures did not prove too successful and Oxford continued to be more attractive to the troops and airmen.

During November 1943 further negotiations took place with the LMS who somewhat reluctantly ran another special from Oxford to Bicester using their own engines and rolling stock. The set of compartment coaches used was strengthened to eight vehicles, allowing a high passenger carrying capacity. A BMR engine worked the train from Bicester (LMS) stopping at all stations to Piddington.

The numbers of passengers still continued to rise and finally it was agreed the Army should provide a Sundays only train to and from Oxford, using their own locomo-

tives, rolling stock and crew. Thus train crews from Targets 1 and 2 commenced 'learning the road' (familiarising themselves with the route and its signalling, together with the civilian rules and operating procedures). For this purpose they were issued with special permits to travel on the footplates and brake vans of LMS trains from which they could observe the signals and other essential features of the route.

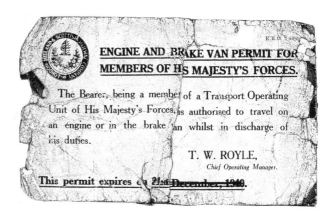

A rather war-torn example of the engine and brake van permit issued to Royal Engineers military railway personnel.

This enabled the soldier railwaymen to 'learn the road' from passenger and freight trains. Such permits were in use between Oxford and Bicester.

After a period, a locomotive inspector from the LMS motive power depot at Rugby conducted a series of driving examinations which included knowledge of the line, rules and operating instructions. Those Army drivers passing the examination were then allowed to sign the route card and were permitted to run trains to and from Oxford (Rewley Road) and Bicester. Similar arrangements were made for the brakesmen/shunters who carried out the guard's duties.

The War Department engines and rolling stock were also examined by technical staff from the LMS to ascertain their suitability for running over the route. Excellent co-operation and willing assistance was given by all the LMS staff during this period. This service commenced in 1944, departing from Piddington at 13.20hrs, the engine running tender first, calling at all stations to Exchange Sidings where the engine uncoupled and ran round the train. Although the service was shown in the timetables as running to Langford Farm station this was never carried out as the platform was too short for the seven or eight coach Oxford trains. Instead passengers travelling to the town of Bicester alighted in Exchange Sidings and proceeded, on foot, alongside the tracks to Langford Lane and London Road to gain access to the town. This was hardly a practice that would be condoned today by the Department of Transport or British Rail!

In the meantime the brakesman/shunter carrying out the guard's duties proceeded to the LMS ground frame, obtained clearance from Bicester No. 2 signal box, set the road from the sidings to the trailing connection and pulled off the short arm upper quadrant semaphore for the LMS

White Cross Green level crossing on the Arncott loop. Trains from MT Yard use the left track and the line to the right is the main route from Arncott.

E.R. Lawton

'down' line. The train, now engine first, ran onto the main line stopping clear of the connection and picking up the brakesman/shunter. The train then ran non stop to Oxford (Rewley Road). After the passengers had detrained at Rewley Road station the signalman at the station signal box operated a gong situated at the buffer stop end of the arrival platform. This was an indication to the driver that the road was set for the carriage siding and the engine propelled the empty stock into the siding, clear of the main line. The locomotive then proceeded to the small running shed situated on the 'down' side of the line, a few hundred yards beyond Rewley Road station, for turning and servicing.

The return journey departed from Oxford at 22.15hrs running non stop to Bicester (LMS) where the engine ran round and worked the train to Piddington, calling at all stations. Arrival in Piddington was scheduled at 23.19hrs.

On 30th December 1944 a Piddington to Oxford passenger train, consisting of eight former LMS double-bogied compartment coaches hauled by 'Dean Goods' No. 70095 running, as usual, with tender leading, was approaching 'A' blockpost. The flagboard was exhibiting two green indications but unfortunately the hand-worked facing point connection to the Sorting Sidings was wrongly set for the yard. Another 'Dean Goods', No. 70094 was standing in the Sorting Sidings' connection awaiting for the passenger train to clear before running light engine to Arncott. The inevitable collision damaged both engines with the front end of No. 70095 overriding the leading brake/third vehicle, crushing the brake section and the leading two passenger compartments.

Fortunately, owing to the length of the train the first two coaches had purposely stopped clear of the platforms at Arncott, Ambrosden and Graven Hill and the leading compartments were not occupied. No deaths or serious injuries resulted but both locomotives were taken out of service. They were sent to Swindon Works for heavy repair on 24th February 1945. After receiving attention at Arncott locomotive shed, enabling it to be hauled in a scheduled freight train, the tender of No. 70094 was also

despatched to Swindon on 3rd March 1945. No. 70094 arrived back on the BMR on 27th April and No. 70095 on 8th May 1945.

With the addition of the military operated train, the BMR Oxford services that were worked by motive power from the LMS, GWR and War Department could be summarised as follows:

Saturdays only - 1944

Dep. Oxford (Rewley Road)	Dep. Bicester (LMS)	Notes
21.00	21.30	Worked from Bicester by WD Locomotive and crew
21.40	22.10	GWR locomotive to Exchange Sidings. WD locomotive and crew to Piddington.
22.30 (formerley 22.45)	23.02	GWR locomotive to Exchange Sidings. WD locomotive and crew to Piddington.
23.30	23.59	GWR locomotive to Exchange Sidings. WD locomotive and crew to Piddington.

Sundays only

21.15	21.50	Worked from Bicester by WD locomotive and crew.
22.15	22.47	Worked throughout by WD locomotive and crew.
23.05 (formerly 22.30)	23.34	GWR locomotive to Exchange Sidings. WD locomotive and crew to Piddington.

Saturdays only - 1944
Dep. Piddington

13.20	Via Exchange Sidings	GWR locomotive from Exchange Sidings to Oxford.
14.20	Via Exchange Sidings	GWR locomotive from Exchange Sidings to Oxford.

Sundays only - 1944

Dep. Piddington	Dep. Bicester	
14.20 (later 16.30)	Via Exchange Sidings	Worked by WD locomotive and crew, throughout.

Early in 1945 alterations were introduced and the trains worked by military engines and crews were extended to run from Mondays to Thursdays, departing from Piddington at 18.30hrs with the return from Oxford leaving at 22.45hrs, both trains running via Bicester (LMS). The sight of GWR motive power at Rewley Road raised the curiosity of railway enthusiasts, one of which in 1943, sent a query to the *Railway Magazine*. The official reply being as follows:

Oxford - Bicester Service

The 10.45pm (10.30pm on Sundays) passenger train from Oxford to Bicester (LMS) is not run for the use of the general public and for this reason, like many regular passengers trains, is not advertised. It is worked by GWR locomotive power as a matter of convenience. Censorship regulations forbid the printing of information as to new lines, branches, connecting spurs, or widenings brought into use since the beginning of the war.

(This extract is reproduced by kind permission of the Editor, *Railway Magazine*.)

The rolling stock used on the services worked by Royal Engineer crews consisted of seven or eight double-bogied compartment coaches acquired from the LMS Railway. One of the seven-coach sets included three clerestory roof vehicles of Midland Railway origin and four former LNWR coaches bearing Wolverton Works plates dated 1912.

The motive power employed on the trains worked by military crews was confined to the 'Dean Goods' and the sole A12 class 'Jubilee' 0-4-2, which retained the "Southern" lettering on the tender throughout its War Department service. Both classes performed well on the heavily loaded Oxford trains. Very few failures were experienced and it is considered this could be attributed to the engines being confined and used by only six crews from Targets 1 and 2, each of which took a pride in the running and servicing of their charges. In fact it became a point of honour that the "Oxfords" should never run late and early arrivals were commonplace. The near twelve miles run from Bicester to Oxford was scheduled to take twenty minutes for the WD worked trains, but this was rarely adhered to and the usual running time was 15 to 16 minutes.

On VE Day, 8th May 1945, with many members of the Garrison being granted an extra day's leave, the 22.45hrs from Oxford had three additional coaches added, bringing the load to eleven vehicles all packed to capacity. The 'Dean Goods' hauling the train managed to reach Bicester (LMS) in 19 minutes and after having completed the run to Piddington and disposing of the empty coaches, arrived back at Arncott locomotive shed with the tender completely devoid of coal.

The comparative young age of the Army enginemen resulted in the inevitable speeding. On one occasion in late 1944 dense fog descended and visibility over much of Oxfordshire was reduced to a few yards. An off duty driver joined the enginemen at Oxford (Rewley Road) to assist the rostered crew in observing signals. With a driver on each side of the cab and the foreman confining his energies to the shovel and attendance of the injectors, the well loaded 22.45hrs arrived in Bicester three minutes before time, much to the horror of the LMS operating authorities. Action, by the Signalman's Inspector followed and the signalmen were instructed to maintain their distant signals at caution to slow down the military trains. Despite this precaution 'on time' arrivals continued to be the order of the day.

By 1959 the Saturday services were withdrawn but a Sunday only train, leaving Oxford at 22.20hrs remained until 1960 when the service terminated at Bicester (London Road). After Nationalisation of the railways in 1948 the former LMS station was re-named Bicester (London Road) and the ex-GWR station became Bicester (North).

During 1946, at the insistence of the railway trade unions, the military crews were replaced by regular LMS enginemen and guards. BMR engines and crews continued to run into Bicester (London Road) until the special Oxford trains were finally withdrawn. Withdrawal of all passenger services on the Oxford-Bletchley line took place on Saturday 30th December 1967, the last passenger train being the 22.50hrs from Oxford to Bletchley.

In May 1987 a limited passenger service was re-introduced between Oxford and Bicester, details of which are shown in Chapter 8.

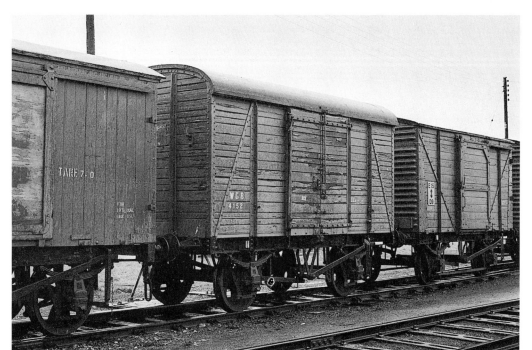

A train of internal user vans being marshalled in the Sorting Sidings including No. 4152, a former Southern Railway box van.

Peter Nicholson

61

Services to London

Troops posted to and from Bicester or proceeding on leave were often obliged to travel via London using scheduled train services. These, during the war years, were generally overcrowded with the corridors, vestibules and often the toilet compartments full with standing passengers. The trains between Bicester and London were no exception despite two routes being available, one to Paddington and the other via Bletchley to Euston.

Bicester being a particularly large garrison presented special problems of overcrowding, and on the 27th October 1944 the LMS consented to run a special military service commencing its journey on the BMR and running via the South Curve at Bletchley non stop to Euston. No additional motive power was required on the military system as the London train replaced an internal service.

The 'up' train ran on Friday and Saturday evenings departing from Piddington at 18.03hrs calling at all stations on the BMR to Bicester (LMS) and then running non stop to London (Euston) arriving at 20.42hrs.

The return train departed from London (Euston) at 21.40hrs (Saturdays) stopping Bicester and departing at 23.38hrs for Piddington where arrival was scheduled at 00.19hrs (Sunday mornings). On Sundays a later departure from Euston was at 22.00hrs the service running twenty minutes later throughout and arriving in Piddington at 00.39hrs (Monday morning).

In all cases the LMS locomotive was attached or detached in the Exchange Sidings with the BMR engine, usually a vacuum-equipped saddle tank, working to and from Piddington.

For the first few months this new service was very popular with very heavy loadings on Sunday nights where it became necessary to increase the composition to twelve coaches. A train of this length could not be accommodated at the various BMR stations. This was resolved by dividing the train in Exchange Sidings, the first six coaches being worked non stop to Arncott and terminating at Piddington. The second portion followed five minutes later calling at Graven Hill, Ambrosden and Arncott. The two portions were then re-formed either in Arncott Yard or Exchange Sidings and worked by the LMS locomotive to Bletchley Yard. On several occasions when motive power was in short supply a single saddle tank worked the empty train of twelve coaches from Arncott to Exchange.

When a twelve-coach train was provided the station announcer at Euston would inform passengers that the first portion of the train would call at Bicester, Arncott and Piddington only and the last six coaches at Bicester, Graven Hill and Ambrosden only although, in fact, the last portion also stopped at Arncott. These announcements often caused much astonishment from other seasoned travellers at Euston who had never heard of such destinations!

Despite its earlier success the number of military passengers using the 18.03hrs Piddington to Euston train on Saturday evenings decreased rapidly and after the 17th February 1945 was withdrawn. In its place the 14.25hrs service from Piddington to Oxford (Rewley Road) was terminated at Langford Farm and the 16.22hrs Piddington to Langford Farm was extended to Oxford. The latter then provided a connection, by changing stations, with the 17.50hrs Oxford (GWR) to London (Paddington).

At various times plans were also discussed to run military passenger specials on British Railways (Western Region) tracks via Oxford into London (Paddington) but at the times required by the military authorities it was not possible to find a suitable path through Oxford. On reflection it would have been quite delightful to hear a train announcer in London broadcasting a Paddington-Piddington service!

A partial solution was found in 1950 when, on Friday evenings, a relief train departed from Bicester (North) at 18.15hrs arriving in Paddington at 19.43hrs. On Saturdays this left Bicester (North) at 12.20hrs while on Sunday evenings a relief service departed from Paddington at 23.15hrs calling at Blackthorn, Bicester (North) 00.46hrs, Ardley and Banbury.

Internal Works Trains

Trains for the exclusive use of troops travelling to and from their places of work within the confines of the Depot were run seven days per week during the war years. Some were scheduled for a few weeks only before changes in the work pattern necessitated their withdrawal and replacement by trains running to and from different sites.

The following list shows examples of such internal services which enabled the Depot to function efficiently with a flexible passenger transport system which could be adapted quickly to meet the ever-changing military requirements:

Examples of Works Trains in 1944/45

Dep.	From	To	Rolling stock	Notes
07.15	'E30'*	Piddington	Nine ferry vans.	Returns from Piddington 17.50
07.30	Langford Farm	Piddington	Seven coaches.	Returns from Piddington 18.00
07.35	Piddington	'C2'	Six or seven coaches.	Returns from 'C2' at 18.05
07.40	'B3'*	'C2'	Six-wheeled set.	Returns from 'C2' at 18.15
12.05	'C2'	'B37'*	Nine ferry vans.	Returns from 'B37' at 13.00
13.00	Piddington	Graven Hill	Six-wheeled set.	Returns from Graven Hill at 14.10 conveys REME personnel Mondays to Fridays only.
18.05	'C2'	Piddington	Six or seven coaches.	
21.05	'C2'	Piddington	Six-wheeled set.	'Q' train - runs if required.

* No platforms built at these points.

To ease the general labour shortage which was acute in the early 1950s a number of European Voluntary Workers (EVWs), refugees from the wartime occupied countries, were recruited. Many of these were given living accommodation at Graven Hill and a passenger train service conveyed them each day from Graven Hill to Ambrosden, Arncott and Piddington. A corresponding service returned in the evening.

The cost of running these trains was shared by the War Department and the workers themselves and it was agreed that if the trains ran late for any reason the EVWS would not lose any pay. As a consequence the BMR Operating Officer had to report on the timekeeping of the service and the reason for any delay that occurred.

Between the North and main running lines just south of 'B' blockpost there is a pond on which, each year two swans alight, raise a family and later depart for pastures new, returning during the next season.

One day a 'down' EVW passenger train had been checked at 'B' blockpost and was running at a low speed towards Arncott. Near the turnout leading to 'C9' shed the driver noticed a cygnet caught between the check rail and the frog of the points. Owing to the low speed he was able to halt the train, alight and attempt to free the bird, only to be attacked by the furious mother swan. The brakesman/shunter carrying out the guard's duties on the train came to the rescue and managed to hold back the adult bird with a shunting pole. The cygnet was released and the train proceeded on its journey leaving an embarrassed Operating Officer to explain why the service had been delayed some twenty minutes!

The return service of these trains from Piddington also created a problem as three or four times over a period of one year the leading coach became derailed at the junction of the Up and South Running Lines between No. 5 TP and Arncott platform. These incidents were somewhat mystifying as passenger trains had used the junction, without trouble, for over sixteen years. All the track and sleeper marks made by the derailed bogies indicated split points. After consultation with the Divisional Permanent Way Officer, Nick Napier and a detailed examination, the point operating mechanism and the switch blades were renewed but the derailments still continued. The Operating Officer then conducted a series of tests using a diesel locomotive and one empty bogie coach running backwards and forwards over the junction. After several attempts at successively higher speeds it was discovered that at the points connecting the Up and Down Running Lines from Piddington the coach buffers rode over the engine buffers and were carried forward in this fashion, leaving no marks on the track or sleepers until arriving at the next set of points where a derailment took place. It appeared that track creep on the 1 in 90 down gradient and the 1 in 8 turnout had combined to cause the situation. This was resolved firstly by a 10 mph speed restriction over the junction and finally by substituting the junction with a 1 in 12 turnout.

Internal Scheduled Services

In addition to the works trains a regular service of internal passenger trains ran for military personnel travelling individually or in parties to duties in all parts of the system, posted to other units or proceeding to and from leave or off duty activities.

A series of 'Passenger Public Timetables' were

New rolling stock for the London Transport 'Underground', Piccadilly Line stored in the Up Sidings in 1977. The freight rolling stock is standing in the Sorting Sidings, the 'up' and 'down' running lines being sandwiched between the two yards.

Lt Col. G.K. Gillberry

BICESTER MILITARY RAILWAY

PASSENGER PUBLIC TIMETABLE COMMENCING 11th NOVEMBER 1944

'UP TRAINS'

Station		MONDAYS TO FRIDAYS							SATURDAYS ONLY							
		05.30	09.00	12.30	B. 18.00	F.O. 18.03	F.X. 18.35	19.42	09.00	13.20	14.25	16.22	17.11	18.03	19.33	22.10
PIDDINGTON	DEP.	05.30	09.00		18.00	18.03	18.35	19.42	09.00	13.20	14.25	16.22	17.11	18.03	19.33	22.10
ARNCOTT	ARR.	05.38	09.08		18.08	18.11	18.43	19.50	09.08	13.28	14.33	16.30	17.19	18.11	19.41	22.18
ARNCOTT	DEP.	05.39	09.09		18.10	18.14	18.45	19.52	09.09	13.30	14.35	16.32	17.20	18.14	19.43	
AMBROSDEN	ARR.	05.45	09.15		18.16	18.20	18.51	19.58	09.15	13.36	14.41	16.38	17.26	18.20	19.49	22.24
AMBROSDEN	DEP.	05.46	09.16	12.30	18.18	18.23	18.53	20.00	09.16	13.38	14.43	16.40	17.27	18.23	19.51	22.25
GRAVEN HILL	ARR.	05.49	09.19	12.36	18.21	18.26	18.56	20.03	09.19			16.43	17.30	18.26	19.54	22.28
GRAVEN HILL	DEP.	05.50	09.20	12.37	18.23	18.28	18.58	20.05	09.20			16.45	17.31	18.28	19.56	
LANGFORD FARM	ARR.	05.54	09.24	12.40	18.27	18.31	19.02	20.09	09.24	13.45	14.50	16.49	17.35	18.31	20.00	22.30
LANGFORD FARM	DEP.			12.41		18.35				13.50	15.05			18.35		
BICESTER	ARR.			12.45		18.40								18.40		22.35
BICESTER	DEP.					18.45								18.45		
OXFORD	ARR.									14.10	15.25					
EUSTON	ARR.					20.42								20.42		

'DOWN TRAINS'

Station		MONDAYS TO FRIDAYS							SATURDAYS ONLY					
		11.30	F.X. 18.25	19.10	B. 22.10	F.O. 22.45	23.45 (Thur.O.)	00.25	21.00	21.40	22.30	23.30	21.40	22.00
EUSTON	DEP.												21.40	22.00
OXFORD	DEP.	11.30	18.25	19.10	22.10	22.45			21.00	21.40	22.30	23.30		
BICESTER	ARR.	11.34	18.33	19.14	22.14	23.03			21.18	21.58	22.50	23.48	23.33	23.53
BICESTER	DEP.	11.35	18.35	19.16	22.16	23.15	23.45		21.30	22.10	23.02	24.00	23.38	23.58
LANGFORD FARM	ARR.	11.38	18.41	19.19	22.19	23.20	23.48		21.35	22.15	23.07	00.05	23.43	00.03
LANGFORD FARM	DEP.	11.39	18.43	19.21	22.21	23.25	23.50	00.25		22.23	23.12	00.10	23.48	00.08
GRAVEN HILL	ARR.		18.46					00.29					23.53	00.12
GRAVEN HILL	DEP.		18.48					00.31					23.54	00.14
AMBROSDEN	ARR.	11.45	18.52	19.27	22.27	23.32	23.56	00.34	21.42	22.30	23.19	00.17	24.00	00.20
AMBROSDEN	DEP.	11.46		19.29	22.29	23.35	23.58	00.36	21.45	22.33	23.22	00.20	00.02	00.23
ARNCOTT	ARR.					23.41		00.42	21.51	22.39	23.28	00.26	00.10	00.30
ARNCOTT	DEP.					23.44		00.44	21.54	22.42	23.31	00.29	00.12	00.32
PIDDINGTON	ARR.	11.54		19.37	22.37	23.52	00.06	00.52	22.02	22.50	23.39	00.37	00.19	00.39

NOTES: - 'B' - Runs eight minutes earlier Fridays. 'F.X.' - Friday excepted. 'F.O.' - Fridays only. 'THUR.O.' - Thursdays only.

'UP TRAINS' — SUNDAYS ONLY

Station		10.30	13.20	14.20	16.30	20.15
PIDDINGTON	DEP.	10.30	13.20	14.20	16.30	20.15
ARNCOTT	ARR.	10.38	13.28	14.28	16.38	20.19
ARNCOTT	DEP.	10.39	13.29	14.30	16.40	20.21
AMBROSDEN	ARR.	10.45	13.35	14.36	16.46	20.24
AMBROSDEN	DEP.	10.47	13.36	14.38	16.48	20.26
GRAVEN HILL	ARR.	10.50	13.39		16.51	20.32
GRAVEN HILL	DEP.	10.51	13.40		16.53	20.34
LANGFORD FARM	ARR.	10.55	13.44	14.45	16.57	20.42
LANGFORD FARM	DEP.			15.00		
OXFORD	ARR.			15.20		

'DOWN TRAINS' — SUNDAYS ONLY

Station		21.15	22.00	23.05
EUSTON	DEP.	21.15	22.00	
OXFORD	DEP.	21.33	22.15	23.05
BICESTER	ARR.	21.50	22.35	23.23
BICESTER	DEP.	21.55	22.47	23.35
LANGFORD FARM	ARR.	22.02	22.52	23.40
LANGFORD FARM	DEP.	22.05	22.59	23.45
GRAVEN HILL	ARR.	22.11	23.02	23.52
GRAVEN HILL	DEP.	22.14	23.08	23.55
AMBROSDEN	ARR.	22.22	23.11	00.01
AMBROSDEN	DEP.		23.19	00.04
PIDDINGTON	ARR.			00.12

Bill Bracewell

Probably the longest serving member of the BMR staff was the late William 'Bill' Bracewell. He arrived at the fledgling system in 1941 with the original detachment of RE railway troops.

Bill Bracewell was born on 15th March 1918 in Miles Platting, Manchester and was first employed by the Blue Circle Cement Company. He was mobilised in the Royal Engineers Transportation section at the outbreak of the Second World War. Throughout the war years he worked as a brakesman/shunter, during which period the position involved long and strenuous duties, marshalling and running the thousands of freight trains which formed part of the vital link in supplying the armed forces. Part of his work also entailed being a guard on the frequent passenger train services, including the Piddington to Oxford trains.

At the termination of hostilities civilian staff gradually replaced the former railway troops and after being demobilised Mr Bracewell was appointed Yard Foreman. Because of his lengthy and varied experience his knowledge of the Depot rail system was invaluable. Until his death on 1st September 1979 he was a well-known figure both in Arncott and throughout the whole of the Depot area. In his younger days he often played football with the local Ambrosden team.

In April 1979 he was awarded the Imperial Service Medal to commemorate his long service. This was presented to him by the Superintendent, Army Department Railway Staff, Major M.W. Sackett, ISO.

Other members of his family were also connected with the Central Ordnance Depot, his wife Marjorie being a stores supervisor for very many years and his son Tony, a chargehand in the C&W Workshops until appointment as Yard Master at the military railway, Kineton.

The accompanying photograph shows Bill Bracewell (right) outside the Arncott Regulators Cabin sometime during the mid 1950s.

published at regular intervals and displayed on the notice boards of the military units 'Company Offices' throughout the Garrison. The term 'Passenger Public Timetables' was somewhat of a misnomer as the trains were intended solely for authorised military passengers or civilians employed by the War Department, but it is known that a few local inhabitants 'in the know' travelled without charge. The table on page 64 shows a typical timetable of the period and illustrates the schedules for November 1944.

In 1943 an interesting double bogie passenger coach was transferred from the Longmoor Military Railway to Bicester. This was one of a pair originally built by R. & Y. Pickering of Wishaw, Scotland for the former Kent & East Sussex Railway in 1905 and numbered 18 and 19. In 1912 both were acquired by the Woolmer Instructional Military Railway (later the Longmoor Military Railway) and after approximately ten years in service were re-built, No. 18 becoming an officers' saloon and receiving the number 111. The former No. 19 became No. 110 and used

The boilerhouse at 'E14' site showing a train of BR HEA wagons entering the discharge plant.

Peter Nicholson

as a 'saloon/brake'. Both vehicles were employed on inspection trains and it is believed conveyed HM King George V on a visit to Longmoor in the late 1920s.

No. 110 was destroyed in an air raid on Longmoor Garrison in 1941 and two years later No. 111 was transferred to the BMR. During its wartime duties at Bicester it carried no running number but was maintained in an immaculate condition for VIP and similar visits. It was also used occasionally to convey the crew of the Arncott breakdown train when called out to attend accidents and derailments. The end windows provided an excellent view of the track and lineside features, thus providing an ideal vehicle for inspection parties.

In 1945 the coach was converted for use as a 'push-pull' unit although no mechanical controls to the engine, an 'Austerity' saddle tank being used. A wooden partition with a door was fitted at one end and communication between driver and fireman was maintained by an electric bell. A chain linkage enabled the whistle to be sounded from the coach driving cab and a brake van type of vacuum brake lever operated the brakes, the signal to re-create vacuum being given on the electric bell. This somewhat primitive type of 'push-pull' unit successfully replaced several of the more lightly used internal passenger services and was operated by two men.

On Tuesday 30th July 1946 the 'Pickering' coach was again patronised by royalty when the 11-years old King Feisal of Iraq and his entourage visited the Central Ordnance Depot. Saddle tank No. 75133, resplendent in highly polished khaki livery, red side rods and gleaming footplate fittings, provided the power. The highly excited young King travelled on the footplate from the Signals and Wireless sub depot to 'C2'. This was his first ride on a steam hauled train and the highlight of his visit to the Garrison. His military ADC Brigadier Abdul Wahab, his tutor John Pitt-Rivers, the Officer Commanding military railway detachment Captain White RE and Major J. Marsh RAOC also travelled on the train.

To commemorate the visit engine No. 75133 was named *King Feisal of Iraq* with the name painted on the tank sides. Later a brass nameplate was fitted with the name abbreviated to *King Feisal*. This was eventually transferred to No. 75118 (AD No. 134). Today the plate is preserved in the Graven Hill Headquarters of the BMR. Tragically, on 14th July 1958 the young King and other members of the royal household were assassinated in Iraq.

In post war years the crest of the Royal Engineers was affixed to each side of the 'Pickering' coach, the push-pull equipment and driving cab partition removed and the coach used, once more, for VIP and inspection purposes. It was scrapped at Bicester but the date of its withdrawal from service has not been traced.

The operation of the steam-hauled passenger services proved to be a harder task for the engine crews than may be imagined at first. Careful vigilance was necessary by the drivers. The number of level crossings, many without gates, were a constant source of anxiety as were the hand-worked facing points. Although the speed limit on the main running lines was a mere 20 mph this was rarely adhered to. The large numbers of passengers alighting and boarding at intermediate stations usually resulted in the scheduled stopping times at stations being exceeded, and in maintaining the running times throughout, speeds frequently reached 30 to 40 mph.

Firemen were constantly engaged, not only in their normal duties of firing, in operating the injectors, taking water etc. but also in uncoupling and coupling trains at each end of the comparatively short journeys. They were also engaged in picking up and handing over of the operating tickets at the blockposts, in obtaining permission to proceed when halted at TPs and in protecting the trains at some of the principal level crossings. Every effort was made by the Regulators to give passenger trains a clear passage but in cases when traffic was particularly heavy, clearance could only be given to the next TP. This necessitated another stop to obtain permission to enter the next section.

When the engine finally reached the end of the shift and entered the locomotive depot the bunker or tender had to be coaled by hand, water taken, fire, ashpan and smokebox cleaned and defects recorded in the repair book.

Restarting the well-loaded 'down' passenger trains from Oxford and Euston after the scheduled stop at Arncott platform called for good driving ability. The seven or eight-coach trains were faced with a short 1 in 90 gradient on a tight curve. On many nights this occupied some five to ten minutes, particularly with a wet rail as, despite sanding, slipping often took place. Assistance was

A spectacular derailment in 1946 as an 'Austerity' 0-6-0ST comes to grief in the Arncott shed ashpit! This resulted from a derailment on the crossover leading from the shed road to the South Running Line. This incident required the assistance of the LMS breakdown train from Rugby. After repair, including a new set of wheels and side rods, the engine continued in service for many years.

David Mowbray

available sometimes from the Arncott yard pilot, usually a saddle tank, but often this was fully occupied on yard and trip duties and the 'Dean Goods' or A12 hauling the passenger trains had to manage unaided.

The hazards of running frequent trains over hand-worked facing points can be illustrated by an incident which occurred in 1945. The actual date was never reported or recorded and the event merely remembered by one of the co-authors. During one late evening a packed passenger train consisting of six bogie compartment coaches hauled by a 'Dean Goods' was travelling between Langford Farm and Piddington. Target 4, the Arncott Yard pilot working in 'C9' storage shed, had withdrawn a string of empty wagons and re-entered Arncott Yard to clear the running line for the approaching passenger train. Both doors to the shed had been left open to facilitate the positioning of loaded wagons after the passenger train had cleared the section. Unfortunately the facing points had also been left open inadvertently! After surrendering the 'Line Clear' ticket at 'B' blockpost the 'down' passenger train was accelerating along the almost straight stretch of track leading to Arncott station. The driver was alarmed by the engine taking a violent right turn onto the spur leading into 'C9'. He immediately made an emergency application of the brakes but by this time the engine and leading coaches were entering the shed. A quick glimpse revealed the track to be empty and after releasing the brakes the entire train passed through the shed, ran through the trailing points at the opposite end and proceeded into Arncott station. Afterwards harsh words were exchanged between the respective crews and months later sarcastic comments were still made about the .... tunnel which had appeared between 'B' Blockpost and Arncott station!

This highlighted the problem of running passenger trains, in particular, over so many unlocked facing points (with two-way levers) which demanded that brakesman/shunters on freight trains working a shed should remember to reset the points for the main line. A decision was taken that all points on passenger routes should be replaced by one-way spring points, set for the main line. However, over the years it was found that one-way spring points caused even more problems of derailment and route setting. On one cold and snowy night at the north end of Sorting Sidings where three such points appeared in rapid succession they were a major element in the derailment of a train of ten 'Warflats' loaded with Bren carriers. By the mid-fifties it was decided to remove all the one-way spring point levers and return to the two-way levers. By this time the train crews were more experienced, night working virtually eliminated and the standard of vigilance vastly increased.

VJ Day on 15th August 1945 was announced throughout the length and breadth of the BMR by all the locomotives sounding the morse code 'V' (three short and one long blast) on their whistles. Shortly after, demobilisation of troops began, including many of the military railwaymen. At first a mere trickle, it soon became a flood and daily long-service personnel began their final journey over the BMR and onwards to the 'Demobilisation Centres'.

This soon had an effect on the passenger carryings, the army-worked Oxford trains reverted to civilian crews. During the ensuing years with the run down of requirements many of the internal passenger trains were either withdrawn or replaced by Wickham or Drewry railcars.

Privately owned bus services had commenced serving the Depot from 6th November 1944 and they too resulted in fewer passengers using the trains. The buses stopped much nearer the various camps and ran direct into Bicester town. Trains still provided a much quicker service into Oxford and continued to be used by troops until the early 1960s.

Four ex-London & South Western Railway dining cars converted and used as ambulance train vehicles during the war period were received on the BMR in the early 1950s. Unofficial sources stated these had previously been stationed at Netley, Hants. They carried Army Department numbers 3016 to 3019 having been built during 1906/1907. Numbers 3016, 3017 and 3019 were eventually sold for scrap to a local dealer and dismantled on site. The sole survivor, No. 3018 remained as the last passenger coach on the system and was stored at Graven Hill in 1987.

This vehicle was used to convey HM Queen Elizabeth II on her visit to the Depot on 16th May 1978. A plate affixed to the interior panelling commemorated the occasion and the special chair used by Her Majesty is preserved in the Headquarters building at Graven Hill.

In its role as an ambulance coach eleven first class seats were provided at one end for sitting patients, together with a Ward Room for the nursing Sister. This space included a cooker, refrigerator, sink, work tops and locker. At the opposite end were fold-up tiered beds in stacks of three to accommodate 36 patients. It was then converted in the Bicester workshops and fitted with observation windows at each end with the seating retained. The opposite end was converted into a conference area with tables and chairs.

Another royal visit took place on 28th September 1978, when HRH The Duke of Gloucester GCVO visited the Depot. His Royal Highness travelled on D3 class No. 624 *Royal Pioneer* and was presented with a working model of this diesel locomotive.

The number of passenger trains continued to dwindle and by 1963 only two services remained. One of these departed from Graven Hill at 07.15hrs calling at Ambrosden (07.22), 'C2' (07.30), Cannons platform (07.38), H.Q. sites (07.50) and arriving in Piddington at 07.55. The service returned from Piddington at 16.29, stopping at H.Q. sites (16.40), Cannons platform (16.48), 'C2' (16.54), Ambrosden (17.08) and arriving at Graven Hill at 17.13hrs. On Fridays this train ran 29 minutes earlier throughout. Both these trains reversed at H.Q. sites, the engine running round with six minutes being allowed in the timetable for this purpose.

The second train left Cannons platform at 07.25hrs calling at 'C2' (07.21), Ambrosden (07.31), 'D4' (07.37), Graven Hill (07.42), 'E2' platform (07.49) arriving at 'D6' platform at 07.55hrs. Departure from 'D6' was scheduled at 16.30hrs, 'E2' platform (16.38), Graven Hill

(16.46), 'D4' halt (16.51), Ambrosden (16.59), 'C2' (17.07) arriving in Cannons platform at 17.13hrs. On Fridays this train ran 30 minutes earlier throughout. During this period no passenger services ran on Saturdays or Sundays.

In June 1965 only twelve passenger coaches remained on the system ie:

Three of the former ambulance coaches Nos 3016, 3017 and 3018, and:

Army Department No.	BMR	
3306	No. 6	Ex-LNER 7-compt. third
3302	No. -	Ex-LNWR bogie van
3303	No. 2	Ex-LNWR 8-compt. third
3304	No. 3	Ex-LNWR 7-compt. first
3305	No. 4	Ex-LNWR 7-compt. third
3310	No. 14	Ex-LNWR 7-compt. first
5301	No. 7	Ex-LNWR brake third
5020	—	Ex-District Railway
3200	—	Ex-Midland Railway

With the exception of No. 3018 all were scrapped after 1967.

The remainder of the passenger coaches had been withdrawn earlier and the bodies burned. The bogies and frames were cut up and scrapped. No record can be found of the scrapping dates, vehicle numbers or types. Several coaches were set on fire in the Armaments Gun Park enabling the steelwork to be salvaged. On at least two occasions the fire brigade was called by persons with good intent who believed a train had accidentally caught fire.

Surprisingly no specific date was recorded when the last passenger train ran on the BMR. The WRAC trains between Piddington and 'C2' were withdrawn in January 1959 and all passenger services were withdrawn in 1967.

The Suez Crisis

During the October/November 1956 Anglo/French offensive against military targets in Egypt troops to man the Base Ordnance Depot were formed at Bicester. Two special trains were provided to convey the Royal Army Ordnance Corps personnel to Southampton/ Each train was split into three portions picking up at various places on the BMR. The portions were recoupled in the Sorting Sidings and handed over the British Railways for the journey to the Port. On return it was planned for the train to halt near the level crossing at Pioneer Road where the troops would alight and be addressed by a senior RAOC officer.

The Movement Control staff at Southampton had, however, loaded the baggage on one side of the coaches and had locked the doors. When the train arrived at Bicester the troops could not alight on the correct side. Consequently considerable delay occurred until the doors were closed, the train was drawn clear and the men were able to gather round the General and be given a 'Welcome Home' speech.

Specials for Enthusiasts

The BMR has always attracted the interest of railway societies and several special trains have been permitted to run over the system. One of the earliest of these ran on Saturday 22nd October 1955 and was organised by the Railway Enthusiasts' Club. The trip commenced at 11.00hrs from Bicester (London Road) and consisted of the 'Pickering' observation coach hauled by a saddle tank. The special traversed the main line through to Piddington and some of the sub-depot lines. A visit was also made to the Central Workshops were a re-railing demonstration was provided using a 45-tons steam crane.

On the following year the Birmingham Locomotive Club visited the railway using what was believed to be the very first diesel multiple unit charter train. This started in Birmingham and ran via Oxford to Bicester on 3rd June 1956. From London Road station a military train was provided with one of the ex-LSWR ambulance coaches and an ex-Southern Railway brake van hauled by saddle tank No. 113 *Royal Pioneer* which ran the special over the main line to Arncott.

The last steam locomotive built by British Railways, Class 9F 2-10-0 No. 92220 *Evening Star* headed a Locomotive Club of Great Britain charter train from London (Paddington) to Bicester on 3rd April 1960. A military train carried the members on a tour of the system, but particulars of the engine and rolling stock are not known.

The first special hauled by a diesel locomotive over the BMR ran on Saturday 14th September 1968. This conveyed members of the Railway Correspondence & Travel Society and started from London (St Pancras) in a four-car diesel multiple unit, via Cricklewood Junction, Neasden South, Princes Risborough, Aylesbury and Claydon to Bicester. Here the passengers joined a train formed of two compartment bogie coaches, one of the ex-LSWR ambulance coaches and four ex-SR brake vans. Motive power was supplied by Army Department, Class D3 diesel locomotive *Waggoner*. A visit was made to the Graven Hill complex and the Central Workshops at Arncott.

The three societies of the Merchant Navy Locomotive Preservation, The Bulleid Pacific Preservation and the Southern Locomotive Preservation travelled over the portions of the BMR of Saturday 16th October 1971.

Their charter train ran from London (Waterloo) via Oxford to Bicester. In the Exchange Sidings the 'Western' class diesel hydraulic locomotive was exchanged for *Sapper*, No. 197, 0-6-0 saddle tank which hauled the special over the main line to Arncott, where a visit to the Central Workshops had been arranged.

Members of the Industrial Railway Society travelled on the system in 1969 and 1972. The first visit was made in No. 3018, the 1907 ambulance coach, hauled by a saddle tank whilst the 1972 trip took place in a special composed of ex-SR brake vans.

The West Midlands Branch of the RCTS visited the railway on 10th September 1977 and were given a conducted tour of Graven Hill depot, together with a journey over the main line to Arncott. They were hauled by Class D3 0-8-0 diesel hydraulic No. 622 *Greensleeves*.

The RCTS made another visit to the network on Saturday 11th October 1980. This commenced at London

(Paddington) and ran via Princes Risborough, Aylesbury, Quainton Road and Clayton to Bicester. At Graven Hill they noted four Barclay 0-8-0 diesel hydraulic locomotives, two of the original fleet of six, Nos 621 and 615 having been transferred to Kineton in 1977 and 1978. Two 4-wheel Vanguards, Nos 252 and 253 were also seen in Graven Hill depot. Many passenger and freight vehicles, including two US Transportation Corps vans, were also in evidence, many of them regarded as worthy examples for preservation.

The return journey was via the former LMS line to Oxford where, after reversal, the three-car dmu retraced its steps to Bletchley and via Bedford, Silkstream, Brent, Dudding Hill and Acton Wells Junctions to Paddington.

A special diesel multiple unit charter train was also used by the Oxford Publishing Company for a tour of the BMR on 16th May 1981.

From time to time parties from the Branch Line Society have also visited the system, but it is understood that visits are to be restricted severely in future.

David Assists Goliath

Mention had already been made of the excellent relations which have always existed between the pre-Nationalisation railway companies, and later British Rail, and the military railway organisation. From its inception the BMR has enjoyed the full co-operation and assistance from the 'Big Brothers' but sometimes has been able to offer its assistance to the national network in turn.

In the late 1950s, on the occasion of the Royal Show at Oxford, officers of British Railways, Western Region, were concerned with the lack of siding accommodation in the Oxford area to hold several hundreds of wagons bringing prize cattle to the Show. Evidently it was essential the cattle returned to their departure points in the same wagons in which they arrived. The BMR Operating Officer held a meeting with the BR officials and promised

every help in this respect, stating he would accept five hundred wagons without question and, if pressed, could make special arrangements to handle a maximum total of one thousand vehicles. When asked whether he would require the assistance of BR staff, they were surprised to learn the only help required at Bicester was the attachment of a Traffic Inspector to supervise the marshalling of outgoing trains. The Army would also expect reimbursement of any additional expenses incurred and should it become necessary, military traffic would be given priority.

From the military point of view this request provided an excellent opportunity to study and practice the BMR's ability to handle an emergency mobilisation situation with many extra trains and marshalling arrangements. In the event the whole operation was carried out efficiently and, despite the staff working particularly hard, it provided a valuable lesson and exercise whilst achieving a worthwhile operation.

On a date which has not been traced but thought to be in 1969, a British Rail Class 47 diesel locomotive, No. 1730, hauling a freight train became derailed at Calvert. The incident occurred on an embankment and the locomotive came to rest out of reach of the railway breakdown cranes.

The (then) Ministry of Transport were asked for assistance which they were unable to give but suggested contacting the military railway group. Bicester possessed Deutschlander re-railing equipment which consisted of sets of alloy beams of several sizes and various associated gear, together with four hydraulic jacks operated from a power base with a control panel, enabling one man to control each jack individually or in combination. The military break-down train proceeded to the site and parked alongside the BR train, the crew set up the gear and then slowly but surely lifted No. 1730 to within reach of the British Rail heavy lift cranes. It was understood at the time that BR were impressed and decided to invest in similar equipment.

Two views of the accident at Calvert in 1969 when Class 47 No. 1730 was partially recovered by BMR re-railing equipment.

M.W. Sackett

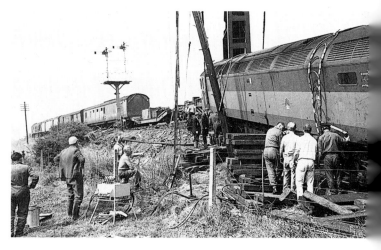

4

Motive Power

The task of documenting the locomotives used on the BMR has presented considerable problems. The biggest obstacle has been the lack of official records relating to the steam era, many of which had been destroyed during the change from military to civilian administration. Other difficulties included the necessary but continual transfer of engines between the various military railways. Some of the locomotives transferred worked only a few weeks before a temporary increase in traffic elsewhere resulted in them being again transferred. This was, of course, particularly prevalent during the frantic years of the Second World War when flows of traffic changed rapidly in accordance with the demand for supplies from forward area units. At Bicester more pitfalls for the chronicler were added following construction of the Central

Workshops in 1947. The movement of locomotives from other installations received for repairs resulted in many being used temporarily for traffic or running-in purposes on the BMR. Some of these engines, after overhaul, were placed in store pending request for power in other areas.

More confusion arose from the practice of transferring nameplates from one engine to another, such as the example of *Sapper* with no less than six steam and three diesel locomotives bearing this name at various times. During the history of the line four re-numbering schemes have been encountered, which all added to the problems of identification and the resultant compilation of the motive power records.

In past publications of the BMR system some observers made valiant attempts to differentiate between the locomotives allocated to the running depots at Arncott and eventually Graven Hill, and those in store and waiting attention in the Central Workshops. As the Workshops were also situated at Arncott and engines from there were also placed in traffic occasionally it was considered too confusing to attempt separate records. Instead, it has been decided to make a single list of all engines, in building date order, which have been used on the line, passing through the Workshops or kept in store for emergency. Readers wishing to note the engines used more or less on a permanent basis on the BMR can therefore select these from Appendix A.

Classification and Numbering

The majority of locomotives used on military railways were originally given numbers in a single War Department series. As can be seen later in this account, the first batch of saddle tanks used at Bicester appeared with four-digit numbers in the 5xxx series.

In 1944, when the invasion of the Continent was being planned, it was thought desirable to give WD engines numbers which would not duplicate those of locomotives in countries where the Army was likely to be on active service. Accordingly, most military locomotives were given the prefix '7', the only exceptions being a few engines on loan from the main line railways which retained their original numbers throughout their military service. An example was the Southern 0-4-2 'Jubilee', A12 class 0-4-2 tender engine, No. 625, which worked at Bicester and retained its original number and Southern Railway livery.

The 7xxxx series painted in 6 in high numbers formed

'Dean Goods' 0-6-0 No. 70156 showing the name *Flying Fortress* painted on the smokebox door. This view taken in December 1941, shows the partly completed state of the track.

Jimmy Higgins collections

the basis of the numbering throughout World War II, but in the early 1950s a decision was taken to again re-number all existing WD engines within a scheme whereby the running number would also indicate the type of locomotive and which would allow for expansion, where necessary. At the same time it was ordered that all items of plant, including railway rolling stock, should have a small plate affixed, showing a three-letter prefix code, indicating the type of plant, followed by an individual number for each type of equipment. The plates were intended for more strict stock control and book keeping purposes. The prefix for railway locomotives was to be 'LOC' and it was desirable the number should be the same as the painted, running numbers; the prefix letters only appeared on the identity plates and did not form part of the running numbers nor were they used for railway operating purposes. Tenders also received the registration plates prefixed by the code 'TR1' followed by the running number of the engine to which attached.

As a guideline it was recommended the running numbers be painted in yellow, either on the tank sides or, in the case of tender engines, or diesels, on the sides of the driving cabs.

The re-numbering scheme commenced in January 1952 in accordance with the following summary, the figures in brackets allowing for possible expansion to the fleets. The steam locomotives of each type were numbered in order of building dates to facilitate mechanical and boiler inspection programmes:

Another view of No. 70156 standing near the temporary watering point on the South Running Line in December 1941. The muddy conditions are apparent and four local children, no doubt thrilled by the sight of the first steam locomotive to appear near their village of Lower Arncott are posing on the footplate. The railway troops with their distinctive dark blue peaked caps and RE badge were a small detachment from 154 Railway Operating Coy RE.

Jimmy Higgins collection

Steam Locomotives
'Austerity' saddle tank 0-6-0
100-299 (1000-2999)
'USA' side tank 0-6-0*
300-399 (3000-3999)
'Austerity' tender 2-8-0*
400-499 (4000-4999)
Ex-LMS tender 2-8-0*
500-599 (5000-5999)
'Austerity' tender 2-10-0*
600-699 (6000-6999)
'USA' tender 2-8-0*
700-799 (7000-7999)

Diesel Locomotives
Diesel mechanical up to 60hp
800-819 (8000-8199)
Diesel mechanical 100 to 195hp
820-869 (8200-8699)
Diesel electric - 350hp
870-889 (8700-8899)
Diesel electric - 650hp*
890-899 (8900-8999)

Railcars
900-999 (9000-9999)

Miscellaneous (Non standard types)
Tank engines*
010-039 (0100-0399)
Tender engines*
040-079 (400-0799)
* = Not in use on BMR.

The regulations governing the re-numbering scheme stated that in no circumstances were the building plates or

Ex-LSWR Class O2, 0-4-4 tank No. 225 passing Kennington Junction near Oxford on 12th July 1943. The engine was being returned to the Southern Railway following use on the BMR.

R.H.G. Simpson

former railway companies registration plates to be disturbed or altered as these provided the basic evidence of the origin and history of each unit. In the case of locomotives employed at Bicester the old and new numbers are shown in Appendix A.

The 1951/2 scheme thereby tidied up the World War II aftermath, making identification easier for the, then, predominantly steam fleet. By the 1960s, however, the situation had altered drastically with the number of steam locomotives down to a mere handful having been replaced largely by diesels of various types. The time was again opportune to introduce a new classification scheme, and after considerable and lengthy discussion, it was decided to dispense with the small registration plates used as the Engineers' Stores record and introduce a fresh system of identifying diesel locomotives according to horsepower. Locomotives were then classified under four letters:

A - Below 150hp
B - 150 - 250hp
C - Above 250hp but under 350hp
D - 350hp upwards

The initial letter to be followed by a number indicating type, as follows:

Type 'A'
1. 44/48hp Ruston & Hornsby
2. 44/48hp Ruston & Hornsby second series
3. 44/48hp Fowler
4. 60hp Fowler
5. 80hp Ruston & Hornsby
6. 80hp Hibberd
7. 102hp Barclay

Type 'B'
1. 153hp Barclay/Drewry with type 5036 final drive
2. 153hp Barclay/Drewry with 5055 final drive
3. 153hp Barclay/Drewry with 5088 final drive
4. 153hp Barclay/Drewry with worm gear final drive
5. 153hp Hunslet
6. 160hp Fowler as built
7. 150hp Fowler with McLaren engines
8. 150hp Fowler rebuilt by Thos Hill with Rolls-Royce engine
9. 204hp Hunslet
10. 153hp Barclay with type 50/2B final drive
11. 153hp Barclay with 5088 final drive, and 195hp engines

Type 'C'
1. 275hp North British as built
2. 275hp North British fitted with 6RPHL Paxman engine
3. 275hp Ruston & Hornsby
4. 275hp Ruston & Hornsby - vacuum-fitted
5. 300hp Barclay with Cummins engine
6.
7. 250hp Thos Hill/Rolls-Royce

Type 'D'
1. 350hp English Electric
2. 600hp Sentinel Rolls-Royce
3. 600hp Barclay with Cummins engine

The letters 'SA' were to be added where a dry type of spark arrestor was fitted and 'EQ' where the exhaust was water quenched.

The number of steam locomotives continued to decline, various diesel locomotives were also scrapped, new designs were introduced and by 1968 thoughts were given to a numbering scheme taking into account the reduced number of motive power units and the general changing situation.

New groups of numbers were allocated to the diesel fleet:

Horsepower	Numbers
44-100	1xx
153-250	2xx
275-300	4xx
350-600	6xx

The remaining steam locomotives under the jurisdiction of No.1 Railway Group, Royal Corps of Transport were all 'Austerity' saddle tanks and these were re-numbered as follows:

No. 196 *Errol Lonsdale* and No. 197 *Sapper*, the latter being the last steam locomotive used at Bicester, were not re-numbered. Both engines were earmarked for preservation and the existing numbers were considered more appropriate for such a role.

The new numbers allocated to individual diesel locomotives can be seen in Appendix B.

For clarity the motive power is described under the various classes:

Dean Goods ex-GWR 0-6-0 tender engines

The first engines to work over the partially completed system arrived in late 1941 and consisted of two 0-6-0 tender engines of the renowned GWR Dean Goods or 2300 class. This type of locomotive was widely used by the military authorities in both world wars in the UK and overseas theatres, and over one hundred were acquired by the War Department in 1940.

Contemporary reports suggest both of the engines sent to Bicester were in indifferent condition and bore the unofficial names of *Flying Fortress* and *Alexander* respectively, painted on the upper part of the smokebox door. From an early, somewhat blurred wartime snapshot *Flying Fortress* is identified as No. 156 (later 70156) which must be the most photographed of all the 'Deans', having appeared in many publications over the years. Some of these show the engine fitted with Westinghouse brake

equipment but this and the GWR Automatic Train Control gear had been removed before arrival at Bicester. Before transfer to the BMR this locomotive had been intended for use in France but was returned to the GWR, presumably for overhaul in September 1940, and then to the Longmoor Military Railway.

The identity of *Alexander* is harder to determine. No photographic proof has been unearthed and the name, being unofficial, has resulted in no written evidence being traced. It is likely, however, this was No. 173 (later 70173) as it was observed working on the BMR early in 1942 and was eventually allocated permanently to Bicester, working passenger services and freight trips throughout the war years. This engine had also worked at Longmoor before arriving on the BMR.

The two 'Deans' provided the sole motive power for the first few months and handled construction trains together with the ever-increasing intake of military stores to the Depot.

At a much later date Nos 70156 and 70173 were joined by a further two engines of the same class, Nos 70094 and 70095. At one time the former bore the name *Monty* but this has been erased and no names were carried during their service at Bicester. Engine number 70094 had previously been on the Cairnryan Military Railway, and during its service there, an extended cab roof supported by two vertical posts of angled-steel was fitted. This was intended to provide added protection to the enginemen from sea spray which evidently was a hazard of the CMR. Its sister engine, No. 70095, also came from Cairnryan and had been used in France during the First World War. No extension was fitted to the cab roof.

Three of the 'Deans' received heavy repairs at Swindon during WWII. Nos 70156 in March 1943, 70094 from October to December 1944, and 70095 in February 1945.

All were fitted with Swindon pattern injectors which were very reliable in service. A GWR single-glass sight feed lubricator with separate condensing apparatus mounted under the cab supplied high viscosity oil to the steam chests and cylinders. A single brake handle controlled the large ejector and steam-brake on the engine, with equipment for applying the vacuum brakes simultaneously on the trains. A crosshead driven pump maintained the vacuum whilst running and this

Ex-GWR 'Dean Goods', No. 70094 being conveyed on a freight train, approaching Kennington Junction on its way to Swindon Works for repair in 1945. The extended cab roof fitted on the Cairnryan Military Railway can be clearly seen.

R.H.G. Simpson

emitted the familiar 'phut-phut' noise so characteristic of GWR steam locomotives.

In 1941 and early 1942 no engine servicing facilities existed at Bicester and the 'Deans' ran with civilian pilotmen to Oxford GWR locomotive shed for boiler washout. Watering and coaling facilities were also basic and a two-inch standpipe at Exchange Sidings and Arncott were the only means of filling the tenders. A surviving member of the operating staff has stated "it took all night to fill the tank". Coaling was achieved by the simple expedient of running a wagon alongside and throwing the fuel into the tender by hand.

Certainly this type of locomotive was ideal for the conditions applying on the newly-laid railway. Whilst the track was consolidating on its ash ballast the 'Deans', for the most part, remained on the track and the tender capacity of five tons of coal and 3,000 gallons of water enabled them to work for fairly lengthy periods, an important feature on a busy pioneer railway with limited servicing facilities.

All the 'Deans' stationed at Bicester steamed well despite the sometimes low quality wartime coal and the heavy loads. They were the mainstay of the intensive internal passenger services and the through trains to Oxford.

Southern Railway and Industrial Classes

Late in 1941 and early 1942 more and more track was being laid to serve the increasing number of storage sheds. During some weeks over 9,000 wagons and over 20,000 passenger journeys were recorded. More power was called for and three industrial and one Southern Railway tank locomotives were despatched to the BMR in an attempt to prevent further traffic thrombosis. These measures proved largely unsuccessful as three of the engines concerned proved completely unsuitable for the strenuous duties involved. Their limited coal and water capacities resulted in delay to trains during the frenzied constructional period and they were quickly banished from the scene.

The first of the 'industrial' type of engine arrived in December 1941 and was an 0-6-0 saddle tank with inside cylinders, 13 in x 20 in bearing the name *Staines* and WD number 69. This had been built by Hudswell, Clarke (No. 1513), completed on 20th March 1924 for Sir Robert McAlpine & Sons Ltd, the well-known civil engineers, and had previously carried their number 42. Its stay was short and had left Bicester by the middle of 1942.

Another Hudswell, Clarke engine, No. 1102 constructed in 1915, was noted working on the line in 1942. This was numbered 211 in the WD series and was an 0-6-0 side tank with outside cylinders 16 in x 24 in with 3 ft 9 in coupled wheels. This had been owned by the Port of London Authority (No. 46) for shunting duties at Tilbury Docks and was given an extensive overhaul by Hudswell, Clarke in April 1942 before arriving on the BMR. Whilst it appeared to cope reasonably well with some of the freight trips higher authority decreed its services were required elsewhere, and it was despatched to Sinfin Lane, Derby in November 1943, later working at Long Marston and on the Melbourne Military Railway.

Probably the most successful of the industrial locomotives was WD No. 71 a new 0-6-0 side tank with outside cylinders, 16 in x 24 in with 3 ft 9 in diameter coupled wheels. This was built by Hudswell, Clarke (No. 1737) on 23rd March 1943 for the Port of London Authority. One of the NCOs working at Bicester alleges this engine was sent "by mistake". In the event it was reported as on loan to the PLA (Royal Docks Group) in July 1943 and was later purchased by that Authority and re-numbered 77.

The first Southern Railway representative was Adams O2 class 0-4-4 side tank No. 225 which arrived in 1942, the actual date being unknown. This class of ex-London & South Western Railway locomotives was well-known on the Southern, hauling suburban trains and they were a firm favourite on the Isle of Wight railways. The steaming capabilities were generally good but its limited water capacity of 800 gallons was a decided liability in the conditions applying at Bicester in the early years. It was returned to the Southern Railway in July 1943 and continued in service, hauling passenger trains until the 1960s. A sister engine, No. 213 gave sterling service on the Longmoor Military Railway, where more established conditions, including more watering points were available.

The other Southern locomotive was an Adams 0-4-2 of the A12 or 'Jubilee' class which, at first sight, may appear to have been another example of motive power which was unsuitable for working on the BMR. Conditions had, however, changed drastically by 1944 when the 'Jubilee' appeared. It had previously been employed on the LMR with three others of the same class. The main and running lines at Bicester had, by this period, become consolidated and improved. The number of passenger trains had increased enabling engines to be allocated purely for passenger duties. No. 625 proved eminently suitable, the wheel arrangement coping well with the tight curvature, its steam capabilities and reasonable turn of speed proving useful in hauling the well-loaded eight-coach passenger trains between Piddington, Bicester and Oxford.

The A12 was fitted with lever reverser on the right side and Stephensons link motion. Steam brakes were fitted to the engine and vacuum/steam combination apparatus worked from the large ejector handle enabled the engine and train brakes to be worked simultaneously. Front-end lubrication was provided by a rather early type of displacement lubricator mounted in the cab. This had no sight feed glass and the rate of delivery was controlled by a valve with graduations numbered 1 to 4. The only indication of the reservoir being empty was a complaining groan from the pistons. Two non-lifting injectors with controls on either side of the cab were fitted. These possessed a non-explained peculiarity which was a tendency to cease delivery and blow steam through the overflow pipe when making stops with the tender leading. This occurred even with the tender tank full and when slow, easy brake applications were made.

By the end of 1944 the boiler needed urgent attention and No. 625 was sent to Eastleigh Works on 23rd November of that year. By January 1945 it was noted still working passengers trains on the BMR, but was finally returned to the Southern Railway on 25th July 1945.

LNER and LMS Tank Engines

Little is known of the work performed by two LNER F4 class 2-4-2 side tank engines formerly used on armoured train duties on the South Coast. No. 7077 of this class was recorded hauling freight trains on the BMR in February 1943 but was sent to Stratford Works, for repair, shortly afterwards. It does not appear to have returned to Bicester. The locomotives in the armoured train fleet received letters instead of WD numbers and No. 7077 carried the letter 'F'.

Another F4, No. 7111 was sent to Bicester, as a replacement on 13th March 1943 after repair at Stratford. It did

Ex-LSWR A12, 'Jubilee' class 0-4-2 No. 625 crossing Liphook road level crossing on the Longmoor Military Railway shortly before being transferred to the BMR.

H.N. James

Saddle tank No. 75039 shunts a freight train in the yard at Arncott. The prefix 'W D' and the wartime style of numbering can be seen on the cab side.

Authors' collection

Built by Hunslet in 1953, No. 197 *Sapper* was the last steam locomotive used on the BMR. It is now named *Northiam* on the Kent & East Sussex Railway. Behind is Thos Hill 'Vanguard' 4-wheel diesel No. 252.

Roy Holford

not remain for very long and was returned to the LNER in June 1943. In the absence of documentary evidence it must be assumed these engines, which had worked some of the world's most intensive steam-hauled suburban passenger train services to and from London (Liverpool Street), and elsewhere on the Great Eastern, and later LNER tracks, had proved unsuitable for the conditions applying to the BMR.

The LMSR contribution was yet another 2-4-2 side tank, No. 6725, which was hired by the War Department, as a temporary measure in March 1943. The arrival of the first three saddle tanks in May 1943 soon made this redundant and it was returned to the LMS, the precise date unknown.

Hiring of Locomotives

The hire of No. 6725 from the LMS raised the question of costs and it is interesting to note the charges for the hire of engines by the War Department in 1943 and 1944. The weekly hire charge was £16 15s (£16.75) which covered renumeration, renewals and all repairs. All other costs were borne by the military authorities and these included crew, fuel, lubricants, water and boiler washing. The civilian railways were reimbursed £1 2s 6d (£1.12½) if they undertook the boiler washing tasks. These charges were based on steam locomotives of unspecified types weighing up to sixty tons empty. Additional charges were made for larger locomotives as follows:

	Additional charge per week	
Over 60 tons and up to 65 tons	£1 4s	(£1.20)
Over 65 tons and up to 70 tons	£2 7s 9d	(£2.39)
Over 70 tons and up to 75 tons	£3 11s 6d	(£3.57½)
Over 75 tons and up to 80 tons	£4 15s 6d	(£4.77½)
Over 80 tons and up to 90 tons	£5 19s 6d	(£5.97½)

Diesel locomotives were also included in the hiring arrangements, the charges being:

| 150-250hp | £30 15s (£30.75) per week. |
| Over 250hp | £32 10s (£32.50) per week. |

These costs covered renumeration, renewals and all repairs, the military railway supplying crew, fuel, lubricants, etc. Where the Army carried out running repairs as well as the cost of crewing, fuel and lubricants the hire charges were reduced, as follows:

| 150-250hp | £22 per week |
| Over 250hp | £27 per week |

When the hired steam locomotives were returned to the civilian railway for boiler washing and a replacement engine was required, the charges were:

Up to 60 tons empty	£2 16s	(£2.80) per day
Over 60 tons to 65 tons	£3	(£3.00) per day
Over 65 tons to 70 tons	£3 4s	(£3.20) per day
Over 70 tons to 75 tons	£3 8s	(£3.40) per day
Over 75 tons to 80 tons	£3 13s	(£3.65) per day
Over 80 tons up to 90 tons	£3 17s	(£3.85) per day

'Austerity' 0-6-0 Saddle Tanks

The early years of the Second World War and the subsequent invasion of the Continent by the allied forces brought about, amongst other things, the need for a sturdy, short trip and shunting locomotive which could be mass produced utilising the minimum of labour and materials. First choice lay in the well-proven Class 3F 0-6-0T of the LMS Railway. Further consideration, however, decided in favour of the Hunslet 0-6-0 saddle tank which had its roots in a 1923 design further improved and modified in 1937 and 1941. As a basic design this type of locomotive could be manufactured more easily and quickly than the LMS side tank. A detailed description of the reasons behind this decision can be found in *WD Locomotives* written and published by R. Tourrett in 1976.

In 1942 the then Ministry of Supply let a contract to the Hunslet Engine Co. Ltd, Leeds to modify their 0-6-0ST for military requirements. The coal, water and diameter of coupled wheels were all increased over the civilian version. In view of the urgent need for the locomotives

Hunslet completed the first engine and carried out intensive testing by 1st January 1943, only a few months after the order had been placed. The new class, with its design modifications carried out under the direction of R.A. Riddles, Head of the Ministry of Supply, Transportation Materials Directorate, proved to be an outstanding achievement. So successful was the design that, in the passage of time, 485 of this type were built both for military and civilian use. Its capabilities were also recognised by the National Coal Board (now British Coal) who adopted the class as its standard type.

Whilst the Hunslet Engine Co. Ltd were the principal

Although not a regular BMR locomotive 'Army 92' *Waggoner* is a well-known example of the famous saddle tank fleet in the Army's green and red livery. It received repairs in the Central Workshops during 1959 and 1960 and has been exhibited on several occasions at the Army Display in Rushmoor Area, Aldershot. Visitors were allowed to view the footplate whilst the engine was in steam. It is now permanently displayed in the Museum of Army Transport, Beverley, Humberside.

MOD, Shoeburyness

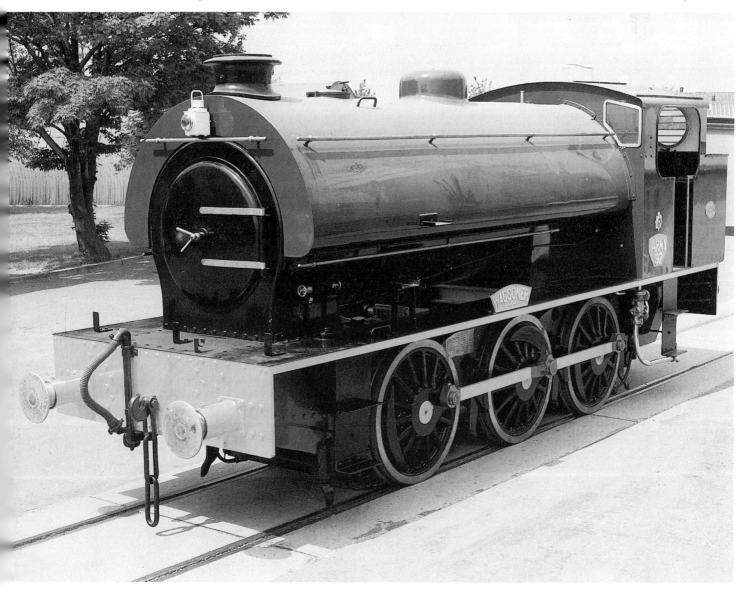

Principal Dimensions of Steam Locomotives
Main Line Railways

	Dean Goods 0-6-0 Tender Locomotives Ex-GWR	0-4-2 'Jubilee' A12 Class Tender Locomotive Ex-Southern Railway	0-4-4 Class O2 Tank Locomotive Ex-Southern Railway
Coupled wheels diameter	5' 2"	6' 1"	4' 0"
Idle wheels	–	4' 0"	3' 0"
Wheelbase	15' 6"	16' 10"	20' 4"
Cylinders (ins)	17½" x 24" (Two)	18" x 24" (Two)	17½" x 24" (Two)
Boiler length	10' 3"	11' 0"	9' 5"
Boiler diameter	4' 3"	4' 4"	4' 2"
Boiler pressure (pounds per square inch)	180	160	160
Total heating surface (sq. ft)	1,142 (Superheater)	1,233 (saturated)	987 saturated
Firegrate area (sq. ft)	15.45	16.9	13.83
Coal capacity (tons)	5		1 ton 10 cwt
Water capacity (gallons)	3,000	3,300	800
Weight in working order			
Weight (Engine)	36 ton 16 cwt	44 ton 3 cwt	46 ton 18 cwt
Weight (Tender)	36 ton 15 cwt	35 ton 17 cwt	–
Tractive effort (85% boiler press.)	17,120 lb	15,900 lb	17,245 lb
Valve gear (inside)	Stephensons	Stephensons	Stephensons
Front end lubrication	'Swindon' type single-sight feed with separate condenser	Displacement lubricator in cab (no sight feed glass)	Sight feed in cab
Brakes (when on BMR)	Vacuum/steam combination One large ejector and crosshead driven pump	Vacuum/steam combination One large and one small ejector	Vacuum steam combination One large and one small ejector
Reverser	Lever – right side	Lever – right side	Lever – right side

	F4 2-4-2 Tank Locomotives Ex-LNER	J68 0-6-0 Tank Locomotive Ex-LNER
Coupled wheels diameter	5' 4"	4' 0"
Cylinders (ins)	17½" x 24"	16½" x 22"
Boiler pressure	160 psi	180 psi
Weight in working order	53 ton 19 cwt	42 ton 9 cwt
Tractive effort	15,618 lb	19,091 lb

0-6-0 'Austerity' Saddle Tanks

Principal Dimensions
Cylinder (Inside) 18" x 26"
Boiler pressure 170 psi
Weight in working order 48.2 ton
Tractive effort at 75% boiler pressure 21,060 lb
Tractive effort at 85% boiler pressure 23,870 lb
Maximum axle load 16.35 ton
Tank capacity - 1,200 gallons
Regulator and steam brake control valves - arranged for control at either side of footplate
Wheelbase - 11'
Length over buffers 30' 4"
Sanding - Steam sanders to leading and trailing coupled wheels.
Grease nipples to: Spring hangers and links, cylinder cock gear, brake linkage

Wheel diameter 4' 3"
Heating surface 960 sq ft
Grate area (Flat) 16.8 sq ft
Injectors - Two Gresham & Craven (non-lifting)
Water gauges - two
Valve gear - Inside Stephensons, lever reverser right side
Bunker capacity - 2¼ ton
Tubes - 181 - 1¾" dia 10' 6¼" between tubeplates
Lubrication: Worsted tail trimmings to piston rod and valve spindle glands.
Worsted tail trimmings to axleboxes and horn cheek with pad in axlebox keeps.
Plug trimmings in big ends and eccentrics. Open oil reservoir with stop valve for brake cylinders
Front end - Wakefield displacement single sight feed mounted on left side of cab. Some fitted in addition with two Furness lubricators mounted on front running plate for cylinder lubrication.

contractors, the demands of their wartime commitments, which included armaments, necessitated sub contracts being given to five other locomotive builders:
Robert Stephenson & Hawthorns Ltd, Newcastle-upon-Tyne
W.G. Bagnall & Co. Ltd, Stafford
Vulcan Foundry Ltd, Newton-le-Willows
Hudswell, Clarke & Co. Ltd, Leeds
Andrew Barclay Sons & Co. Ltd, Kilmarnock

Hunslet supplied fully detailed working drawings and was responsible for the bulk buying and allocation of restricted materials.

At Bicester the first three saddle tanks arrived on 18th May 1943 and before the steam age had run its course

DIAGRAM OF AUSTERITY LOCOMOTIVE.

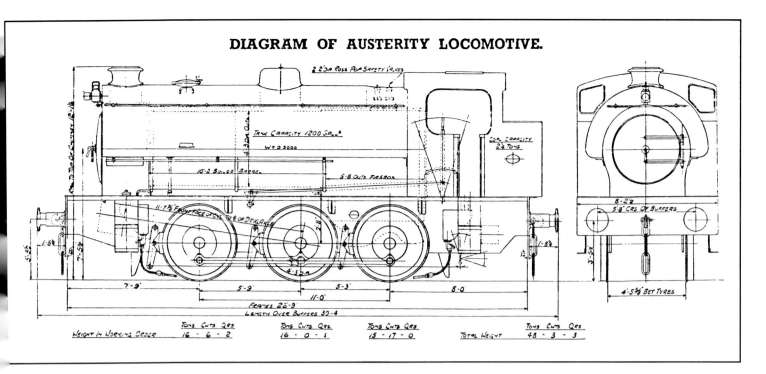

	Tons	Cwts	Qrs
Weight in Working Order	16	6	2
	16	0	1
	15	17	0
Total Weight	48	3	3

nearly ninety of this class had, for one reason or another, run over BMR metals either in service, for overhaul in the Workshops or held in reserve for emergencies.

A final batch of fourteen were built for military use in 1952/3 and were classified as War Reserve Locomotives and were held in case of emergency, initially in the engineers Stores Depot at Longmoor. Twelve were eventually transferred to the BMR and finally some were sold to enthusiast societies, restored railways and museums, details of which can be found in Appendix A.

It is an inescapable fact that the saddle tanks 'saved the day' for the Bicester Central Ordnance Depot. It is doubtful whether any other locomotive of this wheel arrangement and size could possibly have coped with the extremely strenuous duties imposed upon them. With today's railways concentrating more and more on bulk load, company and Freightliner trains with the lessening importance of wagon load traffics, it is hard to visualise the immense effort involved in sorting and delivering a seemingly never-ending stream of separate wagons bound for a multitude of destinations, each with its vital cargo of armaments, miscellaneous stores and vehicles needed to supply a vast army in the field.

The saddle tanks, described by many of the Royal Engineer crews as 'an engine and a half' carried out these heavy duties, twenty-four hours per day, seven days a week with power to spare. Their superb steaming qualities and rugged construction certainly contributed, in no small way, to solving the tremendous supply problems of a nation at war.

With the benefit of hindsight various improvements could have been made. Wartime fuel supplies necessitated frequent fire cleaning and emptying of ashpans. Rocker bars and hopper ashpans would have eased the labours of the crews and improved availability for traffic. Mechanical lubricators for the steam chests and cylinders would have saved time waiting for the displacement lubricators to cool down and be refilled. A means of access to the front lower end of the boiler barrel might have solved scaling problems. Auxiliary oil wells mounted on the running plate with siphon pipes to the axleboxes, keeps

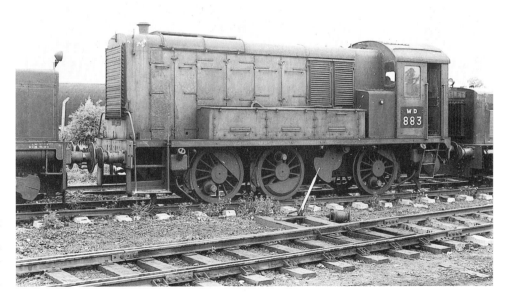

Armstrong Whitworth 0-6-0 diesel electric locomotive built in 1935. This view shows No. 883 lying out of use at Arncott on 3rd June 1956. A sister engine, No. 882, was the first diesel locomotive to work on the BMR.

John Edgington

and horn cheeks would have made preparation easier and reduced the continual problem of water entering the open reservoirs on top of the axleboxes, and the difficulty of replacing trimmings. Insulation and lagging of the boiler back plate might have made conditions in the cab more comfortable in hot weather, but all in all these were minor points of criticism and would certainly have added to the cost and increased length of production schedules.

In 1947 it was decided that because of the continuing heavy passenger traffic and peace-time conditions it was necessary to ensure that all such trains should be run as continuously-braked trains and to this end steps were taken to acquire sets of vacuum ejector equipment to enable all BMR locomotives to be interchangeable for duties. All but one or two coaches were equipped with vacuum brake gear and these were through-piped and run in between braked coaches.

The vacuum ejector gear and associated piping was another set of equipment to be removed before a 'Bicester' locomotive could be transferred to another Depot.

The Diesel age

The first diesel locomotive to work on the BMR was a 1935 Armstrong Whitworth, 400hp, 0-6-0 diesel electric, one of a batch of ten built for the LMS Railway. Its numbers were 7062 (LMS), 70215 (WD) and later 882. The locomotive was fitted with jackshaft drive and arrived in 1945.

The Sulzer six-cylinder engine was in urgent need of attention when it arrived and it was fortunate that six ex-railwaymen were amongst the large number of German prisoners of war held at Bicester Garrison. The six prisoners had received workshop training on the German railways and had been diesel fitters in the Wermacht. They completely overhauled the engine whilst the locomotive was standing, in the open, alongside the South Running Line at Arncott, just opposite the original steam locomotive shed. This was the only covered accommodation available, but of course it was in constant use by steam locomotives.

The Operating Department was eagerly awaiting this locomotive, since it would provide them with an immediate reserve of power to cater for sudden and unexpected flows of traffic. After repair No. 882 was given a thorough testing hauling a lengthy train of 'Warwell' vehicles. It passed the test with flying colours but was transferred to Kineton sometime in 1950.

In 1955 a sister locomotive, LMS No. 7063, WD No. 70216, later 883, arrived from the CMR. From all accounts this was in a poor state of repair and was seen, partially dismantled, outside the Central Workshops in June 1956. This engine was also repaired and put into service until 1963 when it was sold, out of service, to E.L. Pitt (Coventry) Ltd. Following a further overhaul it was later hired to the Central Electricity Generating Board, Hams Hall Power Station, Birmingham where it was finally scrapped in 1967.

From the conception of the plan to completely equip the Railway Group with diesel locomotives it had been intended that the remaining steam locomotives would be utilised on the BMR until they were life expired. However, a change in the type of stores held at Bicester and the increased risk of fires caused by spark emissions from steam locomotives led the RAOC to press Railway Group to change over to diesel power earlier than planned.

As a result, in 1965 six 0-8-0 diesel hydraulic units of 600hp, manufactured by Andrew Barclay Sons & Co. Ltd, Kilmarnock, Scotland were obtained and allocated to the BMR. These were numbered 891 to 896, later Army 620 to 625, and classified as D3. They received names taken from the saddle tank 0-6-0s they displaced. The D3s were fitted with two 300hp Cummins engines so arranged that the driver could select either 'A' or 'B' engine to give a 300hp locomotive, or when necessary, could engage both engines, giving a combined 600hp output. In full working order they weighed 61 tons with an axle loading of 15 tons on a wheelbase of 16 ft 6 in, the overall length being 35 ft 11½ in. The theoretical maximum speed with tyres at full profile and maximum engine revolutions from both engines was 25 mph running light engine. The tractive effort at 25% adhesion was 34,100lb. The engine arrangement of the D3s gave great flexibility in operation and they represented the most powerful locomotives ever to work on the BMR. The D3s tended, however, to be sluggish for the kind of continual loose shunting required. A major disadvantage was the long fixed wheelbase of 16 ft 6 in which, coupled with the 75lb/yd flat bottom rail, laid on poor sub-soil with ash ballast, resulted in the track being pushed out, curves distorted and an unusually high number of derailments.

The first of the class was tested with a train, made up at Graven Hill, weighing approximately 600 tons gross and some 1,450 ft in length. To avoid running round and obstructing level crossings, the test special was routed down the main line through the Arncott loop to Piddington Branch Junction and returned to the Sorting Sidings via the main line. The route was cleared for a non-stop run. One of the authors was riding in the driving cab and as the test train approached Arncott Main level crossing, alighted at Arncott platform. He remembers vividly the expression on the face of a Colonel in a staff car stopped at the crossing gates. On seeing the locomotive approach his driver started the car engine and then the train came on, and on, and on, seemingly endlessly!

Mainly because of the problems of length, tests on subsequent locomotives were carried out with trains of 500 tons. The working load for the D3s was fixed at 500 tons on the level and 350 tons on 1% grades.

Direct air-brakes with a proportional valve and exhauster for working vacuum-braked trains were fitted. All six locomotives passed a variety of strenuous tests with one exception and this was discovered when the first locomotive was passing Ambrosden platform, taking part of the coping with it. Subsequent checks revealed that whilst the units had been designed within the BR 'L1' gauge, allowance had not been made for the 'overhang' between leading and trailing wheels and the respective buffer beams on the tighter curves of the BMR resulted in the buffer beams passing out of the 'envelope'. This was resolved by reducing the width of the buffer beams and chamfering back the running plates.

One result of the tests was a decision that the D3s would be confined to the BMR and would not be used on other military railways within the Railway Group. The sole exception to this ruling applied at the Central Ammunition Depot at Kineton, Warwicks. This military installation was situated on the former Stratford upon Avon &

Midland Junction Railway at Burton Dassett between Woodford and Stratford upon Avon. Portions of this line had been closed and the tracks terminated at the Depot. British Rail had requested the Army to work their trains over the remaining portion between Burton Dassett and Fenny Compton, a distance of 3½ miles. Steep gradients, one at 1 in 100 existed, and D3 class No. 625 was sent to Kineton in 1977 for this purpose only and was not to work in the confines of the Depot. Another D3 was later despatched to Kineton for this duty in 1978.

No. 894, later Army 623, had the distinction of working a Royal train when HM Queen Elizabeth II visited Bicester on 16th May 1978.

These locomotives were the principal haulage units on the system for nearly twenty years. Their high horsepower enabled them to deal, with ease, the freight and passenger services, which although considerably reduced compared with the war years, still provided the occasional heavy haul. All were out of service and scrapped by Marple & Gillott Ltd of Sheffield before July 1985.

In addition to the 400hp and Class D3 locomotives some fifty or so diesel locomotives of various types and horse-power were noted on the system between 1948 and 1977. Many of these were sent from other military railways throughout the country to the Central Workshops for major overhauls. It was the policy of Railway Group that, as far as possible, a locomotive having passed through the Bicester Workshops should remain for approximately seven to eight years at its home base. Routine maintenance and minor overhauls, including engine repairs being carried out 'in the field' by travelling fitters based at Divisional Headquarters. These consisted of a mechanical inspector, two diesel fitters and one boilermaker. Only the major systems such as the BMR, Kineton and Bramley (Hants) etc. had fitters and carriage and wagon personnel on their establishments. To reinforce this policy an arrangement was made between the Central Workshops and the Operating Department at Bicester that before a locomotive, having received its overhaul, was passed to its

April 1972 saw Barclay built No. 236 in store at the Sorting Sidings. It was built in 1945 and acquired Drewry style 'bonnet' plating, the original Barclay design not having louvres. The rear end of the cab on No. 111 to the left, is an interesting comparison in size.

G.P. Roberts

Old soldiers will recollect that '252' was the form used when personnel were charged with some misdemeanour, but Army 252 was also a 'Vanguard' 4-wheel diesel, shown here outside the locomotive shed at Graven Hill on 16th May 1981. This Class C7 locomotive was later named *Greensleeves*.

Bill Simpson

own military railway or placed into store as serviceable, it would run for a week over BMR metals, handling the heaviest trains within its capacity. The Locomotive Foreman then reported directly to Central Work-shops any faults or defects noted for rectification. Thus before leaving Bicester, the engine had been proved under traffic conditions rather than the short light engine run so often given. The details of these miscellaneous locomotives which passed through the Central Workshops are given in Appendix B.

Almost complete standardisation of spares had been achieved with the 'Austerity' 0-6-0 saddle tanks and the motive power department were keen to achieve a similar situation with the diesel fleet. The number of varying types, however, gave the Stores Department many problems until levels of standardisation were reached.

In an earlier part of this chapter the classification method of identifying diesel locomotives is shown in some detail but it may be remembered there were four main classes ie ranging from 'A', below 150hp to 'D', 350hp and upwards.

Class A were useful in depots where the tracks were level, comparatively short and trains were light. The great bulk of the military railways were provided with the versatile and useful Class Bs, with the larger systems using Class C units and the BMR the Class D. It was

against this background that consideration was given to nominating the 'C' types with a multiple unit capability and in 1974/5 plans were laid for implementing this decision.

Authority was obtained and finance allocated to allow the purchase of six 'Vanguard' Class C7 0-4-0 locomotives. These were built by Thomas Hill (Rotherham) Ltd with Rolls-Royce C6FL engines of 250hp. Two locomotives were able to work, in multiple, giving a combined 500hp.

The first two 'Vanguards' were delivered to the BMR in 1977, followed by one in 1978, two more in 1981 and the sixth in 1983 receiving numbers 252, 253, 257, 258, 259 and 267. All received names, in accordance with Bicester tradition, with the exception of No. 257 which was named *Tela* after it was transferred to Kineton on 19th January 1981.

By 1986 the BMR motive power fleet was represented by five 'Vanguards': Army Nos 252 *Greensleeves*, 253 *Conductor*, 258, *Sapper*, 259 *Royal Pioneer* and 267 *Storeman*. No. 253 was formally named by Her Majesty Queen Elizabeth II on 16th May 1978.

Outside the story of the BMR but perhaps of general interest is the fact that there are now 18 'Vanguards' in use throughout the military railway organisation. Owing to recurring problems with clasp brake rigging and springs the basic specification for the latest batch was changed to disc brakes, chevron rubber suspension, hydraulic dampers and the MHA 855L Cummins engine. They are physically very similar to the earlier units but have carden shafts replacing the chain final drive and sliding axle boxes. They can be coupled to and interoperate with the original fleet.

Since 1984 all the existing 'Vanguards' have been fitted with an extra compressor (Sherry V 2. 35 cubic feet per minute) to permit full train air-braking on trains of 1,000 feet in length when coupled in multiple unit formation. The newer locomotives also have this facility and five other locomotives in the organisation have also been so-fitted in order that all Army locomotives working trains of hazardous stores comply with Health and Safety at Work Act and British Rail safety regulations. Thomas Hill (Rotherham) Ltd, now part of RFS Engineering Ltd, introduced a development of their 'Steelman' class designated the 'Royale' type and this was considered by all concerned to be a superior unit to meet the MOD requirements and to be the subject of future buys. The locomotive is powered by a Cummin NTA 855L six-cylinder turbocharged engine with three-stage type torque converter to a direction gear-box with forward/reverse mechanism and axle-mounted final drive reduction boxes; chevron suspension provides a reliable fully floating wheelset. The fuel tank capacity is 250 gallons (1,090 litres). Straight air-brakes are provided on the locomotive which is also capable of hauling fully air-braked trains up to a maximum speed of 25 mph (40 kph).

The first 'Royale' - No. 270, arrived on the BMR on 13th February 1987, followed by Nos 271 on 4th March, 272 13th May and 275 on the 29th January 1988.

These were the first locomotives to receive the MOD (Ministry of Defence) prefix replacing the 'Army Dept' or 'Army' prefix used formerly.

Naming of Locomotives

During the war years many military locomotives had been given names by the troops, some unprintable, often chalked or painted on the tank sides or smokebox. Elsewhere in this account the *Flying Fortress*, *Alexander*, *King Feisal* and *Sapper* are all mentioned at some time, bearing painted unofficial names.

In 1947 it was decided to do the job properly and after much discussion, it was agreed to name locomotives after the principal Corps stationed at Bicester. The first of this series was No. 105 *Sapper*, the name being painted on the saddle tank by the Depot's signwriter. This was replaced later by brass plates made in the Central Workshops. The others were *Storeman*, *Craftsman*, *Royal Pioneer*, and for the WRAC, *Greensleeves* after their regimental march.

Each plate was surmounted by the appropriate Corps badge and the opportunity was taken to have a naming ceremony when a senior officer was visiting his or her unit.

The nameplates remained 'Bicester property' and when locomotives were moved away the plates were removed and given to another BMR engine.

Eventually the steam locomotives were replaced by diesels and it was decided to perpetuate the naming system. By this time money was scarce and it was not possible to obtain brass for the plates. They were consequently made in aluminium. As the replacement diesels, the Class D3 0-8-0, were new and likely to remain on the BMR, fresh naming ceremonies were arranged and perhaps one of the most memorable was that for No. 622 *Greensleeves*. The ceremony took place on Tuesday 4th October 1966, the naming to be performed by Brigadier Dame Mary Railton DBE, Deputy Controller Commandant of the WRAC. The new locomotive was standing in one of the storage sheds where many WRAC and RAOC personnel were employed, with its nameplate covered with a curtain. The Depot Commandant, Brigadier Young, with troops and WRAC personnel stood in front. Dame Mary was to join the train with an observation coach, hauled by the 0-6-0ST *Greensleeves*. The BMR Operating Officer was to welcome Dame Mary at Graven Hill station and accompany her on the train to the shed where No. 622 was waiting to be named. He fondly thought it would be a simple, enjoyable trip along the line. The train had barely moved when Dame Mary, looking down at the track asked "Do you think the pre-stressed

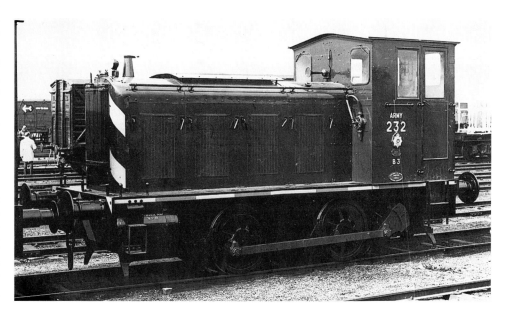

Standard Class B3, No. 232, built by Vulcan Foundry in 1945. The photograph shows the 0-4-0 diesel stored in the Sorting Sidings in April 1972. This locomotive was given a new 195hp engine and re- classified B11.SA and afterwards transferred to Long Marston.

G.P. Roberts

concrete sleepers are preferable to reinforced concrete"?, and continued in the same vein with many technical questions until arrival at the naming point. She had really done her homework and deserved full marks!

Following the naming ceremony Dame Mary then went into the driving cab of the new diesel locomotive which then pushed the saddle tank out of the way, symbolising the replacement of steam by diesel traction.

Another notable occasion took place on 16th May 1978 when HM The Queen carried out a visit to the Garrison. The Class C7 'Vanguard' locomotives had arrived to replace the D3s and Her Majesty had consented to name No. 253 *Conductor*, an RAOC title which dates back to the days of the Wagon Trains. The ceremony took place at the original Graven Hill station which was subsequently re-named Queen's Halt. The route from the nearest storage shed to the station was lined by RAOC Conductors. Following the naming ceremony HM The Queen travelled in observation coach No. 3018 hauled by D3 class locomotive No. 623 *Storeman* from 'D' sites to HQ sites with the Commander Bicester Garrison Brigadier M.B. Page. To enlighten his description of parts of the Depot en route he had arranged demonstration activities. At Ambrosden, for instance, where it is said Ambrosius Aurelianus had a camp, there was a short line of Roman soldiers, elsewhere dog handling by the Ministry of Defence Police, bomb disposal demonstrations etc. One scene in particular showed the importance of a dress rehearsal. The Army

Summary of Locomotive Names					
Name	*Type*	*Nos*	*Named*	*Removed*	*Notes*
Alexander	0-6-0	173			
	Dean Goods	70173	1940	1943	Name painted on smokebox door
Basra later		72220			
Chittagong	0-4-0DM B3	829			
		222	N/K	N/K	
Black Knight	0-6-0ST	75250			
		171	6/1954	6/1956	
	0-6-0ST	91			
		191	6/1956	5/1959	
	0-6-0ST	75191			
		153	N/K	N/K	
	0-6-0ST	75100			
		127	1959	N/K	
Caen	0-6-0ST	75035			
		102	N/K	N/K	
Conductor	4-wheel DM 'Vanguard'	253	16/5/1989	8/1988	Named by HM Queen Elizabeth II
	4-wheel DM 'Steelman'	276	19/8/1988		
Craftsman (The)	0-6-0ST	75151			
		142	17/6/1954	2/1956	
	0-8-0DH D3	896			Named by Maj. Gen. L.H. Atkinson OBE, DEME
		625	25/2/1966	1985	
Greensleeves	0-6-0ST	71444	22/10/55	4/57	
		158			
	0-8-0D D3	893			
		622	4/10/66	-/78	Named by Dame Mary Railton DBE Deputy Controller, Commandant WRAC
	4-wheel DM 'Vanguard'	252	-/78	13/5/87	
	4-wheel DM 'Steelman'	270	9/88		
Flying Fortress	0-6-0	156			
	Dean Goods	70156	-/40	-/43	Name painted on smokebox door
King Feisal	0-6-0ST	75133			
		138	8/46	-/54	Name, King Feisal of Iraq, painted on tank sides. Later metal plate fitted (King Feisal)
	0-6-0ST	75118			
		134	1/54	12/55	
	0-6-0ST	195	-/56	7/59	
Monty	0-6-0	70094			
	Dean Goods		N/K	N/K	Name painted on smokebox door Removed before 1943
Matruh	0-4-0DH C2	8205	N/K	N/K	
		405			
Royal Pioneer	0-6-0ST	75186	6/1955	4/1956	
		150			
	0-6-0ST	75078	1956	N/K	
		113			

Summary of Locomotive Names (continued)					
Royal Pioneer	0-8-0DH D3	895 624	11/5/1966	N/K	Named by Brigadier R.D. Austin, Director of Army Pioneer & Labour
	4-wheel 'Vanguard'	259	1978	11/4/1988	
	4-wheel 'Steelman'	272	9/1988		
Staines	0-6-0ST	70069	N/K	N/K	
Storeman (The)	0-6-0ST	75162 145	3/1955	5/1959	
	0-8-0DH D3	894 623	10/12/1965	N/K	Named by Major General G. le. F. Payne CBE, DOS
	4-wheel DM 'Vanguard'	267	N/K	5/10/1987	
	4-wheel DM 'Steelman'	271	19/8/1988		
Sapper	0-6-0ST	75039 105	1948	N/K	
	0-6-0ST	71438 156	1/1954	7/1956	
	0-6-0ST	202 97	7/1956	5/1959	
	0-6-0ST	75113 132	5/1959	6/1961	
	0-6-0ST	75176 169	9/1/1961	11/1964	
	0-6-0ST	197	1965	1/1966	Named by Col. R.C. Gabriel
	0-8-0DH D3	891 620	18/1/1967	1977	MBE Commander No. 1 Rly Group RCT
	4-wheel 'Vanguard'	258	1977	24/4/1988	
	4-wheel 'Steelman'	275	9/1988		
Tela	4-wheel 'Vanguard'	257	N/K	N/K	
Waggoner	0-6-0ST	192 92	N/K	-	
	0-8-0DH D3	892 621	21/10/1965	1985	Named by Major General Potter CBE Transport Officer in Chief

Army Class B5 No. 848 shunting in the Central Workshops area during 1972. It was built by Hunslet in 1940 and was used in its latter days as the Workshop engine.

G.P. Roberts

S.W.G. Daniels >

Stan Daniels commenced his career on British Railways as an apprentice locomotive fitter at North Road Locomotive Works, Darlington in 1956. After two years experience he was transferred to the Motive Power Depot at Bletchley to complete his training.

During the period spent at Bletchley he was employed on the maintenance of many types of steam, diesel electric locomotives and diesel multiple units. At this depot he often deputised as mechanical foreman.

A dual training course at the principal railway works at Crewe followed. There he received instruction on the maintenance of electrical equipment, together with general repair procedures and experience with the construction of the Class 46 Sulzer engined locomotives. Further experience was also obtained at Willesden Motive Power Depot.

In 1964 Mr Daniels left British Rail and joined the Army Railway Organisation as a civilian fitter in the Central Workshops at Bicester. He became Chargehand Fitter in 1966 and was regraded Industrial Supervisor, and some time later was promoted to Group Examiner. The latter post involved the inspection of all equipment passing through the Central Workshops.

In 1976 Stan Daniels was transferred to Shoeburyness as Workshops Foreman where he supervised the maintenance of locomotives, railcars, wagons and cranes.

Further promotion took place in November 1979 when he took charge of the military railway installation at the Central Ammunition Depot at Kineton. After two and a half years another promotion resulted in Mr Daniels being appointed as Depot Railway Officer of the BMR, a post he occupies today.

Fire Brigade were to attend a lorry on fire and as the royal train passed to be actively engaged in fighting the fire. During the rehearsal the fire was already out by the time the Queen's coach passed! The Fire Brigade had seen a locomotive approaching, set the fire and began to put it out. However, the locomotive was the pilot ordered to precede the Royal Train. It did, however, work well on the day with the pilot engine passing first and Her Majesty was able to view the fire fighting exercise in action.

Of the original names there were several that did not conform to the 'Corps' theme, two of these being *King Feisal* and *Black Knight*. The former had been applied in 1946, as detailed previously, when the 11-year old Iraqi King had visited the depot and travelled on saddle tank No. 75133 from the Signal & Wireless Depot to 'C2' platform. The driver at the time being one of the co-authors of this book.

Engine No. 171 *Black Knight* had come about because during this period all BMR locomotives, with the exception of No. 171, were painted in Army green.

Regulations were that steam locomotives had to be painted in unrelieved black and when various Directors of Transportation enquired about this the answer was given that they had arrived from the manufacturers in green and when they were due for heavy repair they would be painted black. On one such visit the Inspecting General remarked "I do like the green locomotives", and on his return to the War Office an immediate instruction was issued to use Brunswick green as the standard colour scheme in future. In consequence the black locomotive, whose contrast with the green had caused the change in attitude, was named *Black Knight*.

On 18th January 1967 Colonel R.C. Gabriel MBE Commander No. 1 Railway Group, Royal Corps of Transport, in the presence of Brigadier A. Young, Commandant, Central Ordnance Depot, Bicester named D3 class diesel (No. 891 later AD 620) *Sapper*. He then drove the last steam locomotive, saddle tank No. 197, to the new locomotive shed at Graven Hill where the name was transferred from steam to diesel. Afterwards the other five Class D3s 'marched past' the saddle tank, each saluting with its whistle the retirement of steam traction.

No. 220 is not an Army locomotive although it carries the same number as Class B 11a a Barclay 0-4-0. Hunslet-built in 1944 this locomotive was allocated to the Royal Naval Armament Depot, Bedenham and was pictured after undergoing repairs in the Central Workshops from October 1971 to May 1972, when it was returned to the Royal Navy.

G.P. Roberts

Railcars

Three, four-wheeled Type 17A railcars manufactured by the well-known firm of D. Wickham & Co. Ltd, Ware, Herts were in use on the BMR from November 1943 onwards. They were accompanied by several four-wheeled open trailers fitted with low sides.

The powered units were all driven by two-cylinder, air cooled JAP (J.A. Prestwich & Co. Ltd) 1,323cc petrol engines with friction disc and duplex roller chain final drive. The engines were hand started with spring-release starting handles permanently fitted. The wheelbase was 3 ft 8 in with 16 in diameter cast steel wheels. The chassis was of mild steel channel 4 in x 2 in x ⅛ in welded electrically. Foot operated brakes were mechanically linked to wooden brake blocks. Sanding gear fed from two small cast boxes, one each side, was fitted.

The railcars were ordered by the then Ministry of Supply and the War Department the numbers of two of the cars being 11993 and 11977, the third number being unknown. The three units were used extensively and covered considerable mileages conveying permanent way and relief train crews to distant parts of the system. Despite the overall speed restriction of 15 mph unauthorised speeds of 40 mph were frequently attained on the main running lines. Before the advent of the mobile and later permanent workshops at Arncott the railcars were also used to convey locomotive components to and from Arncott locomotive shed and the Royal Electrical & Mechanical Engineers workshop at 'D11'.

In January 1944 it was noted the Wickham cars were being overloaded, resulting in undue wear on the friction disc drive and constant engine failures. Instructions were issued by No. 1 Railway (Home) Group Headquarters that the following maximum loads were to be carried, in future:

Level track	40 cwt
Gradients up to 1 in 200	30 cwt
Gradients between 1 in 200 and 1 in 100	20 cwt
Gradients between 1 in 100 and 1 in 60	15 cwt
Gradients between 1 in 60 and 1 in 50	10 cwt

Trailers were not to be hauled on steeper gradients and the maximum load under any conditions was not to exceed 40 cwt.

These small but useful railcars were the only type used on the BMR until May 1945 when a new three-car unit was delivered from D. Wickham & Co. Ltd. This consisted of two four-wheeled power cars with a four-wheeled trailer semi-permanently coupled between them. Each of the powered cars was driven by a Ford V8 30 hp petrol engine with Ford four-speed manually operated gearboxes to a roller chain final drive. Each of the power cars weighed 30 cwt with a wheelbase of 5 ft 2 in and wheel diameter of 16 in. Electric lighting at 6 volts was fitted and transverse wood slatted seats provided on all three units. The engines could not be worked in multiple and the brake lever, direction box, control lever and ignition key were made detachable to prevent interference by unauthorised persons. The trailing engine was therefore put in neutral, the leading engine providing the sole power. Clayton Dewandre quick-release couplings were installed at the rear end of each car.

The trailer unit had a wheelbase of 10 ft with wheels of 16 in diameter and was provided with 32 seats. Sheet metal end screens with a hardboard roof and canvas waterproof side screens were included. The brakes on the trailer was operated by vacuum cylinders controlled from the power cars at either end. An auxiliary hand screw brake was used for stabling.

The power units bore the WD numbers 12091 and 12161 and the trailer was 12336. This Wickham unit gave continually excellent service and towards the end of the war was used to replace several of the more lightly used steam hauled internal passenger services. It came to a sudden end in 1959 when it collided with a steam locomotive standing on the West Curve at Arncott when the hand worked facing points had been left open inadvertently. Fortunately the permanent way gang which it was conveying escaped serious injury. After this incident the power cars were scrapped but the trailer continued to be used for conveying breakdown equipment.

In 1951 the Drewry Railcar Co. supplied several Type A 900R railcars to the order of the Ministry of Supply. They

Ruston & Hornsby No. 305315 of 1952 was Army Class A5.SA and built for the Proof & Experimental Establishment at Eskmeals. It also worked at Inchterf, arriving at Bicester in December 1971 for storage until January 1974.

G.P. Roberts

Ex-LMS No. 7050

The only 0-4-0 from a batch of eight diesel mechanical locomotives ordered by the former LMS Railways from Drewry (No. 2047) in 1933 was No. 7050. The remainder were 0-6-0s but the exception worked at Agecroft and Salford Goods Depot in Lancashire and then at Stanlow, Cheshire. It was withdrawn in 1942. The original engine was an Allen eight-cylinder rated at 180hp which latterly suffered from connecting rod problems.

In 1944 the Vulcan Foundry, Newton-le-Willows fitted the WD's standard Gardner 6L3 engine of 153hp with a Wilson gearbox. As WD 70224 the locomotive commenced its military duty at the Ordnance Depot, Feltham in February 1945 and under the 1951/2 scheme received the number WD 846. From October 1953 it hauled wartime supplies at West Hallam and then Stirling. In 1956 it spent several weeks in the BMR Central Workshops for attention to the final drive. It continued in service on various military railways and once again visited the BMR in 1961 and received its final number, Army 240.

Because of its lengthy service and historic importance the Superintendent of the Army Department Railway Staff, (one of the co-authors) obtained authority to present the diesel veteran to the National Railway Museum, York. It is now on loan to the Army Transport Museum at Beverley, Humberside.

The name *Rorke's Drift* commemorates the famous Zulu battle on the Buffalo River in Natal where, in 1879, several soldiers including one officer from the RE and one serving in the Army Commissariat (later RASC and RCTS) were awarded the Victoria Cross. In this way the name is representative of the two principal army corps involved in the long history of military railway operations.

MOD

A parade of five out of the total BMR fleet of six Class D3 Barclay 0-8-0 diesel locomotives pose on the 'up' main line, adjacent to the Sorting Sidings in 1966. The leading locomotive is No. 896 (later AD 625) *Craftsman*, displaying Target 5. The passenger rolling stock is stabled in the Up Sidings.

Authors' collection

Army No. 258 *Sapper* shunts the Sorting Sidings in January 1988.

Courtesy Bucks & Herts Newspapers Ltd

Graven Hill locomotive depot with 'Steelman Royale' No. 272 on the left. The Locomotive on the left side buffer stops is Army 234 built by Barclay in 1945. This was on short loan to the BMR in January 1988. A 'Vanguard' stands on the right hand road.

Courtesy Bucks & Herts Newspapers Ltd

were powered by Morris 12 hp four-cylinder petrol engines which, much later, were replaced by Perkins P4 diesels. The Type A cars carried 15 passengers on wood slatted, centrally situated seats. The units were used for conveying relief train and yard crews, permanent way maintenance staff and for inspection purposes. The wheels were 24 in in diameter, the frames 13 ft 6 in long, 6 ft 9 in wide with a height of 8 ft, the wheelbase being 7 ft. Several of these railcars were used on other military railways and visited the Central Workshops at Bicester for repairs.

Between 1953 and 1958 Wickham built several batches of four-wheel rail cars for the Ministry of Supply, the majority being of the Type 27 or 27A Mark III variety. Some of these were fitted with Ford 10 hp and others with Morris 13 hp industrial type petrol engines. At least one appeared with a Perkins diesel engine which was fitted later but whether this was for experimental reasons is not

known. Seating was provided for eight to ten persons and the wheelbases were either 3 ft 10 in or 3 ft 8 ½in with wheel diameters of 16 in. The clutch, throttle and brake pedals were duplicated for driving in either direction with the driver facing the direction of travel. Final drive was by roller chains and a 6-volt lighting system with head, tail, interior and warning lamp was fitted. Car Nos 9024 to 9029 (Type 27A Mark III modified) were fitted with a 12-volt system.

The prominent exterior colour scheme was in deep bronze green but car No. 9033 was given a Royal Blue livery and lettered in 4 in Gill Sans 'LMR 9033' on either side. Other departures from the green livery included Type 27A car No. 9043 which was supplied new to the Pontrilas depot in Hertfordshire as a fire tender. This was painted Post Office red with the lettering 'Pontrilas Fire Engine'. This vehicle also received repairs in the Bicester Workshops.

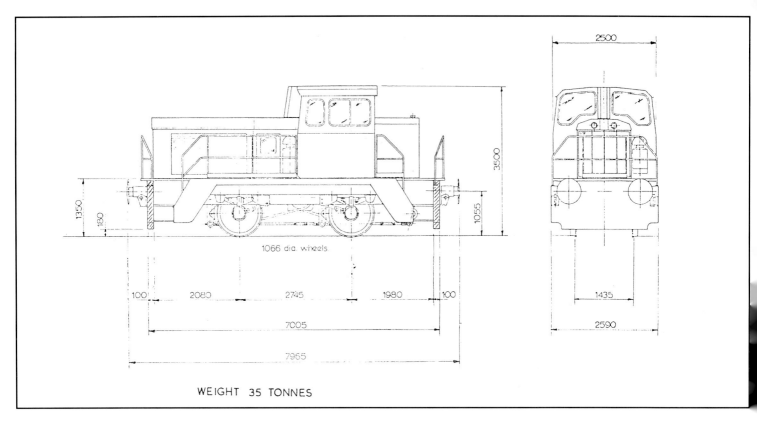

WEIGHT 35 TONNES

Thos Hill 'Vanguard' 4-wheel diesel hydraulic. 250hp.

Driving cab of a 'Steelman Royale' diesel locomotive.

Courtesy Bucks & Herts Newspapers Ltd

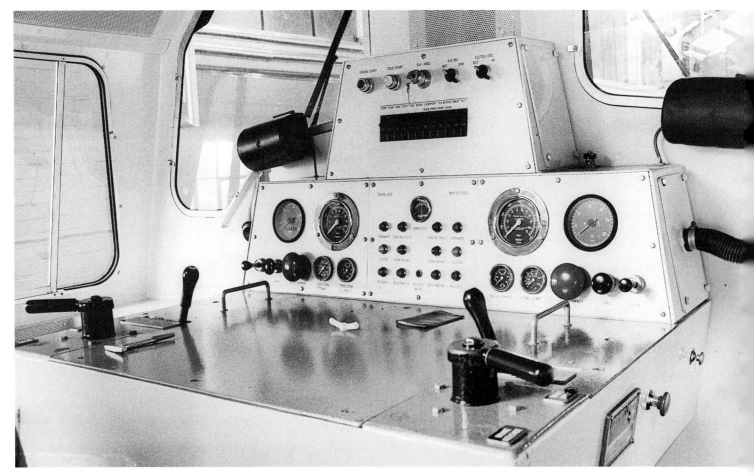

'Steelman Royale' MOD 272 built by Thos Hill (Rotherham) Ltd takes over its BMR duties in May 1987.

E.R. Lawton

Naming of Army 892 *Waggoner* (later No. 621) by Major General Potter OBE on 21st October 1965. Other personnel present were (left to right) Ron Hoyle, Divisional Locomotive Officer, Major M.W. Sackett, then Divisional Railway Officer, Frank Smith, Group Locomotive Officer, Brigadier W.A. Kenny CBE, Commandant COD Bicester, Major General Potter, CBE, Transport Officer in Chief and Colonel R.C. Gabriel, ME, Officer Commanding Railway Group, Royal Corps of Transport.

An unexplained mystery is the designation of the locomotive which is wrongly shown as a 'D1' instead of 'D3'. It can only be assumed this was an error made in the paint shop of the Central Workshops.

Harris Morgan & Son

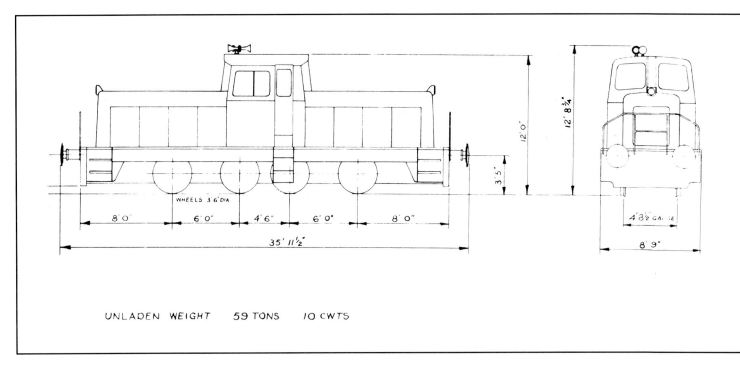

WHEELS 3'6" DIA

8'0"   6'0"   4'6"   6'0"   8'0"

35' 11½"

12' 0"

12' 8¾"

3' 5"

4' 8½" GAUGE

8' 9"

UNLADEN WEIGHT   59 TONS   10 CWTS

Barclay 0-8-0 diesel hydraulic with Cummins engine. 600hp.

Army 624, *Royal Pioneer*, Class D3 SA received its name on 11th May 1966. It stands outside Graven Hill locomotive shed in May 1981. Plenty of elbow grease has been applied to this Barclay 0-8-0 with a Cummins diesel engine.

Bill Simpson

Designation and nameplate of another Barclay/Cummins 0-8-0, Class D3 in 1981.

Bill Simpson

In 1956 and 1957 the Wickham company built three larger type units for military railway purposes at Longmoor, Shoeburyness and Bicester. These were known as Type 40 Mark II and fitted with Ford V8 engines of 30 hp with four-speed gearboxes. The wheelbase was 8 ft 10 in with 245 in diameter wheels. Nine reversible seats were upholstered in Dunlopillo and green hide. Four doors were provided, the body exterior being finished in Brunswick green. Vacuum and hand-operated brakes were used and the tare weight was 2 tons 19 cwt. Rexine blinds were fitted to the side windows and doors.

Appendix C gives particulars of individual railcars and it might appear that an unusually high number of vehicles were used at some installation such as the Central Ammunition Depot, Kineton. This was mainly due to the different nature of work required in the major ammunition depots which had large numbers of storage points connected by many miles of rail track. In addition to the bulk movement of ammunition carried by locomotive-hauled trains many demands were produced for consignments of ammunition for individual military units. It was obviously more economical to utilise railcars, with trailers

The interior of Graven Hill diesel locomotive depot with 'Steelman Royale' MOD 271 *Storeman* and MOD 272 *Royal Pioneer* receiving a routine examination on Wednesday, 5th April 1989.

Peter Nicholson

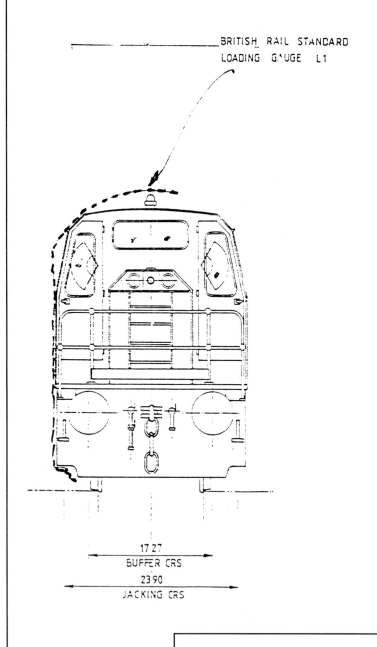

BRITISH RAIL STANDARD
LOADING GAUGE L1

1727
BUFFER CRS
2390
JACKING CRS

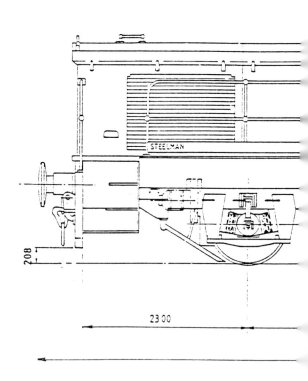

208

2300

4/27 Thos Hill 'Steelman Royale' 4-wheel diesel hydraulic.
(Courtesy Thomas Hill (Rotherham) Ltd)

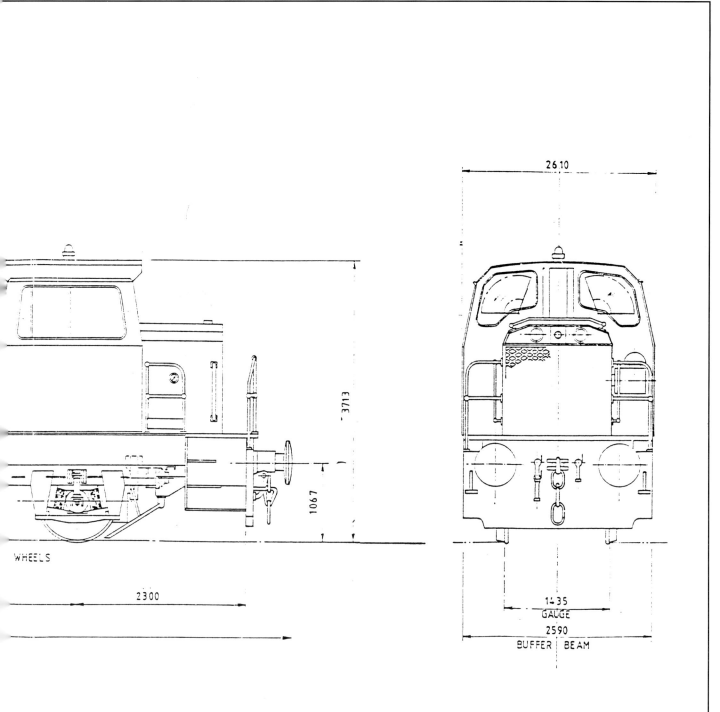

WHEELS

2300

3713

1067

26.10

1435
GAUGE
2590
BUFFER BEAM

BUFFING AND DRAWGEAR TO CUSTOMERS REQUIREMENTS
DISC BRAKE SYSTEM SHOWN
ALTERNATIVE SINGLE OR CLASP TYPE BLOCK BRAKES
MAY BE SUPPLIED TO CUSTOMERS REQUIREMENTS

WD No. 11977, one of the original four-wheeled Wickham railcars supplied to the BMR in November 1943. This vehicle was powered by a two-cylinder JAP air-cooled petrol engine with friction drive. The wheels were 16 in in diameter and the vehicle often reached speeds of 40 mph. Corporal William Mell is on the left and co-author Sgt E.R. Lawton is at the controls. The railcar is standing on the South Running Line looking towards Piddington.

A.L. Tibbs

where necessary, to convey these loads to a central distribution point.

In some military installations there were few roads and railcars were used for ambulance and fire fighting duties. These carried most of the equipment fitted to the more usual road fire tenders with the exception that the pumps had to be portable and easily removed from the railcar to the exact location required. At the Bramley, Hants depot the fire station was designed with a rail and road section. When the fire alarm was sounded the Fire Officer would decide whether road or rail units were appropriate and the crew would board the selected tender.

In 1959 two Baguley built cars, Nos 9112 and 9113, were ordered and sent to the BMR. In conjunction with the Army Fire Service the Central Workshops designed and converted the cars to rail fire tenders. No. 9113 was sent to Bramley, Hants on 16th June 1960. As a result of the experience gained by the use of this unit No. 9112 was modified slightly and was despatched to Bramley on 30th May 1961.

The success of these units led to the purchase of three further fire tenders which were constructed by the Clayton Equipment Co. Ltd, Hatton, Derbyshire in 1968. These were four-wheeled and powered by three-cylinder Perkins diesel engines. Two were transferred to Kineton in 1969 and the third followed later after trials on the BMR. Car No. 9114, the sole survivor of this class, was still lying out of use in the Up Sidings at Graven Hill in 1992. Little is known of their working life and, apart from No. 9114, were scrapped by 1984.

In 1951 an early example of a petrol railcar arrived on the BMR in the shape of a Hudswell, Clarke, four-wheel

Built by D. Wickham & Co. Ltd in 1954, Type 27 Mark III, railcar Army 9033 stands outside Graven Hill shed. This was unusual for the Army, in being a semi-open vehicle fitted with a 13 hp Morris petrol engine.

G.P. Roberts

Baguley-Drewry railcar No. 9113 (builder's No. 3539 of 1959) was converted to a fire tender in the Bicester Work-shops. It was sent to Bramley (Hants) on 16th June 1960 where it was photographed in its bright red Army Fire Service livery.

M.W. Sackett

Clayton fire tender No. 9114 as newly built in 1968.

Authors' collection

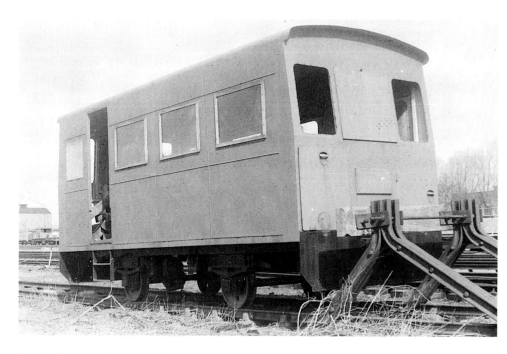

The Clayton railcar abandoned and out of use in the Up Sidings, March 1988.

Authors' collection

Baguley-Drewry twelve-seater railcar AD 9125 leaving 'A1' conveying an inspection party sometime in 1976. This vehicle was transferred to Bramley (Hants) in July 1977.

S.W.G. Daniels

vehicle. This had been built in 1933, builder's No. P265, for the Spurn Head Military Railway in East Yorkshire. This unit, with bodywork by the well-known firm of Charles Roe & Co. Ltd of Leeds, had an overall length of 25 ft, a frame length of 22 ft and a wheelbase of 10 ft. It was originally provided with seats for twenty persons. The car was propelled by a 30 hp four-cylinder, Dorman side valve engine supplied from a 25 gallon fuel tank. A driving cab was provided at each end.

This railcar was conveyed to the Central Workshops at Arncott on a low loader road vehicle. The bodywork was removed and a strong floor and low sides transformed the vehicle into a self-propelled unit for carrying permanent way materials to all parts of the BMR.

Later, when its function in this sphere was no longer needed, the engine and transmission were removed and the long serving unit ended its days as a runner wagon for one of the Depot's steam cranes.

No records have been found to denote when the vehicle was finally scrapped but evidence suggests it was still being used as a runner wagon in the early 1970s.

The final batch of railcars to be repaired or used at Bicester were seven four-wheeled units manufactured by Baguley-Drewry Ltd, Burton-on-Trent, Staffordshire in 1975/6. These were the most powerful of all the units seen on the BMR and were fitted with Perkins Type 4.236 VD, four-cylinder, 75 hp diesel engines. Brockhouse hydraulic transmission was used and the tare weight totalled 6 tons 6 cwt. The overall length measured 4,400 mm height 2,865 mm with an overall width of 2,443 mm. The wheelbase was 1,860 mm with wheels of 686 mm diameter. Accommodation was provided for twelve passengers and sanding gear for both directions of travel was fitted.

All the railcars mentioned gave highly satisfactory service but changing circumstances resulted in all BMR

Drewry Type A 900R 12hp railcar supplied to the military railways in 1951.

(Courtesy Baguley-Drewry Ltd)

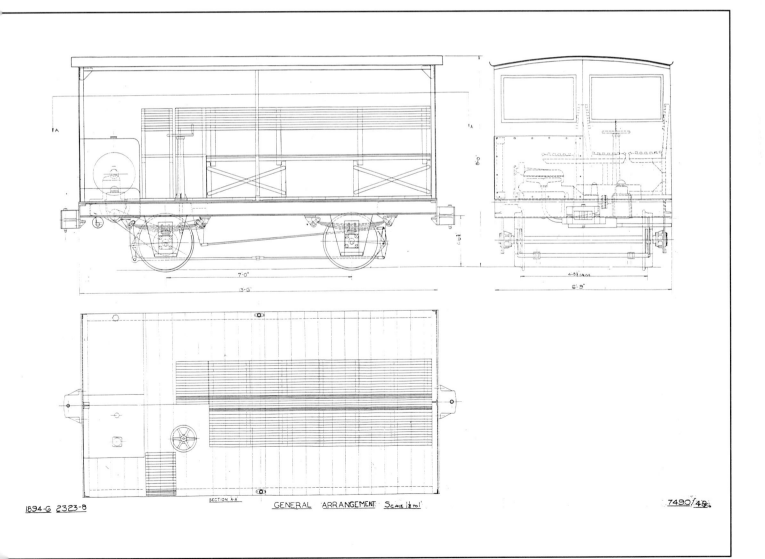

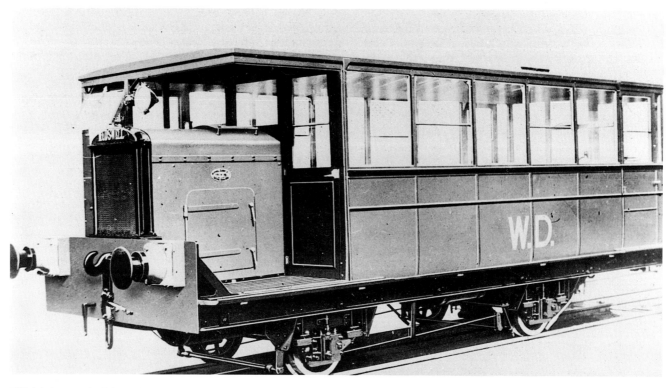

Official photograph of the Hudswell, Clarke railcar, builder's No. P265, built in 1933 for the Spurn Head Military Railway. Shortly before the closure of the Spurn Head line in 1951, this vintage example of a petrol-driven railcar was transferred to the BMR where, in much altered form, it was used to convey permanent way materials. Later it served as a runner wagon for a steam crane.

Courtesy the R.N. Redman/H.M. Frost collection

railcars being withdrawn from service by 1984.

All types of railcar were required to have, in addition to the driver, a qualified brakesman/shunter or other authorised person qualified by the Officer Commanding.

This requirement covered all military railways where:

a. A signalling system of any kind was in use.
b. A Regulator system was used.
c. Any road crossings were encountered requiring lamp or flag protection.
d. Any spring points had to be operated.

The brakesman/shunter was also responsible for carrying out protection (MRRB Rule 85) in the event of the railcar becoming derailed or coming to a halt owing to engine failure.

Maintenance was carried out by the staff from the running shed at Arncott and later Graven Hill. In accordance with military practice a 'Sixteen Task' day to day maintenance programme was carried out for all railcars and different parts of the unit were examined as follows:

1. Engine
2. Engine lubrication
3. Engine cooling system
4. Fuel supply and carburettor
5. Fuel supply and carburettor
6. Ignition
7. Ignition
8. Framing and engine body.
9. Charging system and battery
10. Lights
11. Clutch and gears
12. Wheels, axles and driving chains
13. Framing and engine bolts.
14. Bodywork
15. Brakes
16. Drawgear and trailers

Particulars of individual railcars are given in Appendix C.

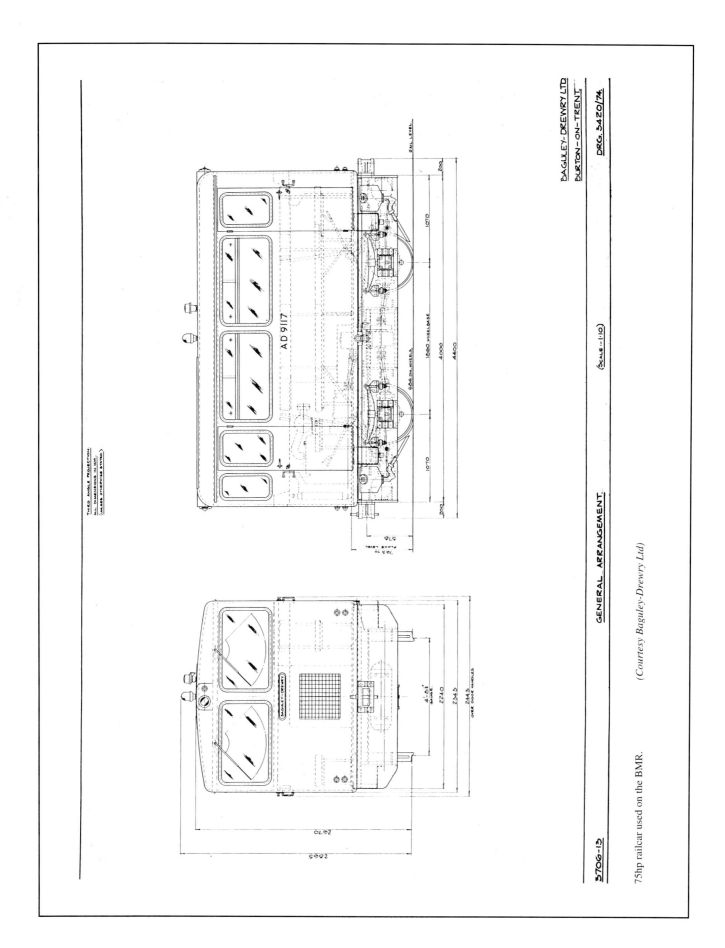

THIRD ANGLE PROJECTION.
ALL DIMENSIONS IN M.M.
(UNLESS OTHERWISE STATED)

AD 9117

RAIL LEVEL.

1070

1060 WHEELBASE
4000
4400

GAUGE ON WHEELS

1070

FLOOR LEVEL
1165 TO

4'-8½"
GAUGE
2240
2345
OVER DOOR HANDLES

2670
2665

5706-13   GENERAL ARRANGEMENT.   (SCALE-1:10)

BAGULEY-DREWRY LTD.
BURTON-ON-TRENT.

DRG. 3420/74.

75hp railcar used on the BMR.   *(Courtesy Baguley-Drewry Ltd)*

Saddle tank No. 158 *Greensleeves*, formerly No. 71444, at Arncott, 3rd June 1956.

John Edgington

WD No. 171 *Black Knight*, the black engine which resulted in BMR locomotives being painted green!

John Edgington

5

Passenger Stations

A total of twelve passenger platforms were eventually constructed on the BMR. Several of these were only used by the works trains conveying passengers between the various camps and working sites. None of the stations were provided with waiting rooms or any kind of covered accommodation.

By 1943 platforms had been provided at Piddington, Arncott, Ambrosden, Langford Farm and 'C2' all being in constant use. The structure at Piddington had replaced an earlier short platform of concrete sleepers on the Arncott side of Piddington level crossing. The second and final site was chosen to serve the nearby large ATS/WRAC camp from which several works trains ran to 'C2', Graven Hill and Langford Farm. Piddington was also used as the terminal station for the regularly scheduled passenger trains and was provided with an engine run-round loop. It

Piddington station in post war years. This was intensively used by thousands of ATS/WRAC personnel travelling to work, proceeding on leave, or being posted to other locations.

COD Bicester

Located on the Arncott loop line 'C2' platform stands empty and unused in October 1987. ATS/WRAC and REME personnel used this platform to reach their places of duty in the vast storage sheds nearby.

E.R. Lawton

was demolished in the early 1970s following withdrawal of the WRAC passenger trains.

Arncott, situated on a tight curve, was the busiest station during the peak passenger carrying years from 1943 to 1946. The platform is still intact and has been used occasionally in recent years for railway society and other special trains. The platform, is substantially constructed in brick and concrete with a steel barrier at the rear.

In the original survey of passenger facilities it was not intended to provide a station at Ambrosden but the construction camps nearby and the movement of civilian workers from adjacent houses proved the need for a platform. This was built with wooden surfaces supported on concrete sleepers, and is still standing.

Approximately one mile from Ambrosden in the 'up' direction is Queen's Halt, so called to commemorate HM The Queen's visit in May 1978. The original station at this point was named Graven Hill and served several adjacent camps and storage sheds. It was constructed approximately one year later than the other stations on the main line and formed a stopping point for the regular internal passenger service plus some works trains from 1944.

Following the construction of the Railway Headquarters building in March 1978 the original Graven Hill platform was re-named 'D4' and the title 'Graven Hill' transferred to a new halt built of wooden beams and sleepers located near the Sorting Sidings. This structure was supplied with a suitable nameboard but was never used extensively. A small building to the rear of the platform was not part of the halt but provided for the use of the Sorting Sidings staff.

Langford Farm, the nearest BMR station to the town of Bicester was constructed entirely of sub standard concrete sleepers rejected in favour of the wooden type. Several months after it was opened an engine run-round loop was laid and used by the scheduled internal trains. This platform was demolished in 1948 and today the site is overgrown.

During the post war period several halts were built on the Graven Hill loop line. One, at 'D6', serving several adjacent storage sheds and workshops. Other halts were erected at Westacott Road and 'E2', both built of concrete sleepers. Westacott Road still remains but is disused. 'E2' and 'D6' were demolished in the early 1970s.

On the Arncott loop a station was provided to serve the 'B' sites complex and named Cannons Halt, but has also been removed. The final halt to be built was situated near No. 3 Telephone Point and is known as 'H.Q. Sites'. It was constructed in the 1950s and consists of a one-coach length platform serving the offices at 'H.Q. 4, 5 and 6 '.

Passenger Stations

Name of Station	Distance from Piddington. Miles	Length in Feet	Date Built	Notes
Main Line				
Piddington	0	366	1943	Removed early 1970s
H.Q. Sites	¾	70	1950s	Still in situ
Arncott	1½	291	1943	Still in situ
Ambrosden	2½	347	1943	Still in situ
Queen's Halt	4	120	1944	Still in situ
Graven Hill	4½	167	1978	Still in situ
Langford Farm	5¾	390	1943	Removed 1948
Graven Hill Loop				
'D 6'		Not known	1960s	Removed early 1970s
Westacott Road		226	1950s	Still in situ
'E 2'		Not known	1960s	Removed early 1970s
Arncott Loop				
'C 2'	2	311	1943	Still in situ
Cannons Halt		Not known	1960s	Removed early 1970s

The platform is still in existence but has seen only occasional use over the past few years, mainly for inspection specials.

During the first two years no lighting was provided at any of the stations and this created many problems associated with the judging of distances and the stopping of trains in the correct position during the hours of darkness. Several of the platforms were too short for the well-loaded seven and eight coach trains and this necessitated pulling up or stopping with several coaches away from the platforms. At Arncott an added difficulty was the necessity for 'down' trains to clear the Arncott main level

Once named Piddington Branch Junction the main line to Arncott with the small HQ Sites halt is on the right. The line from Arncott loop runs in from the left.

E.R. Lawton

crossing which resulted in the first two or three coaches stopping away from the platform. Troops frequently alighted by stepping out of the coaches onto the ballast and several accidents occurred.

An innovation of some note took place in November 1944 when work started on the provision of electric lighting at Langford Farm, Ambrosden, Arncott, Graven Hill and Piddington. By 2nd December 1944 these stations and the principal level crossings were illuminated for the first time, making operations easier for the train crews and safer for the passengers.

Arncott platform looking towards Bicester. The station stands on a short, 1 in 90 gradient and a tight curve. The signals and barriers are controlled from the crossing keeper's cabin situated on the left.

E.R. Lawton

6

Maintenance of Motive Power and Rolling Stock

Locomotive Depots

As will be gathered from the previous chapters the maintenance facilities during the first years of the BMR were very basic. Therefore it is a tribute to the men of the Royal Engineers that the intensively used motive power and rolling stock were maintained in a surprisingly good condition, particularly during the period when peak traffics were carried

Apart from the makeshift arrangements for watering and coaling engines in the shunting neck of the Sorting

Sidings the sole locomotive depot, until the advent of the mobile and permanent workshops, was situated at Lower Arncott, alongside the South Running Line and adjacent to the Arncott South level crossing. This consisted of a suitably modified army Romney hut of corrugated iron construction with low side walls of brick.

The shed could accommodate two tank locomotives if one set of sliding doors was kept open. The single track ran through the shed into a reserved open space at the rear, terminating at buffer stops on the edge of the Arncott-Murcott road. The rear area was used for the storage of firebricks, fire irons, lubricating oils, paraffin and a Kelbus sand dryer. Inside there was a small locomotive foreman's office and a store for engine tools, together with a fitters' toolroom. A bench with hand-worked drilling machine and vices occupied the remainder of the space. A high pressure mains hose was used for boiler washing and an inspection pit ran almost the full length of the shed.

Engines requiring axlebox replacements, spring and motion repairs were jacked up onto wooden packing enabling the wheels and axleboxes to be run out. Replacement of boiler tubes and repairs, together with boiler washouts, were carried out inside the covered portion of the depot. Each engine, irrespective of its duties, was given a boiler washout every twelve to fourteen days in steam. Despite the semi-hard water the interior of all the boilers were maintained in an excellent condition aided by regular injections of DM boiler enamel manufactured by Houseman & Thompson of Newcastle-upon-Tyne. In post-war years boiler examinations were carried out by British Railways' boiler inspectors who were surprised by the high standard in which the boilers were maintained.

Each time a boiler was washed out the locomotive was examined for mechanical defects and cleaned thoroughly by a gang of Italian or German prisoners-of-war. During a period when civilian locomotives were usually

Before heavy lift cranes were provided repairs were carried out with the aid of hydraulic jacks and wooden packing. Here 0-6-0ST No. 75100 (later No. 127) in its original khaki livery is jacked onto packing for attention to the brake gear, motion and axleboxes. This was done in the open, near the original locomotive shed at Arncott.

Authors' collection

Throughout the war years, and up to 1950, the freight and passenger rolling stock was maintained in the open at the north end of Arncott Yard. Here, two RE Sappers are hard at work repairing wagon floors. An ideal task in summer months, but not very pleasant in the winter with equipment covered in snow and ice.

Authors' collection

encrusted with dirt, owing to the shortage of labour, BMR locomotives were always in a very clean condition.

A water column was situated at the east end of the shed yard, between the shed road and the South Running Line, enabling tanks to be filled from either track. Adjacent to the track serving the shed a concrete and brick coaling stage 122 ft long was constructed and supplied by a six to seven wagon spur at the rear of the stage wall. The spur was steeply graded to ensure the wagon floors were level with the brick walling. This considerably eased the labour involved in unloading the wagons, by hand, onto the stage floor.

A pit capable of accommodating one locomotive was used for ashpan, smokebox and fire cleaning. A crossover from the shed road to the South Running line, just before the shed entrance, enabled engines to proceed through the servicing procedures and re-enter traffic without actually entering the covered portion of the depot. In any case, this was continually occupied by locomotives under repair or undergoing boiler washing.

A small wooden hut outside the shed entrance accommodated the Locomotive Supervisor and administrative staff. No toilet or washing facilities were installed but as

the shed was immediately adjacent to No. 3 Camp where the crews were billeted, no further facilities were required.

After completion of a shift drivers entered any defects or parts on their engines requiring repair into a book located on a small desk at the front of the Special Notices board near the door of the Shift Foreman's office.

White metalling of axleboxes and bearings was carried out by Royal Engineer fitters but final turning was sent to the Royal Electrical and Mechanical Engineers workshop at 'D11'. A Wickham railcar was used to convey the parts.

Heavy repairs to engines and rolling stock were dealt with by the main line civilian railways through special arrangements with the War Department. Locomotives ran to Oxford GWR shed or Swindon Works except the A12 'Jubilee' class locomotive which was sent to Eastleigh Works. Coaches were despatched to the LMS shops at Wolverton. Help and technical advice was also rendered by mechanical inspectors attached to the South Midland Division of No. 1 Railway (Home) Group, Royal Engineers. The LMS, GWR and later British Railways authorities always gave every assistance and willing co-operation to the BMR, something which has continued to the present day.

With the end of World War II palliative measures were taken to improve the shed amenities. A boiler, tank sundry piping, control valves, washbasins and showers were obtained from the Royal Engineers Works Maintenance Officer. By dint of hard work and advice a 'Do It Yourself' scheme also resulted in an effective, if somewhat primitive wash-house with two showers and washbasins complete with hot and cold water. A Merryweather steam-driven, high pressure pump was also obtained resulting in more effective boiler washing.

Finance for projects was very hard to obtain and certainly in respect of buildings and amenities the whole

Central Ordnance Depot, consisting of four battalions of Ordnance and REME, plus companies of Pioneers, Royal Engineers and other support services were in the same dilemma of trying to improve the lot of the soldier and civilian workers. Consequently they were in competition with one another for any money that was available.

Whilst conditions were gradually improved during the post-war years it was not until 1960 that financial resources became available to construct a modern locomotive depot. This was built on the north side of the Sorting Sidings and was constructed of brick and concrete by private contractors under the overall supervision of the

The view looking towards Piddington showing Arncott locomotive shed yard. A saddle tank is taking on fuel at the coalstage while one of the 5-ton steam cranes, originally used for loading gun barrels, is standing on the South Running Line, with a newly-acquired ex-Southern Railway brake van. The year is 1950 and civilians are at work on the track.

M.W. Sackett

An April 1972 view of the original locomotive depot and coalstage with the rear wall demolished, is on the left. The erecting, machine, wagon and black-smiths shops forming the Central Workshops, are to the right of the picture. The South Running Line to 'C' sites and the Arncott Loop is in the centre.

G.P. Roberts

Deputy Chief Royal Engineer. The new depot, to which was latter added a Carriage and Wagon and Railcar shed, achieved the desirable object of locating all the mechanical staff in one spot easily under the control of one foreman.

The Graven Hill locomotive depot holds six engines with inspection pits and fitting area, offices, rest rooms and toilets. Two tracks run the full length of the shed. The roof was designed to accept smoke discharge from steam locomotives but with eventual dieselisation in mind the ventilation canopies could be lowered and more reliance placed on electrically operated extractors.

The change to diesel motive power came quicker than expected following a change in the type of stores held in the Central Ordnance Depot and the consequent need for more stringent fire precautions. A request to the military railway authorities for greater safeguards was answered, in the short term, by a ruling that seven empty wagons must be provided between the engine and the vehicles requiring movement in the storage sheds. This obviated the need for locomotives to enter the sheds. The long term solution was however, resolved by the withdrawal of steam traction and the replacement by diesels, which was implemented in 1965.

Rolling Stock

From the beginning the carriage and wagon repair staff fared even worse than their locomotive colleagues. The only facilities were a small wooden hut for jacks, tools and materials located on a spur at the north end of Arncott Yard. For several years, in all weathers, wagons and coaches were maintained in the open using only hand tools. Because of the lack of suitable equipment heavy repairs were sent to the LMS Railway shops at Wolverton.

Later a flat wagon was used as a bench and working area, but for some ten years the rolling stock was maintained under these crude conditions.

In the early 1950s a new workshop was built just west of the South Running Line on a spur leading to the rear of 'C1' storage shed with the advantage of a long loop alongside which could be used for stabling wagons waiting repair. The shed was equipped with office, rest room, stores, washing facilities and toilets. By a stroke of good fortune the BMR authorities were able to acquire a Universal wood working machine and as the Chargeman was an apprenticed carpenter and joiner the standard of repairs improved enormously. He quickly acquired the skills required to deal with underframes, brake rigging, couplings etc., and immediately had available the services of the Central Workshops' blacksmiths shop for work he could not undertake.

The new shop was also equipped with a 5-ton capacity, hand-operated, lifting gantry, and sundry power tools. Only the internal fleet of coaching and freight vehicles was maintained. Each single repair being limited to a budget of £300.

The programme of maintenance and the type of repairs emanating from the 'C1' shop changed from time to time according to circumstances, but many wagons were turned out as almost new, only the metal parts of the original vehicle remaining. For such a small establishment several large and important tasks were accomplished, such as the construction of coaches practically complete from the solebar upwards, railcar bodies for several other military railways, and perhaps one of the most difficult of wood-working tasks, the construction of coach doors which invariably took a beating from the boots of soldiers. These included the re-building of several vehicles of historic interest such as the original Pickering ex-Kent & East Sussex Railway coach and the former London & South Western Railway ambulance coach No. 3028.

The department gradually accepted responsibilities outside its immediate sphere by the supervision of work at Didcot, Marchwood and other Army installations.

In 1973 the RAF wished to acquire a passenger coach for their nine mile long 600mm gauge system at Chilmark, Wiltshire. The coach was required to convey civilian workers and special visitors around the 350 acre site served by this narrow gauge network. Railway Group were asked to assist and the Central Workshops converted a bogie freight wagon from Chilmark and provided the necessary coach bodywork, seats etc. The result was a useful passenger carrying vehicle weighing just over 2½ tons and fitted with central couplers.

After the construction of the new locomotive shed at Graven Hill a C&W shed was added and the depot in 'C' sites closed. The new facility was equipped with a wood store, adequate space for operating the Universal wood working machine while carriage roof level gantries enabled staff to work directly on the tops of vehicles. Its siting brought the C&W Department directly under the control of the locomotive foreman.

With the eventual introduction of new working methods, the reduction of military rolling stock and the closure of the Central Workshops, the responsibility of maintaining rolling stock was transferred to private contractors on 31st March 1986.

The interior of the 'C1' Carriage and Wagon Shop.

Authors' collection

The upper photograph shows the interior of the Graven Hill locomotive shed in the days of steam traction. The smoke vents, later closed off on the introduction of diesel power, can be clearly seen. In May 1981 a charter train organised by the Oxford Publishing Company ran to the depot enabling its passengers to view and photograph the diesel locomotives.

Authors' collection and Bill Simpson

The former Carriage and Wagon repair shop at 'C1'. Rolling stock is now maintained by private contractors.

E.R. Lawton

Exterior view of the Central Workshops showing, on the left the original locomotive shed. The narrow gauge rolling stock off track left, was used on the East Riggs ~~l~~ight railway at Gretna Green.

Authors' collection

The Ransomes & Rapier, 45-ton steam crane outside the Central Workshops, Arncott about 1951.

Authors' collection

The Central Workshops

On 16th February 1944, a few months before the invasion of Europe took place, the 6th Railway Mobile Workshop train, manned by the Royal Engineers, arrived at Arncott. It was stabled on a siding alongside the South Running Line opposite the Arncott locomotive shed. A move to the BMR was designed to give the Workshops personnel added experience of maintaining locomotives and rolling stock prior to supporting the military railway units on the Continent. The train consisted of several covered vans containing machine tools, living quarters and generator van.

The arrival of this train proved a boon to the hard-pressed maintenance staff at Bicester and all manner of repair work was swiftly undertaken. The mechanical condition of all the locomotives was soon brought to a high standard and it was a moment of regret at Bicester when the train departed to take part in the invasion of Europe later in 1944.

In 1946 proposals were made that a fully-equipped workshop to aid mechanical maintenance should be established at Bicester. This was intended to include medium to light repairs on all military motive power throughout the United Kingdom with the exception of the Longmoor Military Railway which undertook its own repairs until the final years of its existence.

Before a permanent workshop building could be established a mobile workshop train was again sited opposite the locomotive shed, in the Arncott triangle. Once there, like the proverbial 'Topsy' it grew and grew ousting all the previous BMR stores and equipment areas including the permanent way stores which had occupied the site for several years. The area occupied by the workshop train made the stabling of locomotives extremely difficult. This problem was particularly acute when the number of traffic shifts were reduced resulting in a greater number of engines being on the shed area at any one time.

To make a clear space for the permanent building the Permanent Way stores were moved to a new location at Graven Hill between the Sorting Sidings and the 'down' main running line. The specific area previously occupied by these stores became the Workshops' blacksmiths and Carriage and Wagon shop.

During the latter few months of 1947 the building had been constructed in the area between the former workshop train siding and the running line at Arncott station. Much of the material for the building was salvaged from a redundant structure at Richborough, Kent. Some of the steelwork was twisted but with considerable ingenuity and self help was straightened and erected. Financial approval was then obtained to clothe the whole structure with brickwork during which time much unwanted rubbish from the war years was buried beneath the foundations. The structure eventually consisted of three buildings, the larger constituting the erecting shop which was provided with an inspection pit approximately seventy feet long. A

5-ton capacity electric gantry crane served the full length of the shop and two sets of four, electric, mechanical screw traversing, jacks each of 15 tons capacity were used for lifting locomotives and rolling stock.

A few years previously the Operating Officer had been advised of a wheel turning lathe surplus to requirements in the RAOC stores. This was obtained and loaded onto an old coach underframe and stored at Arncott under tarpaulin sheets. There it stayed until the Workshop was erected but by this time the springs on the coach underframe had become reversed and the wheel flanges were biting into the coach floor. Fortunately the distance to be traversed was only two to three hundred yards and the movement was made successfully. The lathe was capable of turning the 4 ft 3 in tyres of the 'Austerity' saddle tanks.

A Ransomes & Rapier, 45-ton capacity, steam crane was allocated to the complex, making it capable of dealing with the heaviest loads.

The Workshops then commenced complete medium and light repairs to all the locomotives throughout the Group's military railways. The rolling stock programme included overhaul of the external fleet of main line 'Warflat' and 'Warwell' wagons, vans and open vehicles. The spare parts for these, as opposed to the internal fleet maintained in the 'C1' shop, were supplied by British Railways and

Among the more unusual products made by the Central Workshops was this narrow gauge passenger coach. This followed an approach from the RAF at Chilmark, Wilts, who required a passenger carrying vehicle for their one mile long 600 mm gauge railway.

The RAF supplied a double-bogied freight flat wagon from their existing stock and this was adapted and supplied with a new body by the Bicester Workshops. It is shown here on trial on 24th May 1973, hauled by a 48hp Ruston & Hornsby 4-wheel diesel locomotive. Syd Hopcraft, the BMR Carriage & Wagon Chargeman, is just visible through the leading window.

RAF Wendover

assembled in the Central Workshops. The original steam locomotive shed at Arncott was utilised as the paint shop.

At the time there were 17 steam powered, 45-ton capacity rail cranes in use throughout the country, notably at the Proof & Experimental Establishments. The Workshops completely overhauled many of these including boiler repairs. General repairs to several diesel powered cranes were also carried out successfully.

The Shops adapted easily to the advent of diesel motive power and a few lines of demarcation existed amongst the labour force. Personnel were expected to be interchangeable and, when necessary, assisted on jobs other than their own specified duties.

Locomotives having passed through the Shops were usually given a running in period on the BMR hauling the heaviest trains available. The locomotive foreman advised the Workshops Officer of any fault or defects requiring rectification before despatching the engines to their own depots.

With the decline in the number of military railway locomotives and rolling stock the Works were closed in 1982 and the major repairs to the remaining fleet transferred to private contractors.

Some of the workshop equipment, such as the lathe and jacks were transferred to Long Marston. The buildings today are still in existence but used for non railway purposes.

7

Maintenance of the Permanent Way

The greater proportion of the system at Bicester was laid out utilising flat bottom rail of 75lb to the yard in thirty-foot lengths. This was secured by dog spikes into wooden sleepers. Ash, a readily available waste product of the steam age, was used as ballast. During the hasty construction period this was more easily unloaded and packed by hand shovels than stone ballast which, at the time, was difficult to obtain in large quantities.

The ash laid on the treacherous clay, combined with drainage difficulties, continued to give endless trouble, especially when pounded by the heavy wartime traffic. Gangs of Non Combatant Corps personnel and Italian and German prisoners-of-war supervised by the Royal Engineers were employed on the never-ending task of jacking, lifting and shovel packing the trackwork. This had to be performed without interrupting the frequent train services.

The late 1940s witnessed the demobilisation of many skilled Royal Engineers' permanent way staff and the rehabilitation of prisoners-of-war. The remaining labour force faced an almost impossible task of keeping the network in a reasonable condition. Despite their efforts there were slacks and soft spots, sleepers pumping, low joints, distorted curves and deteriorating sleepers. Weeds and grass were slowly taking over in spurs and sidings and derailments became a daily occurrence.

The authorised establishment included some forty permanent way staff but many were completely untrained and were unable to make much impression on the task which faced them. By a stroke of good fortune the Operating Officer recruited a retired ganger from the Great Western Railway, a colourful character called Jack Cherry. He proved to be a tower of strength, fitter than many men half his age, with a drive and tenacity and range of language that was truly remarkable. Curves began to be aligned and difficult lengths tackled in a professional manner. The renewal of turnout timbers throughout the system was taken in hand and largely completed in 1953.

The track maintenance force was divided loosely into three gangs, allocated to Graven Hill, Arncott and the main line. One of the problems was the impossibility to work consistently on a plan for any appreciable length of time without the gangs having to be moved to the scene of an emergency or derailment. On a system of such a size and nature, in the 1950s, not all the storage sheds would be under pressure at any one time. As an extreme example one particular shed held hundreds of Bren Gun Carriers for which, after the war, there had been no movement. The track leading to the shed had disappeared from view under waist high grass and weeds. There came a time when it

was decided these vehicles would no longer be held at Bicester and would be transferred to a vehicle holding depot. This required many trains of 'Warflat' vehicles but before this was possible all the energies of the gangs were directed to the clearance and upgrading of the spur and connections to the storage shed. Identical problems occurred at other locations on the system as the limited number of personnel available rarely gave opportunity for giving continuous attention to rarely-used spurs.

Attempts to contain the weed growth on the main and running lines were made in 1947 when a six-wheeled tender from a scrapped Dean Goods locomotive was converted to a weed killing unit. Pipe sprays were fitted and fed by gravity to the track. Partial success was achieved but in the mid 1950s a more permanent solution included the fitting of a pump-driven spraying apparatus onto the underframes of the last ex-LNW six-wheeled coach to form the weed killing train. This operated successfully until 1959 when liquid weed killers were replaced by granular chemicals.

The South Midland Division, later Southern Division, of No. 1 Railway Group RE had Permanent Way and Locomotive Officers who could give advice and help to the various railways under their jurisdiction on problems arising in their respective fields of activity. Bicester was fortunate that Nick Napier, the Divisional Permanent Way Officer, was a highly experienced engineer who had gained his training on the Canadian Pacific Railway followed by wartime experience building railways in the Middle East as Officer Commanding with an Indian Engineer Construction Company. He had the ability to detect track defects instantly and also judge the ongoing situation so that preventative action could be taken. For a period the South Midland Division Headquarters was located at Bicester which meant the Permanent Way Officer was readily available when BMR staff wished to discuss any problem.

With these measures the condition of the track continued to improve, but the gains made were still insufficient, particularly as Bicester was regarded as a permanent Central Ordnance Depot. Continued requests to Group Headquarters for additional resources were finally met following an application based on the fact that there were some 80,000 sleepers on the system but they were only being supplied with 8,000 secondhand wood sleepers per year. The secondhand material had an estimated life of seven years and simple arithmetic illustrated the impossibility of achieving any large scale improvement until additional supplies of track materials were made available.

In 1955 this application led to the decision to completely renew all the sleepers throughout the network. It

using surplus channel tracking. This consisted of narrow steel channel linked together to form panels of approximately 8 ft x 4 ft and laid rapidly on soft ground or over sandy areas to form temporary roadways for military supply vehicles operating in battle zones.

Hundreds of lengths of this material were obtained from every available source and laid under the right of way after the ballast had been dug out. This method proved most effective if the channel tracking was laid just below the sleeper level rather than at greater depths.

The most troublesome section of track was on the main line between the River Ray and its tributary just south of Ambrosden. At this location the line is carried on an embankment which had been built of clay dug from pits on either side. During periods when the sluice gates on the River Ray at Oxford were closed, the River backed up along much of its length and, at worst, the water would be less than one foot below the bridge span. The water also flooded the borrow pits resulting in movement of the embankment. On occasions the rails dropped six inches overnight. The situation was not helped by a curve on the embankment and by another very tight curve just past the North end which, from a combination of rail creep and expansion, was liable to move a foot laterally in less than twenty-four hours.

A proposal to rebuild the embankment was submitted to Group Headquarters in 1956 and was approved in general. This task was given to the 8th Railway Squadron, Royal Engineers who, in addition to carrying out the construction, were permitted to operate their own works trains in order to occupy the Squadron's operating and locomotive crews.

The plan involved excavation of the embankment top, creating a camber and to substitute a 2 ft 6 in layer of limestone dust topped with ash ballast. New sleepers and rails were included in the scheme. The theory was that the limestone dust, being impervious to water, would become rock hard thus distributing the weight of track and trains evenly over the clay base. Unfortunately, owing to the financial constraints in force at the time the layer of limestone dust was reduced to a depth of only 1 ft 6 in.

The 8th Railway Squadron duly arrived and began

was also decided the replacements would be pre-stressed concrete sleepers with an anticipated life of twenty-five years. Extra labour was also needed and during the same period of time many European Volunteer Workers (EVWs), or as first described, Displaced Persons (DPs) became available. These were refugees from World War II and some 30-40 were recruited to work on the BMR. A rapid training programme was instituted and many of the EVWs remained at Bicester after completion of the track relaying project and became members of the permanent gangs. Some turned to other railway jobs and were trained as locomotive firemen, brakesmen/shunters and a few were eventually appointed locomotive drivers.

An Assistant Permanent Way Officer was appointed to Divisional Headquarters specifically to oversee the BMR project, for a period of two years.

Initially the new pre-stressed concrete sleepers showed faults, cracking diagonally across the centre portions, which necessitated at first a modified design, and subsequently a change to reinforced concrete sleepers. The re-sleepering programme was completed in 1957 together with work to improve the soft sections of the track. This was done by utilising a stock of the original 1941 concrete sleepers after many had been used for the construction of platforms at Langford Farm and Ambrosden. On one very bad curve the sub-soil was excavated to a depth of two feet and the sleepers laid herring-bone fashion in the base. After restoration of the formation and rails the curve remained firm.

Some four hundred damaged paving slabs were also used on a further curve which was treated in the same fashion. This too held firm and has given very few problems since. Supplies of the original sub-standard concrete sleepers and paving slabs were soon exhausted and further efforts to stabilise the formation were made by preparations not only for the main project but also for other activities to occupy the remainder of their personnel. Ruston Bucyrus (RB19) tracked mechanical excavators were used to remove the crown of the embankment. The Bicester Garrison Engineer was consulted to ascertain the limits of working as it was known that the main 6 in water main serving the Depot ran alongside the railway. The route of the pipeline was duly pegged out but the first excavator broke the water main with considerable loss of water and inconvenience. It was later discovered the pipe run was some ten feet further west than the wartime plans indicated.

The Squadron had possession of the line for seven hours on each working day between the morning and evening passenger train services. On certain days the works was suspended completely to allow any backlog of freight trains to be worked. This entailed close liaison with the Depot Traffic Officer to ensure their storage sheds received any special requirements in the Arncott and Piddington areas to cover the days when there was no through traffic to Graven Hill and Exchange Sidings. The Squadron planned to carry out the required work on two lengths of track, approximately seventy-two feet in length, per working day. This was achieved without any delays to passenger trains despite, on one occasion, a passenger coach on their works train becoming derailed near 'A' blockpost. Fortunately, this was re-railed and cleared with a few minutes to spare.

The task was completed on time but within two years the embankment was again on the move and by cutting a section through the bank it was found it had, once again, forced a saucer shape. The reduced depth of limestone dust had been insufficient to distribute the load, failing to blanket the wet clay. It had broken up allowing water through and had formed a wet 'porridge', the clay making a very poor bearing layer. Added to this the hollows under the track, although filled with ash, had also admitted water. Drainage ways had to be dug from the ends of the sleepers to drain the water down the sides of the embankment.

Approval was gained to carry out remedial work but this time with a full 2 ft 6 in depth of limestone dust topped with stone ballast instead of ash. The task was undertaken by the regular BMR gangs using hand tools. Since carrying out this work the embankment has remained stable, giving little or no trouble.

Similar treatment was carried out on the main line curve near 'A' blockpost in 1957, on the running line curve at 'C3' towards White Cross Green level crossing and at 'B2' loop in 1958.

In Chapter 1 mention is made of 'Mickey's Bridge' carrying the main line over the tiny River Ray and the troubles that occurred in building this structure. By the mid 1950s surface fractures were found across the concrete piers and received constant inspection. Glass tell-tales had been fixed across the fractures to enable the engineers to detect any worsening of the problem. The cross levels on the track over the piers were as much as three inches out and locomotives were plunging and increasing the stress on the piers. Additionally, the track on either side of the bridge was five inches proud of the bridge rails, leading to more serious plunging by locomotives. In co-operation with the Depot Works Organisation

The Late Major Nicholas Napier

Whilst not on the establishment of the BMR but attached to the Southern Division of No. 1 Railway Group, 'Nick' Napier gave invaluable assistance and professional guidance on permanent way affairs at Bicester.

He was born on 23rd April 1906 and attended Bloxham College. At the age of twenty he joined the Canadian Pacific Railway as an assistant surveyor, later becoming a qualified surveyor. In this capacity he had considerable experience of track and work problems in remote regions of the trans Canadian main line, and on new branch line construction.

At the outbreak of WWII he returned to Britain and enlisted in the Royal Engineers, eventually receiving a commission. He served overseas with the Royal Indian Engineers in Haifa, Bierut, Tripoli and on the famous Western Desert Military Railway. Leaving the Army with the rank of Major he joined the Southern Division of No. 1 Railway Group and became its Divisional Permanent Way Officer from which post he retired in 1969.

His vast experience in track design and maintenance proved of immense value to the BMR and contributed enormously to the improvement and upgrading of the system. Major Napier lived in Kingsbridge, Devon, with his wife and son, but passed away in November 1990.

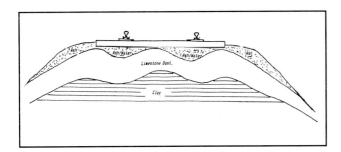

Cross section of Ambrosden Bank two years after first rebuild.

which had replaced the Depot Garrison Engineer, repairs were planned which included removing the steelwork completely, rebuilding the pier seats with rapid hardening cement, fitting new bridge seats, steelwork cleaning and painting, new sleepers and rails, new timbers and a footwalk. It was fortunate that by this time the BMR had become owners of a 45-ton capacity steam crane which was to prove of enormous help in the reconstruction of the bridge.

A detailed works programme was prepared giving precise timings for each operation and naming the personnel responsible for each phase of the operations. Copies of the works programme were also given to all members of the staff involved, both from the BMR and Works Organisation.

The main line was closed after the passage of the last passenger train on a Friday night in 1957 and the crane moved into position to remove the girders. These were immediately put to one side where a gang was detailed to carry out cleaning and painting. As in many such projects there were minor problems from time to time but the work went ahead as planned. On Sunday morning the bridge seats were completed and the freshly painted girders, timbers, track and footwalk were installed. By 14.00hrs the first train with the heavy crane crossed the bridge two hours ahead of the planned time. Since this operation no major problems have arisen. Whilst the work was being done a local inhabitant stated that during the war years the piers had moved and to stabilize them a concrete raft had been floated between the piers, on the bed of the river and walls of concrete filled sandbags were used on either side of the piers. After cleaning away a blanket of silt it was found the concrete raft was still in place and in good condition.

All the level crossings on the BMR were laid in concrete, without check rails and these were a constant source of trouble as the clay formation constantly resulted in rail movement on either side of the crossing. This was further aggravated by the maintenance gangs packing up the track. As a consequence considerable plunging took place when trains traversed the crossing. Furthermore it was almost impossible to maintain the fishplates when they were located within the crossing length. Over the years a lot of time and attention has been given to renewing the crossings using sleeper and check rails with the road surface being made up with tarmac, thus enabling maintenance to be carried out more easily. Some of the crossings were made with such good quality concrete that road drills could not make any impression and explosives were used to break them up!

By the beginning of the 1960s the tremendous amount of time, effort and money expended resulted in the track being in much better condition. Derailments were reduced dramatically by the complete replacement of sleepers and turnout timbers, the realignment and stabilisation of curves, reconstruction of many level crossings and easing of grades. With this vast improvement the BMR had reached a plateau when a fresh look could be taken of the whole layout and a more detailed and specific approach planned to ensure a good standard of maintenance was continued. To this end the track was divided into seventy sections, each numbered and every length, with the aid of Nick Napier, inspected in minute detail and a maintenance programme was instituted. This covered alignment, grades, cross levels, soft spots, drainage and weed clearance.

The whole network was subjected to this form of examination and each ganger was given the specification of work required for his particular length. When the tasks were undertaken, the ganger signed the specification sheet after the Permanent Way Officer had inspected the completed work.

In 1965 it was decreed that all government civil engineering work was to be concentrated in the newly formed Department of the Environment. This included military railway track. Despite protests that the permanent way and its maintenance was an integral part of the Army's railway organisation, the work was transferred on 5th August 1966.

Although the military railway track remains the property of the Ministry of Defence its upkeep is now the responsibility of the Department of the Environment who also absorbed the permanent way maintenance personnel.

In recent years many of the main line curves have been relaid with 109lb to the yard, flat bottom rail with stone replacing the ash ballast, although the latter is still used on running lines and sidings. Many of the turnouts have had their constituent rails welded resulting in lowered maintenance costs. Much of the track maintenance work is now handled by private railway engineering contractors.

An example of this took place on 27th November 1989 when contractors Balfour Beatty were commissioned to relay the single line section between blockposts 'A' and 'B'. The contract also included the re-laying of through roads Nos 4 and 5 in the Sorting Sidings. The work involved renewal of track with 109lb rail and re-ballasting. The main line section was completed on 2nd April 1990 and renewal of the tracks in the Sorting Sidings commenced on the same date and occupied some eight weeks.

8

Main Line Links

Although planned to link both the former Great Western Railway at, or near to, Blackthorn station on the Princes Risborough to Banbury line, and the ex-LMS Railway at Bicester, between Oxford and Bletchley, the double connections at the latter point proved adequate for all purposes.

During the early stages of World War II the Oxford-Bletchley-Cambridge railway was designated as an emergency route in the event of disruption of the LMS Northern main lines or their London termini by enemy action. To this end new connections were installed in 1940 at Sandy with the London & North Eastern Railway East Coast Main Line, and at Calvert/Claydon with the LNER (formerly Great Central) main line. At Oxford a twin-tracked link at Oxford North Junction provided improved

access to the GWR to Wolvercote Junction and beyond.

By August 1942 the South curve at Bletchley was also re-instated enabling trains to and from the South on the West Coast Main Line to gain direct access to Bicester and Oxford without reversal at Bletchley.

With the exception of Bletchley these connections were of course, installed prior to the decision to construct the BMR, but proved timely in facilitating the flows of traffic serving the Depot.

The building of the 660-wagon capacity yard at Swanbourne was an essential prerequisite to the efficient operation of Bicester as the marshalling facilities in the area were previously inadequate to cope with any significant increase in traffic.

At Bicester the signalling was controlled from the

Built by the former LMS Railway to control entry and exit to the BMR Exchange Sidings, Bicester No. 2 signal box stands empty and vandalised in this view taken in 1979. The structure was demolished in March 1980, the facing connection to the BMR being controlled by a six-lever ground frame which can just be seen opposite the signal box, on the right. The view is taken looking towards Bicester (London Road) (now Bicester Town) station on the Oxford-Bletchley line.

Bill Simpson

Closed in October 1973 and replaced by a ground frame the interior of Bicester No. 2 signal box was in a sorry state when this photograph was taken in 1979.

Bill Simpson

station box, an original LNWR structure with a Webb frame and equipment for hand operation of the level crossing. The opening of the BMR necessitated the construction of an additional signal box which was brought into use in 1942. This was located on the 'up' side of the line, some 950 yards to the west of the station and opposite to the junction with Exchange Sidings. It was named 'Bicester No.2.' the station cabin becoming 'Bicester No.1.' later 'London Road'.

The new structure was built of brick with a flat concrete roof known as an ARP (Air Raid Precautions) type, so called because its construction safeguarded the interior from damage by shrapnel or incendiary bombs. The structure measured 26 ft 4 in x 13 ft 7 in x 8 ft and was fitted with a thirty-lever frame, controlling the points and upper quadrant signals. The train crews operated the trailing connection between Exchange Sidings and the 'down' Oxford line from a ground frame with electrical release from No. 2 signal box. A separate small ground-frame on War Department property controlled the BMR junction to the connection and a short arm upper quadrant stop signal outside the entrance to the sidings. In this way trains were protected when leaving Exchange to the 'down' main line. Clearance for trains entering or leaving

the sidings was arranged by telephone between the signalman at No. 2 box and the BMR Yard Foreman. Throughout the war period trains were despatched via both connections, dependant on destination.

By 1948 the number of trains using the trailing connection had fallen to a low level and the track and ground frames were removed. Further reductions in traffic levels resulted in the closure of No.2 signal box and on 23rd October 1973 it was replaced by a six-lever ground frame operated by train crews. The structure was completely demolished in March 1980. Traffic from the Bletchley direction to the BMR ceased in 1965 when all remaining trains to and from the military railway were routed via Oxford.

Other changes took place on the main line when from 1st January 1948 the LMSR became part of the London Midland Region of British Railways. A decade later, the section of line between Oxford and a little beyond Bicester, was taken over and administered by the Western Region. Oxford (Rewley Road) station closed in October 1951, the Bletchley-Bicester passenger trains then using the Western Region station.

The flyover carrying the Oxford to Bletchley line over the BR West Coast Main Line opened in 1962 as a preliminary step to the electrification of the principal routes from London (Euston) and a proposed enlargement of Swanbourne as a major marshalling yard. With the advent of bulk and Freightliner trains and the reduction in wagon load traffics the latter project was not proceeded with.

Passenger services between Oxford and Bletchley were withdrawn on Saturday 30th December 1967 but almost twenty years later, on 11 May 1987, a limited passenger train service was re-introduced. The former London Road station was re-named Bicester Town and the official re-opening ceremony took place on 9th May. The service was revived by the assistance of grants from Oxford County, Oxford City, Bicester and Cherwell District Councils and provided three trains, four on Saturdays, each way at the following times

				Sat.O.		
Oxford Dep.		07.20	11.57	17.43	22.55
Bicester Town	arr	07.45	12.22	18.08	23.20
Bicester Town	dep	08.05	12.25	18.20	23.23
Oxford	arr	08.30	12.51	18.48	23.49

From 15th May 1989 this service was increased and an intermediate station at Islip, costing some £60,000 was planned, replacing one which had closed at the end of 1967. The new service ran on weekdays only including Saturdays with trains departing from Oxford at: 07.29, 08.54, 11.15 (11.10 on Saturdays) 15.12, 17.35 (17.30 on Saturdays) 18.39 and 22.55. Departures from Bicester Town were scheduled at: 07.58, 09.22, 11.48 (11.45 on Saturdays), 15.40, 18.03 (18.01 on Saturdays) 19.08 and 23.25.

The line from Oxford to Claydon is now single and under control of the Oxford panel signal box, being operated by means of the tokenless block system. Portions of this single line were formed from portions of the

The BR line looking towards Oxford with the connection to the BMR on the left. Bicester No. 2 has cleared its upper quadrants for both 'up' and 'down' tracks.

COD Bicester

Reduced to freight only status the former LMS main line from Oxford (Rewley Road) looking towards Oxford Road Junction in June 1970. A dmu approaches the Oxford (Western Region) station.

E.R. Lawton

original 'up' and 'down' roads, making use of the track in best condition.

Prior to the closure of Bicester (London Road) signal box on Friday 6th June 1986 and demolition of the structure on 3rd May 1987, freight trains from Morris Cowley Yard at Oxford ran into London Road, now

Bicester Town station on the former 'up' line, from where the train crews operated two ground frames, both released by Annett's keys, the first for the crossover to the former 'down' line and the second giving access to Exchange Sidings. The BR locomotive then propelled the inwards train to Exchange Sidings, ran round the outward bound

On the right is the BR six-lever ground frame which formerly controlled the connection to Exchange Sidings and the BMR network. This has now been re-sited and is released by Oxford Panel signal box.

Bill Simpson

After the closure of Bicester No. 2 signal box the connections to the BMR were controlled by two ground frames operated by BR train crews, and released by Annett's keys. The first, shown here, operated the crossover from the former 'up' line to the 'down main' linked to BMR tracks.

Following abolition of Bicester (No. 1) London Road signal box on 6th June 1986 the arrangements were again changed, with a single ground frame controlling entrance to the BMR. This frame is now released by Oxford Panel signal box.

Bill Simpson

vehicles and, in turn, propelled them back into London Road. After closing the ground frames and replacing the Annett's key the trains departed for Morris Cowley yard at Oxford where connections were made with BR 'Speedlink' services to Bescot, Harwich (Parkeston Quay), Dover and the military port at Marchwood.

Since closure of the London Road signal box the arrangements have been altered and a single ground frame is now provided adjacent to the BMR connection. This is released electrically from Oxford panel signal box and operated by BR train crews enabling trains to enter a shunting spur, running over the former 'down' line to Bicester Town station. Here buffer stops are located adjacent to the London Road level crossing. The BR locomotive then propels the inwards train through the connection into Exchange Sidings. Whilst the train is inside the spur the main line points can be re-set to allow any other traffic to pass. Outward bound freight trains connected with the former 'Speedlink' services to Bescot and Eastleigh. Since the withdrawal of 'Speedlink' in July 1991 freight traffic to and from the BMR is now containerised.

Whilst no longer catering for military traffic it may be

of interest to recall that when the line between Bicester and Bletchley was singled in June 1985 the section from Bicester to Claydon was worked with the staff and ticket method from Sunday 23rd June to 28th September 1985. This necessitated issuing special operating instructions to train and operating personnel as the staff and ticket method had generally been discontinued throughout BR and no longer appeared in the operating instructions. From 30th September 1985 electric token working was instituted on this section until the closure of London Road signal box when tokenless block was adopted.

Freight trains to and from the Exchange Sidings of the BMR are worked by Oxford-based BR staff. The average train consists of around twelve vehicles, plus empties. The maximum loading for the BR Class 47 diesel locomotives is 1,690 tonnes and Class 31s are limited to 940 tonnes, both classes having a limit of 80 standard length units. The Oxford to Bicester portion of the line is classified 'RA7' and cleared to 25.5 tonne axle loads. Line speed varies from 40mph to 20mph in places.

Following the amalgamation of the BR areas at Oxford and Reading the Area Manager at Reading, through his administrative staff at Morris Cowley yard, maintains daily contact with the Depot Traffic Office at 'E15' site and also, when necessary, with the Army Department Staff Officer, currently Mr S.W.G. Daniels, at the Headquarters Office, Graven Hill.

Rolling stock details for inclusion on the BR computerised Total Operations and Processing System (TOPS) are despatched from Morris Cowley by fax machine to the Area Freight Centre (AFC) at Reading. Particulars of rolling stock on outward trains from the BMR are conveyed by telephone from the Depot to the Reading AFC.

Apart from the BMR traffic the other freight services using the line consist of roadstone from the ARC quarry, running from Westbury to Wolverton or Banbury Road Sidings. Compacted household rubbish from Avon County Council commenced in November 1985 from Bath to Calvert via the Claydon link. These services are worked by Oxford and Swindon based crews.

In the event of accidents or derailments the Oxford to Claydon line is covered by the Reading road recovery vehicle with the Old Oak Common (London) breakdown train with heavy lift crane for more serious incidents.

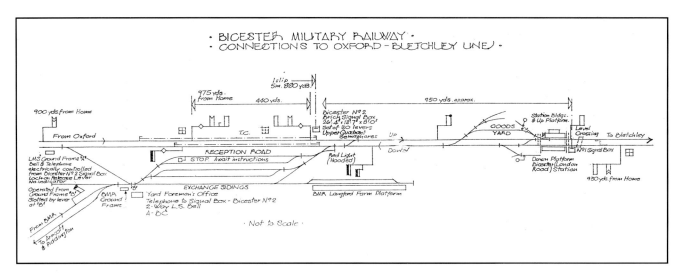

Connection to Oxford-Bletchley Line.

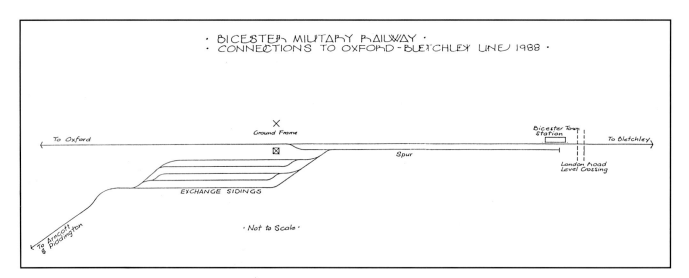

Connections to Oxford-Bletchley Line, 1988

Appendix A
Steam Locomotives

All locomotives known to be have worked on the Bicester Military Railway and/or passed
through the central workshops, Bicester.

Locomotives and Railcar Builders

Sir W. G. **Armstrong Whitworth** & Co. Ltd, Scotswood,
Newcastle upon Tyne
W. G. **Bagnall** Ltd, Castle Engine Works, Stafford
Baguley-Drewry Ltd, Burton-on-Trent
Andrew **Barclay** Sons & Co. Ltd, Caledonia Works, Kilmarnock
Clayton Equipment Co. Ltd, Hatton
Drewry Car Co. Ltd, London
John **Fowler** & Co. (Leeds) Ltd, Leeds
Thomas **Hill** (Rotherham) Ltd, Vanguard Works, Kilnhurst

Hudswell, Clarke & Co. Ltd, Railway Foundry, Leeds
Hunslet Engine Co. Ltd, Leeds
Manning, Wardle & Co. Ltd, Boyne Engine Works, Leeds
North British Locomotive Co. Ltd, Glasgow
Ruston & Hornsby Ltd, Lincoln
Robert **Stephenson & Hawthorns** Ltd, Forth Bank Works,
Newcastle upon Tyne
D. **Wickham** & Co. Ltd, Ware
Yorkshire Engine Co. Ltd, Meadowhall Works, Sheffield

Builder & Builder's No.	Year Built	Original No.	1944 No.	1951/2 No.	Name	Disposal where known	Notes
Hunslet 2850	1943	5001	75001	–	–	Scrapped in Holland 6/10/56	On loan to LMS 4/43. One of the first three saddle tanks to arrive on BMR 18/5/43. Stored LMR -/44. To France 1/45 and then to NS as No. 8802 6/45. Withdrawn 8/56.
Hunslet 2853	1943	5004	75004	–	–	Scrapped at NCB, Linby Colliery 9/72	One of the first three saddle tanks to arrive on BMR 18/5/43. To LMR 8/44 and to France via Calais 11/44. Noted at Calais stored 12/46. Returned to UK 1/47. Sold to NCB, Clifton Colliery and named *Peter*.
Hunslet 2864	1943	5015	75015	–	–	To Strathspey Railway for preservation 6/76	Delivered to BMR 8/43 new. In store MMR 9/44. Sold to MOF&P. Worked at various NCB collieries.
Hunslet 2868	1943	5019	75019	168	-	Preserved at the Rutland Railway Museum, Nr. Oakham, Leics	Delivered to Donnington new -/43. To Shoeburyness 1/44, to Steventon 11/51. To BMR Workshops 8/55 and returned to Shoeburyness 11/55. To Hunslet for rebuilding 9/61 then on loan to BR (WR) for trials with mechanical stoker. Sold to Hunslet and fitted with gas producer system. Rebuild No. 3883 of 1963. Sold to NCB Coal Products Division and worked at Glasshoughton Coking Plant, West Yorks -/63 and Glasshoughton Colliery -/71.
Hunslet 2884	1943	5035	75035	102	*Caen*	Sold for scrap to J.W. Hardwick & Sons, West Ewell, Surrey 8/67	From Kineton to BMR Workshops 11/53. At Shoeburyness 8/55 and returned to BMR. To LMR 2/60.
Hunslet 2888	1943	5039	75039	105	*Sapper*	Scrapped at NCB Wemyss by Connell, Coatbridge 10/69	On BMR throughout WWII. To Long Marston 7/53 then to Donnington 3/54. Returned to Long Marston 9/55. Transferred to CMR 5/56. Sold to NCB Wemyss Private Railway (No. 14) -/60.

Hunslet 2893	1943	5044	75044	109	–	Scrapped at NCB Hafodyrynys Colliery 7/76.	On LMR -/44. Converted to oil firing and loaned to ICI Ltd, St. Boswells. Returned to LMR 6/45 and to CMR -/51 to -/56. To BMR Workshops 6/56 and then Shoeburyness until -/58. Sold to NCB and worked at several Welsh collieries. Rebuilt by Hunslet, No. 3881 of 1962.
Hunslet 2894	1943	5045	75045	121	–	Scrapped on site LMR by J.W. Hardwick & Sons, West Ewell -/70	Delivered to BMR new -/43. To Hunslet for overhaul 1/53 and to SMR 4/54. Returned to BMR -/55. In Workshops 12/57 to 6/58. Transferred to LMR and seen out of use 24/7/70.
Hunslet 2896	1943	5047	75047	122	–	Sold to T.W. Ward Ltd, Grays, Essex 6/59 but not scrapped until after -/60	On BMR from 1943. Stored 4/57 to 6/59.
Hunslet 2897	1943	5048	75048	123	–	Scrapped at NCB Glasshoughton Coking Plant by T.W. Ward Ltd 11/74	Delivered Longtown -/43 and to CMR -/47. To Hunslet for overhaul 4/53 and to CMR -/53. Stored BMR -/58 and also used in service. To Hunslet 10/62. Rebuilt as 3886 of 1962. Sold to NCB, Coal Products Div. (No. 7)
Hunslet 2898	1943	75049	75049	124	–	Scrapped at Shoeburyness 3/59	On BMR during WWII. To Longtown then CMR 5/45. To SMR 9/52 to -/53. Hunslet for overhaul and sent to Shoeburyness 7/56 and to BMR Workshops 10/56 before returning to Shoeburyness 6/57.
Stephenson & Hawthorns 7099	1943	5063	75063	125	–	Scrapped at NCB Mardy Colliery 6/71 by Cashmore, Great Bridge	On BMR during WWII. To Yorkshire Engine Co. for repair 5/8/51. To Honeybourne and to BMR Workshops for overhaul -/57 to -/58. Transferred to SMR -/58 and BMR -/60. Sold to NCB Elliott Colliery, New Tredegar as No. 125 -/61. Worked at several Welsh collieries.
Stephenson & Hawthorns 7108	1943	5072	75072	110	–	Sold to T.W. Ward Ltd, Grays, Essex -/59	Delivered West Hallam new. Also at Marchwood, Bramley, CMR and Sudbury -/57. Stored BMR -/58 to -/59.
Stephenson & Hawthorns 7111	1943	5075	75075	111	–	Scrapped by T.W. Ward, Silvertown 11/60	On BMR during WWII. To Bagnall -/54 and rebuilt as No. 7077 of 1955. Transferred to CMR 5/56 to 5/59 and back to BMR 5/59 until -/60.
Stephenson & Hawthorns 7112	1943	5076	75076	112	–	Scrapped by Wynn & Co. of Shoeburyness 11/64	On BMR during WWII but reported at Chilwell 4/44 and then to CMR 1/50. To Yorkshire Engine Co. for repair 1/51 and to Ridley Shaws for overhaul 6/56 to 4/57. Returned to BMR and stored. To Shoeburyness 7/60.
Stephenson & Hawthorns 7114	1943	5078	75078	113	*Royal Pioneer*	Scrapped at Bicester 1963	At Long Marston and BMR during WWII. Back to Long Marston 1/47 and to BMR -/53 until 11/60. To Hunslet for overhaul 2/56 to 5/56 then returned to BMR.
Hudswell, Clarke 1737	1943	5080	75080	–	–	Preserved Stoom Stichting, Rotterdam	One of the first three saddle tanks to arrive on BMR 18/5/43. To France 2/45, repaired by 155, Rly Workshop Coy RE. Transferred to NS 5/45 becoming NS No. 811. Believed sold to a Dutch colliery at Limberg.

Hunslet 3201	1944	–	71437	116	–	Scrapped by Cashmore, Great Bridge 9/60	Delivered LMR new 1/45. To Chilwell 13/7/45. To BMR Workshops 7/56 and returned to Long Marston -/57.
Hunslet 3202	1944	–	71438	156	*Sapper, Tobruk* and *Mc Murdo* whilst on LMR	Scrapped by Pollock Brown, Southampton 3/68.	On BMR during WWII and transferred Moreton-on-Lugg 3/46. To Kineton -/46. To BMR 8/48, Bramley 12/48. To BMR Workshops 9/52. To Hunslet for repair -/56 to 1/57 and BMR 9/57. To LMR -/59. Used in film *Runaway Children*.
Hudswell, Clarke 1766	1944	–	71490	–	–	Withdrawn 20/11/54 and sold to NV Ijzel En Metallhandel Zwijnorecht, Holland	Delivered new to BMR but not used. Departed for Southampton for the Continent 11/11/44. Reported at 155 Rly Workshop Coy RE 15/2/45 to 21/2/45. Stored at Merelbeke SNCB. Became NS No. 8821 6/45.
Stephenson & Hawthorns 7164	1944	–	71510	–	*Pepper* when in NCB ownership	Scrapped by North Midlands Metal Co. 9/69	Delivered to BMR 17/10/44 new. Sold to NCB 11/49. Used at various opencast sites.
Barclay 2181	1944	–	71527	119	–	Scrapped by Woodhams Bros, Barry -/65	Delivered to Longtown 13/12/44 new. To BMR Workshops 3/54 to 6/54. To Sudbury, Staffs 11/54 and returned BMR 9/61.
Barclay 2182	1944	–	71528	120	–	Scrapped by T.W. Ward, Grays 8/63	Delivered Longton 10/1/45 new. To Donnington 2/50 and to SMR -/50, returned to Donnington by 11/53. To BMR 10/55 and Shoeburyness 12/57.
Hudswell, Clarke 1762	1944	–	75099	126	–	Scrapped by T.W. Ward Ltd. Grays, Essex 1/61	At Shoeburyness (No. 24) 3/44 to 8/55. To BMR 6/56 stored for a period until 1958.
Hunslet 3150	1944	–	75100	127	*Black Knight*	Scrapped at Bicester 12/11/60	Delivered Longtown 3/44, to BMR -/45. Also at CMR -/45, Kineton -/48. Stored BMR 12/49 to Hunslet for over haul 4/54. Returned to BMR 12/54.
Hunslet 3152	1944	–	75102	128	–	Scrapped by Birds at Long Marston -/65	Delivered to LMR 2/44 and to Longtown 3/44. Also at Sudbury, BMR and to Hunslet for overhaul -/49. At Kineton 1/50 and BMR for storage 7/58. Transferred to Long Marston 9/60.
Hunslet 3157	1944	–	75107	130	–	Scrapped by Woodhams Bros, Barry 3/65.	Delivered to LMR 4/44. Also at Tidworth 4/47, SMR 4/52 and to BMR Workshops 12/54. Transferred to Chilwell 8/55.
Hunslet 3161	1944	–	75111	131	–	Scrapped by T.W. Ward Ltd, Ringwood 1/61	Delivered to BMR new 4/44. In BMR Workshops 12/44 to 7/45. To Chilwell 1/52, Bramley (Hants) 7/56. Returned to BMR Workshops 16/5/56 and transferred to Bramley 7/56.
Hunslet 3163	1944	–	75113	132	*Sapper* now *Joseph*	Preserved at the Chatterley Whitfield Mining Museum, Stoke-on-Trent, Staffs.	Delivered to BMR new 28/10/44. To CMR 12/50, Longtown -/52 and stored BMR 4/57. Also used in service BMR. Sold to Hunslet 10/62, used at various collieries until preserved. Took part in 'Rocket 150' Cavalcade, Rainhill 5/80.
Hunslet 3164	1944	–	75114	133	–	Scrapped at Bicester 9/66	Delivered LMR new 4/44. Worked at Marchwood 5/44, Bramley 7/45 and to BMR Workshops 10/55. To Longtown 2/56, Bramley 7/58 and to BMR 9/59.

Hunslet 3168	1944	–	75118	134	*King Feisal* now *Wheldale*	Preserved Embsay Steam Railway, N. Yorks.	Believed delivered to SMR new. Worked at Donnington 5/44. To BMR Workshops -/51 and used in service. Sold to NCB 9/65 and used at various collieries. To Yorkshire Dales Railway (now Embsay Steam Railway) 13/11/82.
Hunslet 3171	1944	–	75121	135	–	Scrapped by Coopers, Chesterfield 9/71.	Delivered Didcot new 5/44. Worked at Sudbury, Steventon, Taunton, Bramley and SMR. Stored BMR 4/57. Sold to NCB 5/62.
Hunslet 3172	1944	–	75122	136	–	Scrapped at NCB, Shilbottle Colliery 4/76 by C.H. Newton	Deliver LMR new 6/44. Worked at Sudbury and on loan to PLA. To BMR 11/54 and then Bramley 2/57. Sold to NCB -/62.
Hunslet 3176	1944	–	75126	137	–	Scrapped by J.W. Hardwick & Sons, West Ewell, Surrey 10/59	Delivered LMR new 7/44. To Bramley -/44 and to Clifford Evans Ltd, Hove for repair 1/45. Worked at Bramley 10/46, Longtown 5/50 and stored BMR 26/6/56. To Kineton -/57 and again stored BMR 7/58 but used also in service -/59.
Hunslet 3183	1944	5133	75133	138	*King Feisal*	Preserved by Hallamshire RPS, Penistone then to South Yorkshire RPS -/83	On BMR during WWII. First saddle tank to be named (*King Feisal*). During 1954 was out of use dismantled. Overhauled in Workshops and worked at Donnington, Longtown and Bramley. Returned to BMR 7/55 until sold to NCB -/63.
Hunslet 3188	1944	–	75137	–	–	Scrapped at West Hallam 10/70	Delivered to BMR new 5/10/44. Evidently loaned to coal industry and worked on opencast sites.
Hunslet 3193	1944	–	75142	140	–	Preserved at the Midland Railway Centre, Butterley	Delivered to Barby new 13/11/44. Noted at BR, Fratton shed 9/51. Worked at Lockerley, Wilts 2/45. CMR -/52, Boughton, Notts 9/53 and BMR for storage 6/58 to 2/60. Transferred to Bramley 3/60 and sold to NCB 3/62. Re-built by Hunslet, No. 3887 of 1964.
Hunslet 3195	1944	–	75144	141	–	Scrapped by T.W. Ward Ltd 1/61	Delivered to West Hallam new 1/12/44. To Kineton 7/55. Donnington, and SMR -/55 to -/60. To BMR Workshops for examination 3/60.
Bagnall 2739	1944	–	75151	142	*The Craftsman*	Sold to T.W. Ward Ltd, Grays, Essex for scrap 6/59	Delivered new to Long Marston 9/44. To Barby 2/46 and loaned to the PLA -/51. Returned to BMR 9/53 and back on loan to PLA 2/55. Returned to BMR and stored.
Bagnall 2740	1944	–	75152	143	–	Scrapped at NCB Ackton Hall Colliery by Wakefield Metal Traders 7/76	Delivered to Long Marston new. Worked on SMR and Donnington -/52 to -/53. To Bagnall for overhaul 3/54 and returned to SMR. To BMR 3/60 and transferred to Long Marston 7/61. Sold to NCB 9/65.
Bagnall 2746	1944	–	75158	144	Now *The Duke*	Preserved by the Peak Forest RPS 4/10/83, now at Peak Rail, Darley Dale.	Delivered to Hilsea new 9/44. To Yorkshire Engine Co. for overhaul -/52. To Bramley -/55 and to BMR Workshops 25/8/55 returned to Bramley 6/56. To BMR 22/7/58. Sold to NCB 9/65.

Builder	Year		Works No.	Fleet No.	Name	Disposal	History
Bagnall 2750	1944	–	75162	145	*The Storeman*	Scrapped at NCB Backworth Colliery by Willoughby, Ashington 10/69	Delivered to Long Marston new 8/44. Transferred to Bramley 29/11/44 and to BMR 7/47 for storage. Also used in service BMR until returned to Bramley 90/59. Sold to NCB -/62.
Bagnall 2753	1944	–	75165	146	–	Scrapped at NCB Woolley Colliery, Barnsley by Wakefield Metal Traders Ltd 11/73	Delivered to Long Marston 9/44 new. To Lockerley, Wilts 21/1/45. To Norton Fitzwarren 14/8/45 and then to Yorkshire Engine Co. for overhaul 10/51 to 3/52. Returned to Long Marston and then BMR Workshops -/57. Then worked at Long Marston and Shoeburyness until 11/60. Sold to NCB -/66.
Bagnall 2759	1944	–	75171	147	–	Preserved at Lochty Private Rly, Scotland	Delivered to Kineton new 11/44. Worked at Donnington -/45, SMR and Bramley. To BMR Workshops 9/55 and to Kineton 6/56. Returned to BMR 8/58. Sold to Wemyss Private Railway 12/64 and re-sold to T. Muir, Thornton but later preserved 6/73.
Stephenson & Hawthorns 7130	1944	–	75180	148	–	Sold ex-Shoeburyness for scrap to Cashmore, Great Bridge 6/67	Delivered to West Hallam ex builders 4/44. Worked at Chilwell and Sudbury -/50. Seen at Oxford en route to Bramley 24/11/50 after overhaul at YE. To BMR 4/54, CMR -/54 to -/58 and returned to BMR -/59. Transferred to Shoeburyness 1/62.
Stephenson & Hawthorns 7131	1944	–	75181	149	–	Sold ex-Long Marston for scrap to Cashmore, Great Bridge 6/63	Delivered Bramley new 4/44. Worked on LMR, Marchwood, Bramley and Kineton. Stored BMR -/49, 1/50 and 10/54. To Ridley Shaw, Middlesbrough for overhaul 6/56. Returned to BMR 10/56 and transferred to Long Marston 3/58.
Stephenson & Hawthorns 7136	1944	–	75186	150	*Royal Pioneer now Warrington*	Preserved at Peak Rail, Darley Dale	Delivered to SMR new 5/44. Worked at Donnington 10/46 and to Hunslet for overhaul 7/9/54. To BMR 4/55 and Kineton 4/56. Sold to Hunslet 9/63 and re-built as No. 3892 of 1969 with Giesl ejector and underfeed stoker. To Dinting Railway Centre for preservation.
Stephenson & Hawthorns 7137	1944	–	75187	151	–	Scrapped at Old Dalby Nr Melton Mowbray -/62	At Old Dalby 5/44 to 1/45. Used on the Continent and was stored for a period at Calais. Returned to UK via Dover 1/47 and sent to SMR 4/47 to -/53. To BMR -/53 and Old Dalby 2/54.
Stephenson & Hawthorns 7141	1944	–	75191	163	*Black Knight*	Left BMR by road for scrapping -/63. Contractor unknown.	Delivered Long Marston new 9/44. Worked at Shoeburyness 6/46 and seen in LMS Works Bow 1/8/46. To SMR 2/47 and Hunslet for overhaul -/54. To BMR 3/55.
Stephenson & Hawthorns 7142	1944	–	75192	154	–	Scrapped ex-BMR -/63. Contractor unknown.	Delivered to SMR new 7/44. Worked at Donnington -/46 and returned to SMR -/46 to -/50. To Yorkshire Engine Co. for overhaul -/54 and to Longtown -/56. To BMR Workshops -/59.

Stephenson & Hawthorns 7143	1944	–	75193	155	–	Sold for scrap ex-Long Marston, by Birds -/69	Delivered to Bramley new 7/44. Worked at Kineton -/45, BMR -/48, SMR -/49 to -/50, Kineton -/55 and to BMR 7/58 for storage. Transferred to Long Marston -/61.
Hunslet 3208	1945	–	71444	158	*Greensleeves*	Sold for scrap to Wakefield Metal Traders 6/74	On LMR 3/45, Thatcham 3/46, Steventon 8/46. To BMR 1/53 and Chilwell 3/60. Sold to NCB Wharncliffe Woodmore Collieries 2/65.
Hunslet 3209	1945	–	71445	159	–	Scrapped at NCB Wharncliffe Woodmoor Collieries 8/68	Delivered to LMR new 4/45. To Westbury 7/47 and BMR 24/7/55. Then sent to Bramley 2/4/57. Sold to NCB Wharncliffe Woodmoor Collieries -/62.
Hunslet 3210	1945	–	71446	160	–	Scrapped -/65 contractor unknown	Delivered to LMR new 4/45. To Kineton 7/45, Westbury 7/47 and to Hunslet for overhaul 3/56. Transferred to BMR and stored 7/56, sent to Long Marston 7/59.
Hunslet 3212	1945	–	71448	161	–	Scrapped at NCB North Gawber Colliery by W. Hazlewood Ltd 4/77	Delivered to Long Marston new 5/5/45. To Shoeburyness 1/46, Sinfin Lane 7/52 and Bramley 7/55. To BMR Workshops 20/9/57 and then to Shoeburyness 12/7/60. Sold to NCB, North Gawber Colliery 4/64.
Hunslet 3214	1945	–	71450	163	–	Sold for scrap to T.W. Ward Ltd, Grays. Essex 1/61	Delivered to Barby new 23/5/45. To Shoeburyness 16/7/45 and BMR Workshops 8/58. Returned to Shoeburyness 3/60.
Stephenson & Hawthorns 7286	1945	–	71477	164	–	Withdrawn before -/63. Scrapping date unknown.	Delivered to Long Marston new 4/6/45. To Shoeburyness (No. 5) 1/46 and BMR 7/46. To Bagnall for overhaul 4/54 and returned to BMR 3/55. To Kineton 8/55 for various periods until 9/61.
Hudswell, Clarke 1783	1945	–	71506	–	–	Scrapped at BR Darlington Works 4/61	Delivered to BMR new 4/5/45. Not used and sold to LNER 5/46 (No. 8026/BR No. 68026). Withdrawn at Langwith 3/61.
Barclay 2184	1945	–	71530	166	–	Scrapped at NCB, Ashington Colliery 5/69.	Delivered to Longtown new 24/3/45. To CMR 12/45. BMR -/47 and Burton Dassett 8/48. Then to CMR -/51. At Ripon 5/4/56 after repair at Ridley Shaw. Back to BMR 6/56 and Shoeburyness 8/57. Sold to NCB, Ashington (No. 50) 8/63.
Barclay 2185	1945	–	71531	167	–	Scrapped at NCB Cadley Hill Colliery 12/70 by Cashmore, Great Bridge.	Delivered to Longtown new 18/4/45. To CMR 15/5/45, SMR -/48, Donnington 8/49 and returned to SMR -/50. To Yorkshire Engine Co. for repair 13/1/51 and Kineton 7/55. To BMR Workshops 5/56, Bramley 7/57 and sold to Hunslet and re-built as No. 3877 of 1961 and sold to NCB Cadley Hill Colliery 4/61.
Bagnall 2764	1945	–	75176	169	*Sapper*	Believed scrapped at Bicester 9/66. Contractor unknown.	To Moreton-on-Lugg -/45 and Kineton 3/46. On loan to Kirkby Outcrop, Notts 8/46. To BMR -/48 and Bramley 12/48. Returned to BMR 8/57 for storage but also used.

Bagnall 2767	1945	–	75159	170	–	Scrapped at Shoeburyness -/69	Arrived at Queensferry, nr Chester 12/44. Also worked at Honeybourne -/51, and Old Dalby. To Yorkshire Engine Co. 5/8/51 for overhaul. To BMR 1/56 and at Shoeburyness 26/10/61.
Bagnall 2773	1945	–	75250	171	*Black Knight*	Reported for sale at Shoeburyness, 1/69. Scrapped on site by E.C. Steele Ltd -/3/69	Delivered to LMR new 3/45. Worked at Ashchurch -/47 and to BMR 10/51. To Hunslet for overhaul 5/56 and returned to BMR -/56. Transferred to Shoeburyness 9/60.
Bagnall 2774	1945	–	75251	172	–	Scrapped by Hunslet	Delivered to LMR new 5/45. Worked at Long Marston and Histon (Cambs) -/45 to -/55. To Hunslet for overhaul 11/55. To BMR 6/56. Kineton 3/58 and Long Marston 7/59. Sold to Hunslet -/63 and rebuilt as No. 3893 of 1965 then used by NCB, Coventry Homefire Plant 9/65. Back to Hunslet 24/5/66.
Bagnall 2775	1945	–	75252	173	–	Sold for scrap to T.W. Ward Ltd, Grays, Essex 10/60. Cut up 3/61.	Delivered to Barby, Nr Rugby new 10/5/45. To Shoeburyness (No. 27) -/46 and then to BMR Workshops, 12/54 to 8/55. Returned to Shoeburyness (No. 27) 23/8/55.
Bagnall 2777	1945	–	75254	175	–	Preserved at the Bo'ness and Kinneil Railway	Delivered Kineton new 5/45. Worked at Thatcham, Long Marston -/46, Kineton 11/47 and to BMR -/49. Used at Barby -/50 and Bramley 8/55. To Hunslet for overhaul -/56. In store BMR 8/56 and to Long Marston 7/59. Sold to NCB 2/2/63.
Stephenson & Hawthorns 7208	1945	–	75278	179	–	Believed scrapped at NCB Bargoed Colliery 4/68	Delivered LMR new 3/45. To Ashchurch 8/45 and BMR 10/51. Between -/52 alternated between Bramley and BMR. Sold to NCB Tredegar Colliery 10/60.
Stephenson & Hawthorns 7210	1945	–	75280	180	–	Scrapped at Bicester -/66	Delivered to Barby new 3/45. To Shoeburyness (No. 28) 16/7/45 and BMR Workshops 11/11/58, afterwards being stored and used in service until -/65.
Stephenson & Hawthorns 7211	1945	–	75281	–	–	Sold for scrap to Cohen, South Bank 8/64	Delivered to BMR new 19/4/45. Stored until 5/46 when sold to LNER (No. 8032/BR No. 68032). Withdrawn at West Hartlepool 5/64.
Vulcan 5273	1945	–	75283	182	–	Scrapped by Motherwell Machinery & Scrap Co. 5/70	Delivered to Long Marston new 9/6/45. On loan to Honeybourne 19/8/45 and Kineton 11/53. To BMR for storage 4/57 and to Old Dalby 3/60. Sold to NCB Wemyss Private Rly (No. 182) 8/67.
Vulcan 5274	1945	–	75284	183	–	Scrapped at Bicester late 1966.	Delivered to Barby new 5/6/45. To Shoeburyness 16/7/45 (No. 29) and also used at other locations until 7/58. To BMR Workshops 12/58 and then used in service.
Vulcan 5275	1945	–	75285	184	–	Scrapped by Cashmore, Great Bridge -/64	Delivered to BMR new 1/6/45. Worked at Chilwell 21/7/45 and Shoeburyness (No. 22) until 23/8/55. To BMR Workshops 17/12/56. To Boughton Notts -/57 and Chilwell -/59. Sold to Hunslet 5/63.

Vulcan 5276	1945	–	75286	185	–		Scrapped at NCB Prince of Wales Colliery 11/72 by Wakefield Metal Traders Ltd	Delivered Kineton new 1/6/45. Worked at SMR 9/52 and to BMR -/57. To Shoeburyness -/58 to -/64. Sold to NCB, Prince of Wales Colliery, Pontefract, Yorks 7/65. Fitted with mechanical stoker 5/67.
Vulcan 5282	1945	–	75292	187	–		Scrapped at NCB Harrington Colliery by T.W. Ward Ltd, 12/71	Delivered to LMR new 10/45. To Marchwood 12/53, Thatcham -/54 and BMR 6/56 for storage. Re-built by Hunslet as No. 3878 of 1961. Sold to NCB, Harrington Colliery 3/65.
Vulcan 5284	1945	–	75294	188	–		Scrapped at Shoeburyness -/68	Delivered new to LMR and stored for a period. To Thatcham -/52 to -/56 and to BMR Workshops 27/8/56. Transferred to SMR 5/57 to 3/60 and returned to BMR. To Shoeburyness 9/62.
Vulcan 5285	1945	–	75295	189	–		Scrapped at Bicester 7/67	Delivered to LMR new -/45. Worked at Thatcham -/46, Steventon -/46 and to Yorkshire Engine Co. for repair 10/11/51. To SMR -/54 to -/56 and BMR -/56. Transferred to Sudbury -/59. Returned to BMR -/62.

1968 No.

Hunslet 3790	1952	190	90	–	Now Castle Hedingham		Preserved on Colne Valley Railway	Delivered LMR new -/52. To Long Marston 6/55 and stored BMR 2/59. Transferred to Shoeburyness -/67 and sold to Stour Valley RPS -/71.
Hunslet 3791	1952	191	91	–	Black Knight. Now Holman F. Stephens		Preserved on Kent & East Sussex Railway	Delivered to LMR new -/52. Stored for a period and transferred to BMR -/56 to 5/62. To Long Marston 6/5/62 - 4/12/67. Transferred to Shoeburyness. Sold to KESR (No. 23) 4/2/72.
Hunslet 3792	1953	192	92	–	Waggoner		Preserved at the Museum of Army Transport, Beverley, Humberside	Delivered to LMR new -/53. To Histon 7/55 and BMR 5/59. Stored at Long Marston 5/61 and to Shoeburyness 4/69. Transferred to Marchwood -/74 and back to Shoeburyness 11/82. To Museum of Army Transport, Beverley, Humberside 29/6/84.
Hunslet 3793	1953	193	93	–	Now Shropshire		Preserved on East Lancashire Railway	Delivered to LMR new. To SMR 2/55 and BMR 10/59. Returned to SMR 3/60. Sold to Severn Valley Railway 8/71.
Hunslet 3794	1953	194	94	–	Now Cumbria		Preserved on Lakeside & Haverthwaite Railway	Delivered new to LMR and stored. Transferred to BMR and stored 8/55 to 10/55. Histon 11/55 until 7/59. To BMR 27/9/59. Sold to Lakeside & Haverthwaite Rly (No. 10) 15/9/73.
Hunslet 3795	1953	195	–	–	–		Not known, but believed scrapped at Longmoor	Delivered new to LMR and stored. Transferred to BMR and stored -/55 to -/56. Also used in service until 11/60. Back to LMR 11/64 to 12/70.
Hunslet 3796	1953	196	–	–	Errol Lonsdale (Named at Longmoor)		Preserved on South Devon Railway	Delivered new to LMR and stored. To BMR 12/9/55 and Honeybourne 9/55. Returned to LMR -/64 - 11/67. Worked last but one passenger train on LMR 31/10/69. Sold to KESR -/70.

Hunslet 3797	1953	197	–	–	*Sapper* Now *Northiam*	Preserved on Kent & East Sussex Railway	Delivered new to LMR and stored. Transferred to BMR 10/55 and was the last steam locomotive to be used on the system. Transferred to Junior Leaders Regiment 9/77, but finally purchased by KESR (No. 25) 10/79.
Hunslet 3798	1953	198	98	–	*Royal Engineer* (Named at Long Marston)	Preserved by MOD, on loan to the Isle of Wight Steam Railway 1992-97	Delivered new to LMR 6/53 and stored. To Steventon 11/55 to 8/58 and to BMR for storage. To Lockinge until -/59 then returned to BMR until -/61. To Long Marston 7/62. Transferred to Isle of Wight 2/92.
Hunslet 3799	1953	199	–	–	–	Not known	Delivered new to LMR and stored. Transferred to BMR and stored -/55. To Thatcham 7/55, Westbury 27/6/56 and BMR Workshops 15/7/59. To LMR -/66.
Hunslet 3800	1953	200	95	–	Now *William H. Austen*	Preserved on Kent & East Sussex Railway	Delivered new to LMR and stored. Transferred to BMR and stored -/55. To Bramley 18/2/56. Returned to BMR 11/60. Sold to KESR (No. 24) 1/71.
Hunslet 3801	1953	201	96	–	–	Scrapped at Shoeburyness by Steel Breaking & Dismantling Co. Ltd	Delivered to LMR new 6/53. To BMR 7/55 and stored. Worked at Westbury and Bramley 2/56 until 21/5/59. Returned to BMR with occasional periods in store. Transferred to Shoeburyness 8/63.
Hunslet 3802	1953	202	97	–	*Sapper*	Scrapped at Shoeburyness by Steel Breaking & Dismantling Co. Ltd	Delivered new to LMR 6/53 and stored. To BMR and stored 8/55 also used in service until 8/66 when transferred to Shoeburyness.

Former Main Line Locomotives

Ex-SR (LSWR) Class A12 'Jubilee' class 0-4-2

Builder	Year Built	Original No.	1951/2 No.	Name	Brakes	Disposal	Notes
Neilson	1893	625	625	–	VBS	Scrapped 1947, contractor unknown.	Believed withdrawn from service by Southern Rly in 1939 but repaired for use by WD. At LMR 1942 to 1944 when transferred to BMR. Waiting boiler repairs 14th Oct. 1944. To Eastleigh Works 23rd Nov. 1944. Returned to BMR 31st. Jan. 1945. Returned to Southern Rly, Eastleigh under own steam 25th July 1945.

Ex-SR (LSWR) O2 class 0-4-4 Tank

Builder	Year Built	Original No.	1951/2 No.	Name	Brakes	Disposal	Notes
LSWR Nine Elms	1892	225	225	–	VBS	Scrapped 1962	Arrived BMR in 1942. Left BMR 12 July 1943. Returned to Southern Rly 11/43 and used at Eastleigh and Plymouth.

Ex-GWR 2300 Class 0-6-0

Builder & Works No.	Date Built	GWR No.	WD No.	Name	Disposal	Notes
GWR Swindon 1199	10/1890	2399	70094	*Monty.* Name removed before arriving BMR	Scrapped 1948	To WD -/40. Used on CMR and to BMR -/43. Swindon Works for repair 10-12/44 and returned to BMR. Swindon Works for repair 22/2/45. Returned to BMR 27/4/45 and to SMR -/46.

GWR Swindon 1376	6/1893	2446	70178	–	To China with 25 other locomotives to complete a £15 million UNRA 1947 programme.	Used on MMMR -/40, to Kineton -/42. Arrived BMR 1/45 and stored until 7/46. Fitted with pannier tanks in addition to tender. Westinghouse brake equipment also fitted. Although given repairs at Bicester this engine was never used in service on BMR.
GWR Swindon 1472	2/1896	2470	70095	–	Scrapped 1948	To WD -/40. Used on CMR -/41 and then to LMR. To BMR -/43. Swindon Works for repair 22/2/45 and returned to BMR 8/5/45. To SMR 12/46.
GWR Swindon 1570	6/1897	2529	70156	*Flying Fortress.* Removed 1943	Scrapped 1948	To WD -/40. Used on LMR and to BMR 12/41. Swindon Works for repair 3/43 and returned to BMR. Swindon Works for repair 7/44 and returned to BMR.
GWR Swindon 1487	1896	2485	70173	*Alexander* Removed 1943	N/K	On LMR 11/39 to -/40 then to Kineton. To BMR 12/41. Swindon Works for repair 10/8/43. Left BMR 1946.

Ex-LNER (GER) Locomotives F4 Class 2-4-2 Tank

LNER No.	WD No.	Brakes	Disposal	Notes
7077	–	WBS	After repair not returned to BMR. March 1943 Returned to LNER	Ex-armoured train locomotive lettered 'F'. To BMR February 1943. LNER Stratford Works for repair 13th March 1943.
7111	–	WBS	Returned to LNER June 1943	Ex-armoured train locomotive. Worked on BMR 13th March to May 1943.

Ex-LNER (GER) Locomotive J68 class 0-6-0 Tank

LNER No.	WD No.	Brakes	Disposal	Notes
7041	85	–	–	On LMR 10/39 to 3/42. Reported working on BMR 1942 but no further records can be traced. Believed to have been sent to No.1 Military Port Faslane.

Ex-LMSR Locomotive 2-4-2 Tank

LMS No.	Brakes	Notes
6725	VBS	Hired from the LMSR March to May 1943. No records exist showing work performed on BMR.

Miscellaneous Industrial Locomotives

Builder & Builder's No.	Year Built	Original WD No.	WD No.	Type	Name	Disposal	Notes
Hudswell, Clarke 1102	1915	211	70211	0-6-0T	–	Sold to NCB Clara Colliery on the Griff Colliery Railway	Former PLA No 46. Given overhaul by Hudswell, Clarke 4/42. To BMR -/42 and to Sinfin Lane 11/43. Used at Long Marston and MMR dates unknown.
Hudswell, Clarke 1513	1924	69	–	0-6-0ST	*Staines*	Sold to NCB 1/1/48 for use at Whitburn & Boldon Colliery. Scrapped 12/59	Built for Sir Robert McAlpine & Sons No. 42. Sold to John Mowlem & Co. Ltd. Arrived on BMR -/41 and left -/42, destination not known.
Bagnall 2652	1941	237	70237	0-4-0ST	–	N/K	At Queniborough ROF as their No.1. Transferred to Stirling -/46 and to BMR Workshops -/49. Returned to Stirling -/50. Used also at Bramley and Kineton -/55 to -/58.
Hudswell, Clarke 1720	1943	71	–	0-6-0T	–	N/K	To BMR from builders 3/43. Loaned to PLA, Royal Docks Group 7/43. Purchased by PLA and re-numbered 77.

Appendix B
Diesel Locomotives

Details of all diesel locomotives known to have been used
in service on the BMR, stored or repaired in the Central
Workshops, Bicester. Locomotives entered in building date order.

0-4-0 Diesel Locomotives

Builder	Builder's No.	Year Built	Nos & Name 1. Original 2. 1951/2 3. Final 4. Name	Class	hp	Weight 1. Working order 2. Empty tons cwts	Length Height Width	Wheel Diameter	Disposal	Notes
English Electric (Drewry)	847 (2047)	1934	70224 846 240 *Rorke's Drift*	B4 DM	153	25 00 24 10	23' 10" 12' 4" 8' 4"	3' 3"	Presented to NRM York 10/79, now at Army Transport Museum, Beverley	For early history see Chapter 4. At Feltham OD 2/45, West Hallam 10/53 and COD Stirling 13/8/56. To BMR Workshops 7/9/56, Hilsea, Hants 7/6/57 and BMR 18/4/61. Also used at Elstow, West Moors, Botley, Hilsea and Warminster.
Ruston & Hornsby	187075	1937	70231 800	A1	–	–	–	–	–	At Marske, Yorks dates unknown. On BMR -/54 to -/56. Transferred to Stirling 4/56
Fowler	22503	1938	– 815 111	A4 DM EQ	60	15 05 - -	19' 7" 9' 7" 7' 8"	2' 6"	Now preserved HQ 179 Rly Sqn RCT Germany	Delivered to Ashfordhy Gun Range, Melton Mowbray 10/39. To BMR 7/68 and stored. Despatched to Germany 10/73.
Fowler	22890	1939	71687 854 243	B7 DM	150	27 01 26 12	23' 2" 11' 2" 7' 6"	3' 3"	Sold to G.Cohen & Son Sheffield for scrap 4/7/77	At COD Hilsea and to BMR Workshops 3/8/56, Also used at Honeybourne, Leeds, Longtown and Botley between 8/56 and 4/66. Rebuilt Hunslet 1958. To BMR Workshops 7/68 and stored until 11/69. To Leuchars -/69 and back to BMR 10/70. On loan to RAF Quedgley and returned to BMR for storage 7/2/76.
Fowler	22889	1939	70228 852 242	B7 DM	150	27 01 26 12	23' 2" 11' 2" 7' 6"	3' 3"	Sold to G.A. Day Ltd, Portsmouth for scrap 10/3/76	Early details not known. Sent to CMR -/43 and also used at Corsham, Harlech and to BMR -/47. to Shoeburyness in -/49 and Queensferry, Chester -/52 to -/56. Back on BMR 30/7/57. Used at Leeds and Longtown -/58 to -/61 and to BMR Workshops 23/10/61. At Rotherwas -/62 to -/66 and to Botley 13/5/66.

Hunslet	2065	1940	71681 847	B5 DM	153	22 22	10 00	20' 11" 11' 5" 8' 3"	3' 3"	Sold to H. Stewart (Metals) Ltd, Manchester 14/12/73	At Branston, Burton-on-Trent and to BMR Workshops 15/2/57. To Branston until -/66 and back to BMR Workshops 28/1/66. Also used at Sinfin Lane, Derby and Branston -/66 to -/73.
Hunslet	2066	1940	71682 848	B5	153	22 22	10 00	20' 11" 11' 5" 8' 3"	3' 3"	Sold for scrap to Birds Commercial Motors, Stratford-on-Avon 4/76	At Branston, Burton on Trent. To BMR Workshops 3/8/55 and transferred to Branston until 3/2/65 when returned to BMR. Used as Works shunter on BMR 2/72 to 2/76.
Hunslet	2067	1940	75519 849	B5 DM	153	22 22	10 00	20' 11" 11' 5" 8' 3"	3' 3"	Sold to T.W. Ward Ltd for scrap 8/67	At Feltham OD and sent to BMR Workshops 12/57. To Sinfin Lane Derby -/58.
Hunslet	2068	1940	75520 850	B5 DM	153	22 22	10 00	20' 11" 11' 5" 8' 3"	3' 3"	Sold for scrap to G. Cohen & Sons -/73	At Wem, Salop and Queensferry dates not known. To Barby 8/56 and to BMR Workshops 29/9/59. To Longtown 10/59 and returned to BMR Workshops 23/10/61. To Duddington 25/4/62 and Branston 2/12/64. Returned to BMR Workshops 18/9/67 and stored. Sold in -/73.
Hunslet	2078	1940	75521 851	–	–	–	–	–	–	–	At Boughton -/48, Feltham -/55. To BMR Workshops 1/58.
Baguley/ Drewry	2157	1941	70030 820 123	A7 DM	153 later 100	24 22	10 00	23' 8" 11' 5" 8' 1"	3' 3"	Sold to Resco Railways Ltd, Woolwich -/79	At West Hallam until -/59 and to BMR Workshops 5/59 to 12/59. To Southampton Docks and Germany. Used by BAOR until returned to BMR for storage 31/1/69. Engine downrated to 100hp and transferred to Birtley 22/12/69.
Baguley/ Drewry	2158	1941	70031 821 124	A7 DM	153 later 100	26	10	23' 8" 11' 5" 8' 1"	3' 3"	Sold to Bristol Suburban RPS Bitton 23/11/78 (now Avon Valley Railway)	At Boughton, Notts until sent to BMR -/53 until -/56. Used by BAOR until returned to BMR for storage 31/1/69. In Workshops 14/4/69 when engine downrated to 100 hp. To Chilmark 16/7/70 until sold -/78.
Baguley/ Drewry	2159	1941	70032 822 125	A7 DM	153 later 100	26	06	23' 8" 11' 5" 8' 1"	3' 3"	Sold for scrap to R.H. Edmondson, Bromley, Kent 5/1/69	At Suez in -/52 and to BMR 3/55. To Thatcham 11/7/56 and sent to BMR Workshops 31/5/67. Returned Thatcham 18/4/68.

Barclay	357	1941	70042 823 220	B3 B11 DM SA	153 later 195	22	00	23' 8" 11' 5" 8' 1"	3' 3"	Sold to ICI Ltd, Powfoot 9/5/80	Early details unknown. At Suez -/52 and to BMR 3/55. To Branston, Burton on Trent 4/9/56. Used on CMR 16/9/57 and to BMR Workshops 12/8/58. Transferred to Hilsea 30/6/59 and to BMR Workshops 29/11/60. Returned to Hilsea 6/3/61 and to BMR 30/7/68. Also used at Botley, Eastriggs and ICI Ltd, Powfoot.
Barclay	358	1941	70043 824 200	B1 DM	153 later 100	22	10	23' 8" 11' 5" 8' 1"	3' 3"	Transferred to Royal Navy, Dean Hill 30/7/80	Early details unknown. At Suez -/52 and to BMR 3/55. Transferred to Hilsea 3/9/56 and returned to BMR Workshops 30/6/59. To Thatcham 21/1/60 and back to BMR Workshops 18/4/68 where engine downrated to 100hp.
Barclay	359	1941	70044 825 221	B3 B11 DM SA	153 later 195	22 22	10 00	23' 8" 11' 5" 8' 1"	3' 3"	Sold for scrap to Shipbreaking Ltd, Queenborough, Kent. 2/5/85	At Boughton, Notts, Lockerley -/55 and to BMR Workshops 2/7/57. To Honeybourne -/58 and to BMR 8/62. Used also at Shoeburyness, Thatcham, Glascoed and returned to BMR Workshops for new engine 1/74. To Long Marston 10/74 until sold.
Barclay	361	1942	70046 826 126	A7 DM	153 later 100	22 22	10 00	23' 8" 11' 5" 8' 1"	3' 3"	Sold to Farthingstone Silos Ltd, Northampton 20/12/78	Early details unknown. At Suez -/52 and to BMR 3/55. To West Hallam -/55 to -/58. Also used by BAOR and returned to BMR 30/1/69 and stored. To Workshops 2/5/69 when engine downrated to 100 hp. Loaned to RN Gosport 11/71 to 3/75 when returned to BMR until sold.
Barclay	362	1942	70047 827 201	B1 DM SA	153	22 22	10 00	23' 8" 11' 5" 8' 1"	3' 3"	Sold to ROF Radway Green 2/8/71	At Barby Nr Rugby until sent to Suez 2/52. Returned to BMR 3/55 and also used at Barby until -/59. Returned to BMR Workshops 7/9/59 and to Marchwood 8/2/60. Back to BMR Workshops 29/6/65 and to Liphook 28/2/66. Returned to BMR 15/6/70 until sold.

Barclay	363	1942	70048 828 127	A7 DM	153 later 100	22 22	10 00	23' 8" 11' 5" 8' 1"	3' 3"	Sold to Farthingstone Silos Ltd, Northampton 20/12/78	Early details unknown. At Suez -/52 and to BMR 3/55. Sent to Thatcham 20/4/56 to -/60. To BMR 3/60 and used by the BAOR until 30/1/69 when returned to BMR for storage. Later to Workshops when engine downrated to 100hp. Also used at Gosport 25/3/71 to -/75 when returned to BMR.
Fowler	22976	1942	70238 853	B7 DM	150	27 26	01 12	23' 2" 11' 2" 7' 6"	3' 3"	Scrapped at ROF Birtley 20/11/69	Early details unknown but believed to have been used at ROF Rearsby during WWII. On LMR -/45 to -/47 then to Shoeburyness 2/49. To BMR -/54, Hilsea /55 and returned to BMR Workshops 18/6/57. To Longtown 6/58 and returned to BMR Workshops 9/61. To ROF Birtley until sold.
Vulcan (Drewry)	4860 (2168)	1942	N/K 862 211	A7 DM	153	22 22	10 00	23' 8" 11' 5" 8' 1"	3' 3"	Transferred to RN Gosport 15/12/80	Early details unknown. At Ruddington, Notts -/61 to -/64. To BMR Workshops 13/5/64 and returned to Pontrilas 22/2/65. Back to BMR for storage 16/12/68 and to ROF Bishopston 21/7/71. Transferred to ROF Leeds 8/3/72 until sent to Royal Navy.
Hunslet	3130	1944	220	–	–	–		–	–	Returned to RN 5/72	Allocated to RNAD Bedenham. To BMR Workshops for repair 10/71 to 5/72.
Ruston & Hornsby	221648	1944	70232 801 100	A1 DM SA	44/48	7 7	06 00	13' 8" 10' 2" 7' 5"	2' 6"	Sold to Mac Williams, Shettleston, Glasgow 25/7/80	At Hilsea, Hants and transferred to Shoeburyness 9/8/56. To BMR Workshops 11/11/58 and to Bramley 6/11/59. Returned to BMR Workshops 8/3/62 and transferred to Inchterf, Scotland 29/10/62.
Ruston & Hornsby	224341	1944	72210 803 101	A1 DM SA	44/48	7 7	06 00	13' 8" 10' 2" 7' 5"	2' 6"	Sold to Track Supplies & Services Ltd, Wolverton, Bucks 26/4/76	At Weedon, Northants and sent to BMR Workshops 5/12/56 and returned to Weedon. Back in BMR Workshops 2/9/58 and afterwards stored. From 1/5/61 to 2/5/68 used at Honeybourne, Long Marston, East Habling and Ashford. To BMR Workshops 2/5/68 and returned to Hessay 7/68 until sold.

Builder	Works No	Year	Numbers	Type			Dimensions	Gauge	Disposal	Notes
Ruston & Hornsby	224342	1944	72211 804	A1 DM	44/48	7 06 7 00	13' 8" 10' 2" 7' 5"	2' 6"	–	At Feltham -/50, Shoeburyness -/53. To BMR Workshops 23/3/60.
Ruston & Hornsby	224343	1944	72212 805 102	A1 DM	44/48	7 06 7 00	13' 8" 10' 2" 7' 5"	2' 6"	–	At Shoeburyness -/53 and sent to BMR Workshops 1/59 to 3/60. To Hilsea 8/61.
Ruston & Hornsby	224344	1944	72213 806 N/K	A1 DM	44/48	7 06 7 00	13' 8" 10' 2" 7' 5"	2' 6"	–	At Shoeburyness and sent to BMR Workshops 2/59 to 3/60.
Ruston & Hornsby	224347	1945	72215 808	A1 DM	44/48	7 06 7 00	13' 8" 10' 2" 7' 5"	2' 6"	–	At Queensferry, Chester and sent to BMR Workshops 6/56. Transferred to Shoeburyness 7/56 and returned to BMR Workshops 23/3/60.
Ruston & Hornsby	224349	1945	72217 809	A1 DM	44/48	7 06 7 00	13' 8" 10' 2" 7' 5"	2' 6"	–	At Lockerley -/55 and sent to BMR Workshops 21/7/59. No further details known.
Vulcan (Drewry)	5256 (2175)	1945	72220 829 222 *Basra* and *Chittagong*	B3 DM SA	153 later 195	22 10 22 00	23' 8" 11' 5" 8' 1"	3' 3"	Transferred to RN Gosport 6/8/84	Delivered new to LMR. To BMR Workshops 25/4/66 and transferred to Shoeburyness 5/9/66. Back to BMR Workshops 28/1/71. When new engine fitted (195hp). Returned to Shoeburyness 13/10/71
Vulcan (Drewry)	5257 (2176)	1945	72221 830 223	B3 B11 DM SA	153 later 195	22 10 22 00	23' 8" 11' 5" 8' 1"	3' 3"	Sold to Shipbreaking Ltd, Queenborough, Kent 23/5/85	At Wem, Salop and transferred to Ashchurch, Glos 12/55. To BMR Workshops 30/7/59. From 5/6/60 used at Honeybourne, Ulnes Walton, Lancs, Liphook and Botley until sent to BMR Workshops 8/69 where new engine fitted (195hp). To Ashchurch 4/70 until sold.
Vulcan (Drewry)	5258 (2177)	1945	72222 831 249	B3 B11 DM SA	153 later 195	22 10 22 00	23' 8" 11' 5" 8' 1"	3' 3"	–	At Highbridge, Somerset and used at Ludgershall, Hants 30/10/53. To Tidworth, Hants 10/8/56 and BMR Workshops 14/2/57. From 25/6/57 used at Lockerley, Ashchurch and returned to BMR Workshops 19/10/67 when new engine fitted (195hp). Transferred to Ruddington 24/7/68 and back to BMR Workshops 17/6/76.

Vulcan (Drewry)	5259 (2178)	1945	72223 832 224	B3 B11 DM SA	153 later 195	22 22	10 00	23' 8" 11' 5" 8' 1"	3' 3"	Sold to Marple & Gillott Ltd, Sheffield 12/83	At Norton Fitzwarren, Somerset and to BMR Workshops 8/1/57. To West Moors, Dorset 6/6/57 and returned to BMR Workshops 11/63. To Stirling, 10/64 and to BMR Workshops 5/69 when new engine fitted (195hp). From 11/69 used at Bramley, Longtown and Donnington until sold.
Vulcan (Drewry)	5261 (2180)	1945	72225 834 226	B3 B11 DM SA	153 later 195	22 22	10 00	23' 8" 11' 5" 8' 1"	3'3"	–	At West Moors, Dorset. To BMR Workshops 18/4/56. Transferred to Taunton 11/7/56 and to BMR Workshops 31/10/62 when new engine fitted (195hp). To Eskmeals 3/5/63 and returned to BMR Workshops 2/5/70. After repair to Stirling 23/11/70.
Vulcan (Drewry)	5262 (2181)	1945	72226 835 227	B3 B11 DM SA	153 later 195	22 22	10 00	23' 8" 11' 5" 8' 1"	3' 3"	–	At Tidworth, Hants and transferred to Swindon 10/8/56. To BMR Workshops 2/7/59 and stored for a period. From 5/4/60 to 11/68 used at Swindon, ROF Bishopton and Sudbury. Returned to BMR Workshops 11/11/68 when new engine fitted (195hp). To Stirling 1/5/69.
Vulcan (Drewry)	5264 (2183)	1945	72228 837 229	B3 B11 DM SA	153 later 195	22 22	10 00	23' 8" 11' 5" 8' 1"	3' 3"	Sold to Marple & Gillott Ltd, Sheffield 22/4/85	At West Moors, Dorset and to BMR Workshops 10/6/57. Stored on BMR for a period then to Wem, Salop 2/6/58, Stirling 30/9/60 and back to BMR Workshops 19/3/65. To Sinfin Lane 7/6/66 and back to BMR Workshops 24/3/71 when new engine fitted (195hp). From 9/73 to 4/85 used at West Moors, Hilsea, Aldershot, Ruddington and Long Marston.
Vulcan (Drewry)	5267 (2205)	1945	72231 840 232	B3 B11 DM SA	153 later 195	22 22	10 00	23' 8" 11' 5" 8' 1"	3' 3"	Sold to Birds Commercial Motors Ltd, Long Marston 5/12/83	At Sudbury and transferred to Ashchurch, Glos 30/10/53. To BMR Workshops 3/8/62 and to Taunton 29/10/62. To Ashford 28/9/66 and back to BMR Workshops 5/5/71 when new engine fitted (195hp). Transferred to Long Marston 24/5/72 until sold.

Barclay	368	1945	72235 841 250	B3 B11 DM SA	153 later 195	22 22	10 00	23' 8" 11' 5" 8' 1"	3' 3"	–	At Queniborough, Leics and to BMR Workshops 18/9/59. Stored for a period. To Shoeburyness 26/4/60 and returned to BMR Workshops 6/66 when new engine fitted (195hp). To Ruddington 20/1/67 and returned to BMR Workshops 15/4/75. Transferred to Ludgershall 9/9/75.
Barclay	369	1945	72236 842 233	B3 B11 DM SA	153 later 195	22 22	10 00	23' 8" 11' 5" 8' 1"	3' 3"	–	At Queniborough, Leics and to BMR Workshops 16/12/58. To Swindon 2/7/59, Elstow 11/8/61 also used at Ruddington and Bromshall. Returned to BMR Workshops 9/68 when new engine fitted (195hp). Transferred to Hereford 14/2/69.
Barclay	370	1945	72237 843 234	B3 B11 DM SA	153 later 195	22 22	10 00	23' 8" 11' 5" 8' 1"	3' 3"	–	At Marske, Nr Saltburn and Wem, Salop 13/8/56. To Elstow, Beds 8/2/61 and to BMR Workshops 17/11/61. Transferred to Ashchurch 1/8/62 and back to BMR Workshops 27/4/70 when new engine fitted (195hp). To Shoeburyness 27/1/71.
Barclay	371	1945	72238 844 235	B3 B11 DM SA	153 later 195	22 22	10 00	23' 8" 11' 5" 8' 1"	3' 3"	–	At Old Dalby and then Sinfin Lane, Derby 30/10/53. To BMR Workshops 19/2/58 and to Shoeburyness 11/11/58. To BMR Workshops 12/59, Thatcham 31/12/59 and Shoeburyness 11/60. Back to BMR Workshops 14/12/64. To Marchwood 30/6/65 and BMR Workshops 11/7/69 when new engine fitted (195hp). To Eskmeals 4/70.
Barclay	372	1945	72239 845 236	B3 B11 DM SA	153 later 195	22 22	10 00	23' 8" 11' 5" 8' 1"	3' 3"	–	At Wem, Salop and to BMR Workshops 8/6/58. To Shoeburyness 9/2/59 and back to BMR Workshops 20/4/65. Returned to Shoeburyness 28/6/66 and to BMR Workshops 14/10/71 when new engine fitted (195hp). Transferred to Ashchurch 7/3/73.

Maker	Works No	Year	Running No	Type	HP		Dimensions		Disposal	Notes
Fowler Re-built Hill	22982 132c	1947 1963	N/K 857 245	B8 DH EQ	150 later 204	N/K	23' 4" 11' 2" 8'0"	3' 3"	Sold to ROF Glascoed 13/5/80	Early details not known but in BMR Workshops 12/54 to 1/55. Sent to Corsham -/55 and Avonmouth Docks 11/8/56 on loan. Back to Corsham 8/57 and BMR Workshops 27/9/58. Returned to Corsham 10/59. In 5/63 sent to Thos Hill, Kilnhurst for rebuilding and new engine. From 22/12/64 to 4/75 used at Melmerby and Eastriggs. To BMR Workshops 4/75 and to Glascoed ROF 17/11/75.
Ruston & Hornsby	305315	1952	112	A5 SA	88	–	–	–	Sold to T.W. Ward Ltd 1/74	Delivered new to P&EE Eskmeals. To P&EE Inchterf -/62. To BMR for storage 12/71 until sold.
North British	27422	1955	401	C1 C2 DH	275	–	–	–	Sold to Track Supplies & Services Ltd, Wolverton -/81	Reported on BMR -/77. To Ruddington date unknown.
North British	27425	1955	404	C1 C2 DH	275	–	–	–	Sold for scrap at Bicester -/78	Reported on BMR -/77. To Ruddington date unknown.
North British	27421	1955	8200 400	C1 C2 DH SA	275	32 00 30 17	22' 11½" 11' 6" 8' 6"	3' 6"	–	At West Moors, Dorset and to LMR 31/5/56. To BMR Workshops 5/10/60.
North British	27424		8203 403	C1 C2 DH SA	275	32 00 30 17	22' 11½" 11' 6" 8' 6"	3' 6"	–	At Moreton-on-Lugg 10/59 to 29/11/60. To BMR Workshops 16/8/62.
North British	27426	1955	8205 405 *Matruh*	C1 C2 DH SA	275	32 00 30 17	22' 11½" 11' 6" 8' 6"	3' 6"	To RAF Leuchars 15/12/80	Stored on BMR and transferred to LMR 2/57. Returned to BMR 10/5/65. To Marchwood 28/6/66 and back to BMR Workshops 8/11/68. Returned to Marchwood 4/7/69 and to Barclay, Kilmarnock for repairs to final drive 4/6/73, afterwards returned to Marchwood. From 18/11/74 to 15/12/80 used at Longtown, Donnington and Leuchars.

North British	27427	1955	8206 406	C1 C2 DH SA	275	32 30	00 17	22' 9¼" 11' 6" 8' 6"	3' 6"	Preserved on South Yorkshire Railway, Sheffield	Stored on BMR and transferred to Kineton 11/58. To BMR Workshops 10/8/62. From 5/63 to 10/72 used at Kineton, Long Marston and returned to BMR Workshops when new engine fitted (Mark 7 Paxman). From 4/4/73 to 7/3/79 used at Kineton and Ludgershall until sold to Mid-Hants Railway 6/85.
North British	27428	1955	8207 407	C1 C2 DH SA	275	32 30	00 17	22' 9¼" 11' 6" 8' 6"	3' 6"	Sold to T.W. Ward Ltd, Sheffield 11/9/81	Stored on BMR and to Workshops 20/11/56. Transferred to Tidworth, Hants 13/1/57 and returned to BMR Workshops 28/11/67. To Marchwood 20/8/68 and sent to Barclay, Kilmarnock for new final drive. From 8/6/73 used at Marchwood, BMR and Eskmeals until sold.
North British	27429	1955	8208 408	C1 C2 DH SA	275	32 30	00 17	22' 9¼" 11' 6" 8' 6"	3' 6"	Sold to Coopers (Metals) Ltd, Swindon 29/4/85	Stored on BMR and to Workshops 7/59 to 8/59. Transferred to Kineton 12/8/59 and returned to BMR Workshops 28/4/64. To Kineton 8/1/75. Yardley Chase 3/9/77, Ruddington 3/81, Ashchurch 10/83 until sold.
North British	27645	1958	8210 410	C1 C2 DH SA	275	32 30	00 17	22' 8½" 12' 2½" 8' 6"	3' 6"	Sold to ROF Bridgwater 13/10/81	At Kineton and sent to BMR Workshops 8/59 and afterwards stored. To Didcot 8/6/60 and to Long Marston 1/2/64. Given overhaul at BMR Workshops 7/9/66. From 7/67 to 7/78 used at Ruddington and Yardley Chase until sent to BMR Workshops for repair 18/7/78. Transferred to Marchwood 8/8/79 until sold.
North British	27646	1959	8211 411	C1 C2 DH SA	275	32 30	00 17	22' 8½" 12' 2½" 8' 6"	3' 6"	Sold to Marple & Gillott Ltd, Sheffield 12/83	Stored on BMR and transferred to Didcot 8/6/60. To BMR Workshops 13/5/64 and sent to Shoeburyness from 6/11/64 to 1/1/67. Returned to BMR Workshops when new engine fitted 7/67. Used in service until 12/72 when sent to BMR Workshops. From 6/8/73 to 3/81 used at Ludgershall, Caerwent, Yardley Chase and BMR.

North British	27647	1959	8212 412	C1 C2 DH SA	275	32 30	00 17	22' 8½" 12' 2½" 8' 6"	3' 6"	–	Stored on BMR and used at Kineton -/59. Transferred to Bramley, Hants 1/4/60. To Didcot 27/5/60, Long Marston 14/4/64 and returned to BMR 8/1/66. From 29/6/67 to 21/2/78 used at West Moors, LMR and Ludgershall. At Barclay, Kilmarnock 21/2/78.

Former LMS 0-6-0 Diesel Electric Locomotives

Builder		Year	Numbers		HP			Dimensions		Disposal	Notes
Armstrong Whitworth	D57	1935	LMS 7062 70215 882	–	400	52 51	00 00	31' 4½" 12' 6" 8' 7"		–	Purchased from LMSR 9/1940. On MMR 1/41 to -/44. On BMR -/45 to -/50. Transferred to Kineton and later Long Marston. This was the first diesel locomotive to work on BMR.
Armstrong Whitworth	D58	1935	LMS 7063 70216 883	–	400	52 51	00 00	31' 4½" 12' 6" 8' 7"		Sold out of service to E.L. Pitt (Coventry) Ltd -/63	Purchased from LMS 9/1940. On MMMR, dates unknown and transferred to LMR until -/52. To CMR 1/52 to 9/55 and BMR 10/55.
LMS Derby		1945	70272 878 601	D1	350			28' 6¾" 12' 4" 8' 9¾"		Sold to Lakeside & Haverthwaite Rly, Cumbria 7/80	Purchased by WD -/45. Worked on LMR -/45 to closure then transferred to Shoeburyness -/70. To US Air Force, Welford Park -/71. To BMR -/77.

Barclay 0-8-0 Diesel Hydraulic Locomotives

Builder		Year	Numbers/Name		HP			Dimensions		Disposal	Notes
Barclay	500	1964	891 620 Sapper	D3 SA	600	59	10	35' 11½" 12' 0" 8' 9"	3' 6"	Sold for scrap to Marple & Gillott Ltd, Sheffield 5/85	Arrived BMR 1/65.
Barclay	501	1965	892 621 Waggoner	D3 SA	600	59	10	35' 11½" 12' 0" 8' 9"	3' 6"	Sold for scrap to Marple & Gillott Ltd, Sheffield 5/85	Arrived BMR 1965. To Kineton 1978.
Barclay	502	1965	893 622 Greensleeves	D3 SA	600	59	10	35' 11½" 12' 0" 8' 9"	3' 6"	Sold for scrap to Marple & Gillott Ltd, Sheffield 5/85	Arrived BMR 1965.
Barclay	503	1965	894 623 Storeman	D3 SA	600	59	10	35' 11½" 12' 0" 8' 9"	3' 6"	Sold for scrap to Marple & Gillott Ltd, Sheffield 5/85	Arrived BMR 1965. Hauled Royal Train 16/5/1978.
Barclay	504	1965	895 624 Royal Pioneer	D3 SA	600	59	10	35' 11½" 12' 0" 8' 9"	3' 6"	Sold for scrap to Marple & Gillott Ltd, Sheffield 5/85	Arrived BMR December 1965.
Barclay	505	1965	896 625 Craftsman	D3 SA	600	59	10	35' 11½" 12' 0" 8' 9"	3' 6"	Sold for scrap to Marple & Gillott Ltd, Sheffield 5/85	Arrived BMR January 1966. To Kineton 17/8/1977.

'Vanguard' 4-wheel Diesel Hydraulic Locomotive

Hill	270V	1977	252 *Greensleeves*	C7 MU SA	250	35.00	7,965 mm 3,500 mm 2,590 mm	1,066 mm	Transferred to Kineton 13/5/87	Received new from builders 25/4/77.
Hill	271V	1977	253 *Conductor**	C7 MU SA	335**	35.00	7,965 mm 3,500 mm 2,590 mm	1,066 mm	Transferred to Donnington 1990	Received new from builders 30/6/77.
Hill	275V	1978	257 *Tela**	C7 MU SA	335**	35.00	7,965 mm 3,500 mm 2,590 mm	1,066 mm	Transferred to Longtown 23/11/78, to Kineton 19/1/81 and to Long Marston 1990	Received new from builders 1978.
Hill	298V	1981	258 *Sapper**	C7 MU SA	250	35.00	7,965 mm 3,500 mm 2,590 mm	1,066 mm	Transferred to Marchwood 24/4/88 and to Hereford 1990	Received new from builders 10/11/81.
Hill	299V	1981	259 *Royal Pioneer**	C7 MU SA	335**	35.00	7,965 mm 3,500 mm 2,590 mm	1,066 mm	Transferred to Ludgershall 11/4/88 and to Long Marston 1990	Received new from builders 13/11/81.
Hill	309V	1983	267 *Storeman**	C7 MU SA	250	35.00	7,965 mm 3,500 mm 2,590 mm	1,066 mm	Transferred to Hereford 5/10/87	Received new from builders 15/12/83.

*   On leaving the BMR name transferred to 'Steelman Royale' locomotives.
**   Fitted with new NT 855 Cummins engines.

'Steelman Royale' 4-wheel Diesel Hydraulic Locomotives

Hill	318V	1987	270 *Greensleeves*	335	35.00 34.00	8,260 mm 3,713 mm 2,590 mm	1,066 mm	Received new from builders 13/2/87.
Hill	324V	1987	271 *Storeman*	335	35.00 34.00	8,260 mm 3,713 mm 2,590 mm	1,066 mm	Received new from builders 4/3/87.
Hill	320V	1987	272 *Royal Pioneer*	335	35.00 34.00	8,260 mm 3,713 mm 2,590 mm	1,066mm	Received new from builders 13/8/87.
Hill	323V	1987	275 *Sapper*	335	35.00 34.00	8,260 mm 3,713 mm 2,590 mm	1,066mm	Received new from builders 29/1/88.
Hill	319V	1988	276 *Conductor*	335	35.00 34.00	8,260 mm 3,713 mm 2,590 mm	1,066mm	Received new from builders 10/2/88.

Appendix C
Railcars

Builder	Builder's No.	Year Built	Type	Engine	Gearbox	Army No.	Seating Capacity	Disposal	Notes
Wickham	3410	1943	17A	JAP 1,323cc	Friction disc drive	11993	8/10	Scrapped at Bicester, date not known.	Delivered new to BMR 19/11/43.
Wickham	3411	1943	17A	JAP 1,323cc	Friction disc drive	11977	8/10	Scrapped at Bicester, date not known.	Delivered new to BMR 19/11/43.
Wickham	3412	1943	17A	JAP 1,323cc	Friction disc drive	N/K	8/10	Scrapped at Bicester, date not known.	Delivered new to BMR 19/11/43.
Wickham	3713 & 3714	1945	18A	Ford V8 30hp (Two)	Ford 4-speed	12091 & 12161	N/K	Scrapped at Bicester after collision in 1957	Two power cars of three-car unit. Delivered new to BMR 1/5/45.
Wickham	3715	1945	Trailer	–	–	12336	32	After collision trailer used for breakdown equipment	Trailer car of three-car unit. Delivered new to BMR 1/5/45.
Wickham	8084	1958	27 Mark III	Ford 105E 10hp	Ford 3-speed	9020	8/10	Sold to Market Overton Rly -/78	Delivered new to Kineton 22/10/58. On BMR 11/66 to 6/67. On BMR 8/68
Wickham	8085	1958	27 Mark III	Ford 105E 10hp	Ford 3-speed	9021	8/10	Sold to Severn Valley Rly 11/77	Delivered new to Kineton 22/10/58. On BMR 10/65 to 3/67.
Wickham	8086	1958	27 Mark III	Ford 105E 10hp	Ford 3-speed	9022	8/10	Sold to Alderney Rly, Channel Islands 8/81	Delivered new to Kineton 22/10/58. On BMR 8/62 to 10/62 and 10/69 to 4/70.
Wickham	8087	1958	27 Mark III	Ford 105E 10hp	Ford 3-speed	9023	8/10	Sold to Severn Valley Rly, 12/78	Delivered new to Kineton 22/10/58. On BMR 11/66 to 5/67 and 9/71.
Wickham	7090	1955	27 Mark III	Morris 13hp. Type 15	Morris 3-speed	9024	8/10	Sold to S.C. Robinson, 8/77	Delivered new to Kineton 11/55. On BMR 9/65 to 11/65 and 7/71 to 9/71.
Wickham	7091	1955	27A Mark III	Morris 13hp. Type 15	Morris 3-speed	9025	8/10	Sold to S.C. Robinson, 8/77	Delivered new to Kineton 11/55. On BMR 8/65 to 12/65 and 9/71 to 10/71.
Wickham	7092	1955	27A Mark III	Morris 13hp. Type 15	Morris 3-speed	9026	8/10	Sold to T.W. Ward for scrap 12/75	Delivered new to Kineton 11/55. On BMR 11/65 to 2/66 and 10/71 to 1/72.
Wickham	7093	1955	27A Mark III	Morris 13hp. Type 15	Morris 3-speed	9027	8/10	Sold to T.W. Ward for scrap 12/75	Delivered new to Kineton 11/55. On BMR 12/65 to 4/66.
Wickham	7094	1955	27A Mark III	Morris 13hp. Type 15	Morris 3-speed	9028	8/10	Sold to Alderney Rly, Channel Islands 8/81	Delivered new to Kineton 11/55. On BMR 2/66 to 4/66.
Wickham	7095	1955	27A Mark III	Morris 13hp. Type 15	Morris 3-speed	9029	8/10	Sold to S.C. Robinson 8/77	Delivered new to Kineton 11/55. On BMR 4/65 to 8/65.
Wickham	8088	1958	27 Mark III	Ford 10hp.	Ford 3-speed	9030	8/10	Sold to Market Bosworth Light Railway 8/77	Delivered new to Kineton 22/10/58. On BMR 8/59.

Wickham	8089	1958	27 Mark III	Ford 10hp.	Ford 3-speed	9031	8/10	Sold 1981. To Swindon & Cricklade Railway -/83	Delivered new to Kineton 22/10/58. Converted to fire tender date N/K. On BMR 8/62 to 9/62, 4/67 to 11/67 and 10/71 to 1/73.
Wickham	8200	1958	27 Mark III	Ford 10hp.	Ford 3-speed	9032	8/10	Sold to Severn Valley Rly, 11/77	Delivered new to Bramley, Hants 11/58. On BMR 5/67 to 10/67.
Wickham	6857	1954	27A Mark III	Morris 13hp.	Morris 3-speed	9033	8/10	Sold to S.C. Robinson 8/77	Delivered new to LMR 23/9/54.. Converted to fire tender date N/K. On BMR 11/69 to 9/71 and 3/72 to 7/74.
Wickham	7397	1957	40 Mark IIA	Ford V8 30hp.	Ford 4-speed	9034	9	Renumbered 9104 8/69	Delivered new to BMR 8/57. Transferred to LMR 2/60. After closure of LMR -/69 returned to BMR.
Wickham	8195	1958	27 Mark III	Ford 10hp.	Ford 3-speed	9035	8/10	Sold to E.W. Betts 10/71. Later to Museum of Army Transport, Beverley	Delivered new to BMR 20/11/58. On BMR to 1/60 when transferred to Tidworth. Returned to BMR 7/65 to 10/71.
Wickham	8196	1958	27 Mark III	Ford 10hp.	Ford 3-speed	9036	8/10	Sold to T.W. Ward Ltd, 4/76	Delivered new to BMR 20/11/58. On BMR 11/58 to 10/62 and 12/68 to 2/70.
Wickham	8197	1958	27 Mark III	Ford 10hp.	Ford 3-speed	9037	8/10	Sold to Quainton Rly Society, 15/8/72	Delivered new to BMR 20/11/58. Worked on BMR 11/58 to 9/62. On BMR 8/70 to 8/72.
Wickham	8198	1958	27 Mark III	Ford 10hp.	Ford 3-speed	9038	8/10	Despatched by road to Cowan's for scrap 5/7/77	Delivered new to BMR 20/11/58. On BMR 11/58 to 7/61. Other locations unknown. On BMR 12/68 to 7/77.
Wickham	8199	1958	27 Mark III	Ford 10hp. later Perkins	Ford 3-speed	9039	8/10	Sold to T.W. Ward for scrap 12/75	Delivered new to BMR 20/11/58. On BMR 11/58 to 11/59. On BMR 2/70 to 7/74.
Wickham	7390	1956	40 Mark II	Ford V8 30hp.	Ford 4-speed	9041	9	Sold to Bird's for scrap 10/69	Delivered new to Shoeburyness 11/6/56. On BMR 11/62 to 11/64.
Wickham	7391	1956	40 Mark II	Ford V8 30hp.	Ford 4-speed	9042	9	Sold to Bird's for scrap 10/69	Delivered new to Shoeburyness 11/6/56. On BMR 11/62 to 11/64.
Wickham	6965	1954	27A Mark III	Ford 10hp.	Ford 3-speed	9043	Fire tender	Sold to Kent & Sussex Railway 3/70	Delivered new to Pontrilas, Hereford 6/1/55. To BMR Workshops 4/64 to 4/65.
Drewry	1894	1951	A	Morris 12hp. later Perkins	N/K	9100	15	Converted to trailer 5/76	At Bramley until -/60. To BMR Workshops 8/72 to 2/73.
Drewry	1895	1951	A	Morris 12hp. later Perkins	N/K	9101	15	Converted to trailer 4/77	At Bramley until 11/60. To BMR 7/62 to 6/66 and 11/70 to 2/71.
Drewry	1896	1951	A	Morris 12hp. later Perkins	N/K	9102	15	Converted to trailer 2/77	At Bramley until 11/60. To BMR 3/62 to 12/63 and 1/70 to 8/70.
Drewry	1897	1951	A	Morris 12hp. later Perkins	N/K	9103	15	Scrapped at Bicester 3/81	At SMR -/58 and Bramley -/59. To BMR 10/65 to 8/68. To BMR 12/73 to 3/74.

Drewry	1899	1951	A	Morris 12hp. later Perkins	N/K	9105	15	Converted to trailer date 11/76. Scrapped at Bramley -/87	At SMR -/56 and Bramley. To BMR 4/60 to 6/62. To BMR 7/73 to 10/73.
Drewry	2328	1951	A	Morris 12hp. later Perkins	N/K	9106	15	Converted to trailer 12/82	At SMR -/56. To BMR 8/56 to 5/65.
Drewry	2327	1951	A	Morris 12hp. later Perkins	N/K	9107	15	Sold privately 9/86	At Bramley and to BMR Workshops 3/3/60. Returned to Bramley -/60.
Baguley	3538	1959	N/K	Perkins No. 2104308	N/K	9112	Fire tender	–	To BMR Workshops -/59. Arrived Bramley 30/5/61. To BMR Workshops 1/70. Other dates unknown.
Baguley	3539	1959	N/K	Perkins No. 2104309	N/K	9113	Fire tender	Rebuilt as 2 ft gauge passenger coach for Leighton Buzzard Railway	To BMR Workshops -/59. Arrived Bramley 16/6/60. To BMR Workshops 9/70.
Clayton	5380/1	1968	N/K	Perkins 3-cylinders	N/K	9114	Fire tender	Out of use and stored on BMR -/89	To BMR -/68 and transferred to Kineton date unknown. Returned to BMR date unknown.
Clayton	5380/2	1968	N/K	Perkins 3-cylinders	N/K	9115	Fire tender	Converted to shelter at Kineton 3/84	To BMR Workshops 5/68 to 1/69. Arrived at Kineton 31/1/69.
Clayton	5427	1968	N/K	Perkins 3-cylinders	N/K	9116	Fire tender	Scrapped, date N/K	To BMR Workshops 5/68 to 3/69. Arrived Kineton 24/3/69 until 8/79.
Baguley-Drewry	3706	1975	N/K	Perkins P4 75hp.	N/K	9117	12	–	Delivered new to BMR, 6/75 to 7/75. To Shoeburyness. On BMR 10/77.
Baguley-Drewry	3707	1975	N/K	Perkins P4 75hp.	N/K	9118	12	–	Delivered new to BMR 7/75. On BMR 6/76 to 7/77.
Baguley-Drewry	3708	1975	N/K	Perkins P4 75hp.	N/K	9119	12	Dismantled at Kineton. Frame converted to trailer	Delivered new to BMR 6/75 to 7/75. Transferred to Kineton.
Baguley-Drewry	3709	1975	N/K	Perkins P4 75hp.	N/K	9120	12	N/K	Delivered new to BMR 6/75 to 7/75. Transferred to Kineton.
Baguley-Drewry	3710	1975	N/K	Perkins P4 75hp.	N/K	9121	12	Scrapped at Kineton, date N/K	Delivered new to BMR 7/75 to 8/75. Transferred to Kineton.
Baguley-Drewry	3711	1975	N/K	Perkins P4 75hp.	N/K	9122	12	Scrapped at Kineton, date N/K	Delivered new to BMR 7/75 to 8/75. Transferred to Kineton.
Baguley-Drewry	3741	1976	N/K	Perkins P4 75hp.	N/K	9125	12	Scrapped at Bramley, date N/K	Delivered new to BMR 6/76 to 7/77. Transferred to Bramley, by road, 4/7/77.
Hudswell, Clarke	P265	1933	N/K	Dorman 30hp.	Bostock & Bramley 3-speed	902	20	Scrapped at Bicester, date N/K	Transferred from Spurn Head Military Railway in 1951. Used to convey permanent way materials and later as a 'runner' wagon for a steam crane.

Postscript

The Bicester Military Railway continues to provide an efficient transport mode for the vast Depot it was built to serve. Like most rail systems it makes little intrusion on the environment and is still capable of moving large quantities of freight without shattering the nerves of the local population or causing damage to their buildings and pathways.

The system has not, however, escaped the attention of the road lobby as in 1976 the Depot itself came under close scrutiny in an attempt to cut costs. In the book *Your Disobedient Servant* by Leslie Chapman, a former regional director of the Ministry of Public Buildings and Works, mention is made that the Railway should be replaced by road which, according to the report, would serve the needs of the Depot at a fraction of the cost.

Obviously the team producing the report had not looked very seriously at the severe congestion on the road network in the area, or taken into account the damage already inflicted on road surfaces and structures by heavy 'juggernauts'. Neither had recommendations been made of the BMR's potential for moving great quantities of equipment for the armed forces in an emergency with consequent savings in manpower and fuel costs.

The *Sunday Telegraph* of 19th December 1976 had also eagerly published extracts from the report which included criticism of the 0-8-0 locomotives which were described as "too big and too heavy" and that part of the £48,000 per year spent on track maintenance was expended on putting right the damage caused by these locomotives.

Again, no comparison was made with the costs of road transport, the purchase of additional fleets of lorries, the increased manpower, the resultant damage to the current road system and the greater likelihood of destruction to life and limb.

Today, new roads serving the area, costing many millions of pounds, have been constructed in the never-ending craze of destroying vast tracts of land to cater for the ever-increasing weights of rubber tyred carriers. Many of their cargoes should be conveyed by rail, the end product of which would actually reduce the overall costs to the nation.

Fortunately better senses have prevailed and after half a century the BMR is still fully operational, a valuable asset in the defence structure of the United Kingdom.

Index

BICESTER MILITARY RAILWAY - THE VIDEO

On sale now, this superb video gives a unique insight into the day-to-day operations at this fascinating and busy Central Ordnance Depot. Not generally open to the public, this exciting programme allows the viewer to explore all aspects of Britain's biggest military railway.

As well as internal traffic flows, featuring many unique and interesting wagon variants no longer found on main line systems, the programme also deals with MOD main line traffic since the demise of Speedlink, as well as a site visit to the Museum of Army Transport at Beverley, Humberside, to look at some other unusual relics used by both MOD and the Army. There's also a close look at the immaculate locomotive fleet, and a cab ride around the extensive site at Bicester.

The programme includes many interesting interviews, not least, the reminiscences of Ernest Lawton, author of this book, who was a driver at the Bicester Military Railway during the Second World War.

This video, made by the producers of the highly acclaimed video series, *Rail Freight Today* - is an essential companion to Ernest Lawton and Major Maurice Sackett's fascinating historical book.

£18.95 from all the usual railway video shops or direct from Tele Rail, 9A New Street, Carnforth, Lancs LA5 9TS.

All five Thomas Hill 'Steelman Royale' locomotives at the Bicester Military Railway, June 1992.

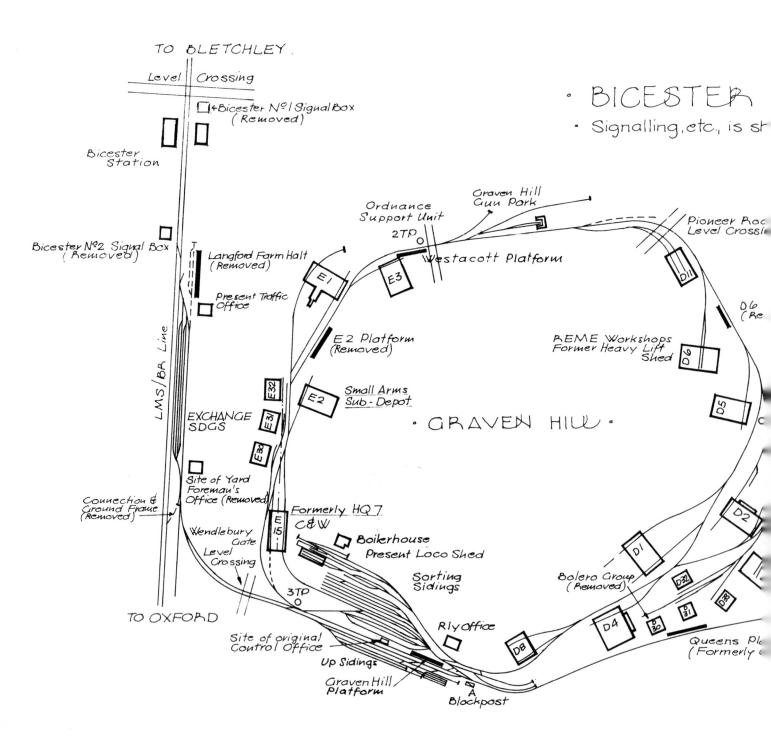

TO BLETCHLEY.

Level Crossing

Bicester Nº1 Signal Box
(Removed)

Bicester Station

Bicester Nº2 Signal Box
(Removed)

LMS/BR Line

BICESTER

Signalling, etc., is sh

Ordnance Support Unit

2TP

Graven Hill Gun Park

Pioneer Proc
Level Crossi

Westacott Platform

D11

Langford Farm Halt
(Removed)

Present Traffic Office

E1

E3

D6
(Re

E2 Platform
(Removed)

REME Workshops
Former Heavy Lift Shed

D9

E32

EXCHANGE SDGS

E2

Small Arms
Sub-Depot

• GRAVEN HILL •

D5

E31

E30

Site of Yard Foreman's Office (Removed)

Connection & Ground Frame (Removed)

Wendlebury Gate Level Crossing

E15

Formerly HQ7
C&W

Boilerhouse
Present Loco Shed

Sorting Sidings

Bolero Group
(Removed)

D2

D1

D3

3TP

TO OXFORD

Site of original Control Office

Up Sidings

Graven Hill Platform

Rly Office

A
Blockpost

D8

D4

D30

D31

D32

D33

Queens Pl
(Formerly